1993

Citizen Machiavelli

Citizen Machiavelli

MARK HULLIUNG

Princeton University Press
Princeton, N.J.

Published by Princeton University Press, 41 William Street,
Princeton, New Jersey 08540
In the United Kingdom: Princeton University Press,
Guildford, Surrey

ISBN 0-691-07661-8

Publication of this book has been aided by the Whitney Darrow
Publication Reserve Fund of Princeton University Press

This book has been composed in Linotron Garamond type

Clothbound editions of Princeton University Press books
are printed on acid-free paper, and binding materials are chosen
for strength and durability. Paperbacks, although satisfactory
for personal collections, are not usually suitable
for library rebinding

Printed in the United States of America by Princeton
University Press, Princeton, New Jersey

TO MAX AND MEG
my favorite Machiavellians

CONTENTS

PREFACE

MY PURPOSE in writing this book is to reopen the question of Machiavelli's relationship to neoclassical, humanist, republican thought—the tradition sometimes called "civic humanism," which began with the Greek and Roman classics, was reborn during the Renaissance, and lived on to the end of the eighteenth century, up to and including the French Revolution, an event owing much of its revolutionary ideology to the classical reminiscences of modern authors.

Many other scholars have written—and with distinction—on the topic of Machiavelli the republican author and devotee of the *studia humanitatis*.* It is not their scholarship that I wish to question, but rather what seems to me their misplaced determination to prevent Machiavelli's thought from being the scandal he intended it to be. Our age, it seems, is too much one of embattled humanism for humanists to be willing to recognize Machiavelli for what he was, the first and one of the greatest subversives of the humanist tradition. We understandably but mistakenly prefer to believe that Machiavelli was a humanist misunderstood, or that his immersion in the humanist tradition proves we have nothing to fear from him, or better yet, that he was, in anticipation of ourselves, a humanist grappling with the problem of "dirty hands," the dilemma of the necessity of doing evil for the sake of the good.

But in truth, as I hope to prove, a Machiavelli so much to our liking is not Machiavelli at all. The real Machiavelli deliberately

---

* A Renaissance "humanist" was educated in the humane studies, the humanities—the study of grammar, rhetoric, history, and ethics. The concept of the *studia humanitatis* is Ciceronian in origin.

inverted the master symbols of Latin literature, and each of his inversions was an intentional subversion of the humanist creed: by turning the Stoicism of Cicero upside down, Machiavelli forced the *studia humanitatis* to give birth to Machiavellism—a Machiavellism born not of "necessity," but of a yearning for the grandeur of conquest, matched by an impatience with—and disdain for—any humanistic sympathies standing in the way of the glory of republican empire. By force and by fraud, the Roman republic of Machiavelli's imagination had devoured the ancient world, and Machiavelli's most heartfelt dream was that Florence might one day do the same for the modern world. The disconcerting brilliance of Machiavelli's subversion of humanism will be the subject of this investigation.

My procedure in interpreting Machiavelli will be to read the texts carefully and to place them in context—context in this case being understood as meaning, above all, the classical republican tradition that made Machiavelli's thought possible and that he remade according to his own audacious specifications. The story of Machiavelli's relationship to "civic humanism" is complex. Sometimes his thought fell flat because his classical learning was so thoroughly Latin that it prevented him from questioning the Roman authors, even when they diluted or failed to appreciate much of what was outstanding in Thucydides, Plato, and Aristotle. At other times he effectively and provocatively called attention to what had always been potentially "Machiavellian" in the classical and neoclassical texts of the ancient Roman and modern Florentine humanists, namely, the theme of the grandeur and glory of imperial expansion. Finally and most remarkably, Machiavelli often creatively imposed a "form" of his own making upon the "matter" of Latin literature. As an alternative to the sexual puritanism of Roman thought, Machiavelli offered a vindication of amorous and seductive activities that are recognized by their perpetrators as games, as mere diversions—as activities belonging to the order of *cose vane* (empty things).

In the order of *cose grandi* (great things), Machiavelli's innovations within the tradition of Roman thought were nothing less than shocking. Briefly put, he took the Roman republicans, whom Cicero had portrayed as pre-Stoics, and turned them into self-conscious power politicians, taking by force and by fraud, by the methods of the lion and the fox, what Cicero had ancient peoples freely giving to the Romans because they were the embodiment of justice, dedicated to the fair and humanitarian treatment of mankind. It was Cicero who invented the imagery of the lion and the fox, the better to congratulate Rome on having disdained their use; it was Machiavelli who maintained that the lion and the fox were evident throughout the history of republican Rome, that the bestial in the Romans was what made them great, and that any modern republic wishing to re-create ancient grandeur had better overcome its denial of the animal inside the man. Not until Nietzsche, perhaps, do we again encounter so deliberate and formidable an attempt to use the *studia humanitatis* for the purpose of inverting its humanitarianism.

I WISH to thank Frank E. Manuel for his comments on the first chapter of this study; George A. Kelly, formerly my colleague but never an ex-colleague, for his remarks on the fourth chapter; James T. Kloppenberg for reading and commenting on the entirety of this book; John H. Geerken for sharing with me his admirable combination of expertise and vision; and Judith N. Shklar for continuing to be my most formidable critic. Of the many distinguished contemporary scholars who have studied Machiavelli, it is Felix Gilbert whose writings I have found particularly indispensable.

Material quoted from *The Literary Works of Machiavelli*, translated by J. R. Hale, is used by permission of Oxford University Press.

NOTE ON SOURCES

NOTES TO Machiavelli refer to *Niccolò Machiavelli: Tutte le opere*, ed. Mario Martelli (Florence, 1971). I have normally used *Machiavelli: The Chief Works and Others*, ed. and trans. Allan H. Gilbert, 3 vols. (Durham, N.C., 1965) when quoting from Machiavelli in English translation. Whenever I offered translations of my own, the notes call this to the reader's attention.

I do not believe this work requires a formal bibliography. My arguments with the interpretive literature in the first and last chapters, together with the notes, provide—I think—a satisfactory enumeration of the interpretive works most relevant to the present study. Here, I wish only to call attention to several surveys of the scholarly literature: Eric Cochrane, "Machiavelli: 1940-1960," *The Journal of Modern History*, 33 (1961), 113-136; Richard C. Clark, "Machiavelli: Bibliographical Spectrum," *Review of National Literatures*, 1 (1970), 93-135; Mario Martelli, *Niccolò Machiavelli: Tutte le opere* (Florence, 1971), "Nota Bibliografica," pp. lxi-lxiv; and John H. Geerken, "Machiavelli Studies Since 1969," *Journal of the History of Ideas*, 37 (1976), 351-368.

Citizen Machiavelli

— I —

CIVIC HUMANISM AND
POWER POLITICS

OVER THE LAST several decades scholarly attempts to save
Machiavelli's name from its popular connotations of immorality,
fraud, and deceit have been untiring in energy and crusading in
tone. The central contentions of this study are that the scholarly
image of Machiavelli is no less mistaken than the popular image,
and that while from his popular reputation he might at least
derive wry satisfaction, his shade would sharply rebuff the absolution ministered by the scholars. Learned friends and unlearned
foes alike bear responsibility for the much-noted sardonic smile
of his portrait, but his friends more so than his foes.

What has happened to Machiavelli in the interpretive literature
of contemporary scholarship is strikingly similar to the fates formerly endured by Rousseau and Nietzsche. To defend Rousseau
from the charges of primitivism and irrationalism, his interpreters
began to write as if he never wrote the *First Discourse*, never
attacked European culture root and branch, never uttered anything not readily assimilated by the "great tradition" of Western
thought. The same is true of Nietzsche. To fend off charges of
proto-fascism, a Nietzsche was manufactured who attacked Christianity but somehow left intact what to him were its nauseating
successors: the Enlightenment, liberalism, socialism, and the humanitarianism common to all three. In the very process of redemption, Nietzsche and Rousseau were lost, shorn of all that
made them great and dangerous. If Machiavelli has suffered from

a similar process of well-intended revisionism, the most fundamental discoveries concerning his meaning and significance may
have yet to be made.

At the center of contemporary discussion among students of
Machiavelli stands the notion of republican political thought.
Puzzlement over the relationship of *The Prince* to the *Discourses*,
long regarded as possibly the most vexing problem of Machiavelli
interpretation,[1] has been resolved by the suggestion that the
monarchical and "Machiavellian" means of *The Prince* have as their
mission the achievement of the republican ends of the *Discourses*.
In no uncertain terms the Machiavelli of the *Discourses* warns the
prince that to wield power for personal ends is to consign his
royal self to the torment of immortal shame in the works of
historians, whereas to build or restore a republican order that will
live on after him is to assure his name immortal glory: infamy
awaits the prince who uses bad for the sake of the bad, fame
awaits the prince who uses bad for the sake of the good.[2] Further
evidence for this interpretation may be found in the *Discourse on
Remodeling the Government of Florence*, an essay addressed to the
Medici and outlining a scheme whereby they could restore the
republic, secure the position of their family and friends as prominent citizens, and attain everlasting glory for overseeing the
withering away of the prince.[3]

With Machiavelli as with other thinkers who have provoked
centuries of controversy, the leading interpretation of today is
usually not without its precursors of yesterday. That the Elizabethan image of a satanic Machiavelli[4] has finally been laid to
rest is largely due to the revival of the Machiavelli of Harrington,
Sidney, Milton, and the English Republicans, the Machiavelli
of the republican *Discourses*. Studies of the transmission of republican ideology from Renaissance Italy to Harringtonian England to the American founding fathers have flourished in recent
times, and the central figure of each such study is inevitably
Machiavelli.[5] As the increasingly recognized and applauded hero

of the republican tradition, Machiavelli's visage has progressively lost its shadowy hue until, at last, a Machiavelli has emerged who is so respectable that the distinguished historian Garrett Mattingly could bluntly assert "Machiavelli . . . was not . . . Machiavellian."[6]

One theme in Harrington's understanding of Machiavelli the republican is consistently overlooked in contemporary scholarship, the theme of empire. When Harrington declared, "the first of these [European] nations that recovers the health of ancient prudence shall assuredly govern the world,"[7] he was not playing the renegade of republican thought; far from it, he was merely repeating Machiavelli's insistence that republics and conquest go hand in hand. Obviously, then, it is not enough to bridge the gap between *The Prince* and the *Discourses* or to point to Machiavelli's republican progeny in order to make a case for an un-Machiavellian Machiavelli. At this point the standard interpretation of Machiavelli ends when it is precisely at this point that it should begin. Why did Machiavelli favor republics over monarchies? If the answer may be phrased in terms of liberty, it may equally well be phrased in terms of power, for his constant principle is that the greatest triumphs of power politics are the monopoly of free, republican communities. The standard scholarly interpretation of Machiavelli is therefore revisionist; it deletes all that is most striking and shocking in his thought; it is Machiavelli expurgated.

Of all republics past and present to choose from, it was the world-conquering Roman republic that arrested Machiavelli's attention. The ancient model he admired and hoped to reproduce in modern times was none other than that singularly expansionary, singularly successful Roman republic whose way of life had been the fulfilment of *virtus*,* an ethic of glory, grandeur, and

* The Latin word *virtus* is in many respects interchangeable with the Greek *areté* and the Italian *virtù*. All three words are thoroughly pagan in their connotations of manliness, valor, and excellence. *Virtù* alone carries additional

heroism. While the individual excellence of the prince may be admirable, the greatest feats of heroism are collective and popular in nature. In its democratic form, *virtus* taps the potential greatness of the common man, his willingness to fight and die for his country, and can claim as its due meed of glory the conquest of all other republics. Machiavelli, then, is admittedly not the prophet of a life "beyond good and evil"—he is not an amoralist; rather, he is one possible fulfilment of pagan morality—but none the less frightening for that.

By no means is imperialism an obscure or occasional topic in Machiavelli's writings. On the contrary, it is a central theme running throughout all his works, from beginning to end. The *Discorsi* deal with the successful empire-building of the Romans, the *Istorie Fiorentine* with the failed empire-building of the Florentines; the "new prince" of *Il Principe* is frequently an old prince in a foreign land, Louis XII of France, whose blundering efforts to annex a chunk of Italy are criticized and superior methods suggested. Alternatively, the methods employed by Cesare Borgia to carve out an Italian empire are praised in *Il Principe* as models worthy of imitation.[8] Not even in his poetry can Machiavelli forget the question of empire: *L'Asino, I Decennali, Dell'Ambizione*, and *Di Fortuna* all bear directly on war and conquest. It is not for want of persistence on Machiavelli's part that scholars have missed the significance of imperialism in his thought.

Nor is the problem a dearth of quality in the secondary literature. Many of the finest minds among contemporary scholars have made contributions to our appreciation of Machiavelli, so much so that bibliographies of Machiavelli studies read like a who's who of contemporary philosophers, political theorists, and intellectual historians. And their findings to date have frequently been remarkable: excellent studies of Machiavelli's vocabulary,[9] of its roots in the vocabulary of the governing circles of his day,[10]

---

associations of Christian virtue. In consequence, a central question of Machiavelli studies asks whether he used this term in its pagan or its Christian significations.

of his biography,[11] and of the use and abuse of his name through the centuries[12] have been placed at our disposal. How, then, are we to explain the whys, the ways, and the means of revisionism? How has his meaning been misconstrued even as the secondary literature has made great strides forward in every other endeavor?

In the case of the philosophers and political theorists an answer is not difficult to come by. Benedetto Croce[13] for the liberals and Maurice Merleau-Ponty[14] for the socialists have been eager to prove that the heirs of the Enlightenment can face up to the harsh realities of power politics. Accordingly theirs is a Machiavelli torn, divided, and tortured by the necessity of doing evil for the sake of the good; to them Machiavelli is that rare man, strong enough to admit that no one can be innocent, that refuge is available to none, not even to those who withdraw from politics or ignore it, inaction itself being action. No one can call himself a humanist and mean it unless he has dirtied his hands politically, for ends are nothing without means. Humanism entails political action, but politics, instead of being humanistic, answers to its own logic, follows its own amoral rules, and judges events according to its own vicious standard of success or failure.

Two eyes on the twentieth century are one too many when writing on a figure of the Renaissance. For all their insight into the dilemmas of liberals and socialists, Croce and Merleau-Ponty show little or none into Machiavelli. They may suffer from *Angst*, he did not. For them the truths of power are terrible; for him they were exciting. As a corrective to such misunderstandings stemming from false modernization, Friedrich Meinecke[15] and Sir Isaiah Berlin,[16] in their different ways, have pointed out that for the Florentine secretary pagan values were one thing, Christian values another; to the former he gave himself heart and soul, joyfully and without misgivings, and hence Machiavelli never had to suspend cherished Christian ethics in order to serve the political order.

The arguments of Meinecke and Berlin are incisive and mark

a clear advance in Machiavelli studies, yet their correctives beg a new round of corrections. Machiavelli's paganism is not the "naive,"[17] innocent, rosy-cheeked and un-self-conscious phenomenon Meinecke would have us believe it is; nor is it necessary to wait, as Berlin implies, for the unfolding of Machiavelli's fame and fortune among the Christian and/or Enlightened thinkers of post-Renaissance times before we encounter the protest that his thought is devastating. Machiavelli's sting has not only been felt by the Christians, *philosophes*, liberals, and socialists of a later age who despise the choice he forced between the community and mankind, power and humanitarianism, virtue and goodness. It was felt within the Renaissance itself and by spirits kindred to his. None other than Francesco Guicciardini, the friend Machiavelli "loved" hardly less than his native city,[18] accused him of being "always extremely partial to extraordinary and violent methods."[19] Hatred of the Catholic church, love of the Florentine republic, an unsqueamish political vocabulary of power and domination, and an admiration of Latin letters closely unite Machiavelli and Guicciardini; yet Machiavelli was sometimes more than his friend could bear. Neither Florentine diplomat-author was a "Christian humanist" in the fashion of Erasmus, More, and the Northern Renaissance; neither was a humanist who was also a Christian in the fashion of the Italian Renaissance; both were genuine pagans, but to Guicciardini, it seems, Machiavelli was an exceptionally disturbing writer. Sir Isaiah Berlin's contrast of pagan versus Christian is inadequate, failing to discriminate, for example, between the contemplative and militarily defensive republic of Plato, which left no impression on Machiavelli, and the activistic and marching republic of Livy, which aroused Machiavelli to commentary.

Why historians have been no more effective than philosophers and political theorists in weeding revisionism out of the literature on Machiavelli is not immediately obvious. On the face of it, all has been going well. Studies of the Italian Renaissance have highlighted the birth and growth of republican ideology, so that we can now view Machiavelli in the cultural context that nourished him. At long last Burckhardt's coupling of humanistic studies with the courts of tyrants[20] has been broken. A humanism that was republican and civic, as Hans Baron, Eugenio Garin, and others have shown,[21] competed vigorously with the humanism that consorted with despots. Around 1400, argues Baron, a "civic humanism" emerged when those intellectuals who studied ancient languages and art forms began to revive ancient political ideals in response to the life and death struggle of the Florentine republic with the tyrant of Milan. Provoked by political crisis, classicism became politicized, patriotic, and republican, and exerted its new-found fervor through reworking the symbols common to the educated. Under the sponsorship of the civic humanists Cicero was restored to his position, lost during the Middle Ages, of citizen and advocate of the *vita activa*;* and Brutus, slayer of Caesar, was rescued from the jaws of Satan, where Dante had placed him, his vacated spot being offered to Caesar, murderer of the republic. At the end of this line of development, more than a century removed from its inception,[22] and standing as its chief beneficiary and culminating point, is Niccolò Machiavelli.

So far as Machiavelli is concerned, Baron's thesis errs by omission; it accounts for intellectual continuity from Leonardo Bruni in the early quattrocento to Machiavelli a century later but says nothing about discontinuity—the differences between Machiavelli and his forebears, which on questions of foreign affairs are especially radical. Juxtaposition of Baron's account of the years 1400 to 1450 with Machiavelli's rendering of that same half-century in his *Florentine History* reveals a great deal. With skill and formidable erudition Baron shows how, in the face of repeated threats from the Visconti, the humanists of Florence united with

---

* The "active life," the life of politics and public affairs, contrasts with the "contemplative life," the *vita contemplativa*. During medieval times, when the contemplative ideal was in vogue, Cicero was misunderstood as a pure sage.

their counterparts in Venice, each republican intelligentsia sounding the phrases of liberty and carrying this theme from the domestic to the interstate realm: the "free peoples" of Italy, a kind
of brotherhood of republics, became a centerpiece of political
rhetoric.[23] Machiavelli, however, sees the same period in an altogether different light. In his account the early quattrocento was
a period of politics-as-usual in which republic confronted republic
fully as often as republic confronted monarchy.[24] What little pride
he takes in the conflict with Milan is local pride, reserved for the
efforts of Florence.[25] And when we finally come upon a passage
in which Machiavelli has Florentines exhorting Venetians to take
up arms in a common republican venture, the Florentines in
question are exiles and very bad citizens. All their eloquence is
disloyal, aimed at fostering foreign intervention in the politics
of their *patria*.[26]

The gap between Baron and Machiavelli widens to a chasm as
we move from specifics to general principles of foreign policy.
To Baron "tyranny was by its nature a dynamic, expansionist
. . . factor in inter-state relations."[27] To Machiavelli, on the other
hand, tyrannies are stagnant and republics aggrandizing.

> As soon as a tyranny is established over a free community
> . . . it no longer goes forward and no longer increases in
> power or in riches; but in most instances, in fact always, it
> goes backward.[28]

With republics it is just the opposite.

> We see that cities where the people are in control grow
> enormously in a very short time, and much more than those
> that have always been under a prince, as Rome did after she
> expelled the kings and Athens did after she freed herself
> from Pisistratus.[29]

In sum, Baron would salvage as much as possible of Sismondi's
simple contrast of liberty with tyranny,[30] while Machiavelli would

make Sismondi* impossible. During the very years when Baron has the republics of Italy proclaiming their solidarity, Machiavelli has the Florentines taking advantage of the debilitation caused by temporary tyranny in Lucca to conquer that republic.[31]

When something fundamental is amiss in the secondary literature, a return to the first principles of interpretation is mandatory: the notion of "civic humanism" must be reconsidered. Contemporary scholarship begins by underscoring the vast distance between Renaissance humanism and the humanism of today; it ends by ignoring that distance. Strictly speaking a Florentine "humanist" could not possibly be an advocate of "humanism," since the latter word was invented by historians of the nineteenth century and then anachronistically read into an era dead and buried for half a millennium.[32] So we initially hear. Soon, however, we are told that the gap between the Renaissance and our age is not so great after all, that the *studia humanitatis*—the revival of classical grammar, poetry, rhetoric, history and ethics—"left a heritage that remained effective at least down to the end of the eighteenth century."[33] So far the footing is still solid, but it becomes unreliable when scholars take a leap into the thin air of faith with the supposition of a teleological development from Renaissance to contemporary humanism. Usually the assumption of a *telos*-at-work is covert but occasionally it dares come out into the open, as in Neal Wood's essay on "Machiavelli's Humanism of Action."[34] After distinguishing between the "cultural humanism" of the Renaissance and the "secular humanism" of today, Wood proceeds deliberately to conflate the two humanisms, the first being regarded as a preparation for the second, and Machiavelli as having a stake in both. Before long his argument becomes a repeat performance of Merleau-Ponty's effort at marrying Machiavellian insights to enlightened modern thought. Unfortunately, what was earlier said of Merleau-Ponty must now be

* Simonde de Sismondi was author of a multi-volume *Histoire des Républiques Italiennes du Moyen Âge*, which began to appear in 1807.

said of Wood: that however desirable it may be for the Enlightenment to learn tough-mindedness, a Machiavelli forcing himself to rise above tender-mindedness is not Machiavelli.

There is, of course, no reason why a link cannot be drawn between the Renaissance and the Enlightenment. The *philosophes* themselves did so in their search for earlier enlightenments. Less self-servingly, modern scholars have noted that an education in the classics and a belief in the *vita activa* form a genuine affinity between the two periods. Without too much stretching of the facts one can say that the humanitarianism of Voltaire drew its inspiration from the *humanitas** of Cicero, with the Renaissance acting as go-between. But though the humanistic studies of the Renaissance may contain the seeds of Enlightenment, they also contain the seeds of one of its most formidable enemies, the ideal of glory which is usually blood-stained. Diderot's project of a theatre of everyday life, the *drame bourgeois*, had very little to do with the much-discussed "rise of the bourgeoisie"; it had a great deal to do with the displacement of Corneille, Racine, and the drama of glory which had held sway in the French classical theatre.

Happily for the *philosophes*, they had only to contend with the heroic ethic in its monarchical guise. Its republican expressions were far more frightening, as can be observed in the contrast of Machiavelli with Castiglione. Writing for the court of Urbino at the same time Machiavelli was composing his works for the republic of Florence, Castiglione would have his ideal courtier seek fame through grace, charm, dress, and style—pacific activities all, for his project of making his self a work of art[35] could only be hindered by militarism. Castiglione disdains those princes who despoil neighboring peoples "and call it virtue [*virtù*]." Princes, he adds, "ought not to make their people warlike out of a desire to dominate, but in order to defend themselves."[36] Machiavelli, by contrast, yearns for the good fight, the fight that is only good

---

* Cicero gave a great many meanings to *humanitas*, one of which was reasonably close to our notion of humanitarianism.

provided its scope is great and its violence substantial. For the mollifying effect of Christianity on the law of nations, he feels nothing but contempt.

> Our way of living, as a result of the Christian religion, does not impose the same necessity for defending ourselves as antiquity did. Then men overcome in war were killed or kept in perpetual slavery . . . ; conquered cities were either laid waste or the inhabitants driven out, their goods taken from them and they themselves sent wandering through the world. . . . Today this fear for the most part has disappeared; of the conquered, few are killed; no one is long held a prisoner because captives are easily freed. Cities, even though they have rebelled many times, are not destroyed.[37]

"Wars they cannot be called," he bitterly complains, "in which men are not killed, cities are not sacked, princedoms are not destroyed."[38]

It would be mistaken to interpret Machiavelli's position as a foreign "form" imposed upon the reluctant native "matter" of civic humanism. Rather might his thought be properly regarded as a finale evoking one of the potentials always present in the humanist tradition. From civic humanism to power politics was a path previously trod by Leonardo Bruni in the early Renaissance, if less vigorously than by Machiavelli near its end. In certain passages Bruni is Baron's man, championing the cause of all free peoples against the king of Naples and the tyrant of Milan, or warning that just as the Etruscans fell to the Romans for want of solidarity among republics, so the Florentines and Venetians may meet their demise should they fail to forge a common front. This same Bruni then turns around and writes his *Historiarum Florentini Populi* without once questioning the propriety of a Florentine empire incorporating all of republic-breeding Tuscany.[39] "Greatness" in the terminology of Bruni was already becoming what it was later to be in Machiavelli's *Istorie Fiorentine*: the list of cities once free and now subject to the yoke of Florence.[40]

The theme of Florentine greatness had been evoked long before the coming of Bruni and humanist historiography in the chronicle of Giovanni Villani, begun shortly after 1300. Imperfectly educated in the Greek and Roman classics, medieval in his most fundamental beliefs, forever in danger of drowning in his knowledge of facts, the simple burgher Giovanni Villani could nevertheless rise to sublime heights when contemplating the *grandezza* (grandeur) of his commune: "Considering that our city of Florence, daughter and creature of Rome, was in its ascent and about to accomplish great things, while Rome was in decline, I judged it proper to record . . . all the doings and undertakings of Florence."[41] Still, there is all the difference of two worlds between Villani's and Bruni's respective conceptions of grandeur, and an appreciation of what separates them on this score is a promising means for proving that the advent of humanism marked a triumph of "Machiavellism" as well as of "idealism." When Villani, swelling with local pride, interrupts his narrative to claim for Florence the fame that is her due, the result is not, as with those later cosmopolitans, the humanists, a list of conquests. Instead his list includes the number of workshops, bakers, apothecaries, lawyers, doctors, and bankers; the figures on the amount of wine, meat, and flour produced; plus statistics on population and public finance.[42] None of the entries in his ledger is very dramatic, all are literally bourgeois, but they have the considerable advantage of not suggesting that the freedom of Florence is bought at the price of the unfreedom of other republics.

By an inexorable dynamic, the humanists of Baron's chosen period, for all their talk about the ideal and ethically best form of government, were driven to build the fortress of power politics that Machiavelli was eventually to command. In common with the ideologues of later revolutionary eras, they magnified the significance of conflict through a process of abstraction.[43] "During the Milano-Venetian War of 1451 and 1452, between Francesco Sforza and Jacopo Piccinino," notes Jacob Burckhardt,

> the headquarters of the latter were attended by the scholar Gian Antonio Porcello dei Pandoni, commissioned by Alfonso of Naples to write a report of the campaign. It is written . . . in the style of the humanistic bombast of the day. . . . Since for the past hundred years it had been seriously disputed whether Scipio Africanus or Hannibal was the greater, Piccinino through the whole book must needs be called Scipio and Sforza Hannibal.[44]

Similarly, at the beginnings of his *History of Florence* Leonardo Bruni compares the Florentine conquest of Pisa to Rome's victory over Carthage. Thus both humanists take a limited conflict and represent it with parallels to what every educated man regarded as the most total war ever fought, the struggle to the finish between the two most powerful republics of antiquity.

Sometimes intellectuals abstract excessively because they are out of contact with their society. Such is not the case with the Renaissance humanists. Often they held public posts, whether as secretaries or chancellors of cities, so it cannot be said they were literary or academic intellectuals and nothing more. Moreover, the humanists were actively concerned to adjust their thought to the needs of the established social order, as may be observed in their willingness to question Cicero's strictures against traders. Praise of work, Praise of the burgher as citizen, were themes frequently on their lips.[45] The simple truth is that the humanists abstracted because it was their self-imposed professional duty to do so. Given their self-conception as an intellectual elite founded upon expertise in oratory and rhetoric, they had to exaggerate.[46] And when their exaggerations were applied to politics, political rhetoric became extreme.

Through abstraction the humanists had become ideologues; what made matters worse was that the content of their ideology crystallized into an ideal of glory which by its very nature was aggrandizing. For Giovanni Villani there could be too many wars: he speaks out against the rulers of Florence when they begin to overburden their citizens and to shock Christian conscience.

> Oh Florentine Signori, what a bad and evil measure it is to increase the revenues of the commune with the substance and poverty of the citizens through imposed taxes, in order to finance insane projects! . . . Temper, most beloved, inordinate desires; thereby you will please God and not overburden an innocent people.[47]

Bruni, on the other hand, is clearly flirting with a glorification of war. His purpose in writing history is the classical one of conferring immortality on great deeds and heroic actions. Hence the history of the Florentines is for Bruni what the history of Rome had been for Livy: an unending succession of battles, wars, and conquests. In writing history, Bruni's mission is to show how the people of Florence "shook all Italy from the Alps to Apulia with the sound of Florentine arms."[48]

That Professor Baron relies so heavily upon Gregorio Dati in sustaining his thesis is telling. This heir to the tradition of the medieval chronicle, a witness to the events of 1380 to 1406, is treated by Baron as a prehumanist, a figure of transition from the chronicle to humanist historiography, whose record of the Florentine republic's heroic stand against the aggrandizing tyrant of Milan foreshadows Bruni's later history of the same period. Once he has settled upon Dati, Baron has no trouble adducing quotations to his liking. "The Florentines," wrote Dati, "live on peace and profit by it as the bee profits by the honey of flowers." Of the Florentines it may be said that "their nature is made for peace, and that war is something forced upon them"—thus reads Dati's *Istoria*.[49] Where Baron goes wrong is in construing Dati's chronicle as an anticipation of Bruni rather than a continuation of Villani—wrong because the pacific emphasis in the writing of

Dati owes fundamentally to what is redolent of the old way of thinking. Villani, the old-fashioned chronicler, had been the nay-sayer to war; the newfangled humanist Bruni, by contrast, was sometimes to be the dramatist of violence between states. As unsophisticated burghers, Villani and Dati knew full well that an imbalance between revenues and expenses is usually the out-come of prolonged wars, to which Dati adds a eulogy of decent, peaceful, middle-class citizens and a tirade against the ambition of tyrants. Calculations of economic profit and loss set limitations on war, unlike the humanistic pursuit of *gloria* (glory), which constantly called out for more.

A scholar of Professor Baron's erudition and brilliance cannot be simply mistaken. Much must be conceded to him: his evidence for the existence of a generation and more of humanists cham-pioning the cause of republican peace against monarchical aggres-sion is powerful, indeed. Missing, however, in his analysis is an appreciation of the extent to which the humanists' goal of peace was the result of their admission of the trader—mercilessly cas-tigated by Aristotle and Cicero—to the rank of citizen in repub-lican theory. By this adjustment in Greek and Roman political thought the humanists were, of course, merely admitting the facts of life (or perhaps the facts of patronage) in the modern city-state of traders as opposed to the ancient city-state of warriors.[50] Yet their revision of classical norms, however pragmatic, was noteworthy for giving the humanists something in common with the nonhumanists Villani and Dati, namely, an economic anchor which prevented the theorized ship of state from becoming an idealized warship.[51] So long as humanistic thought bore even a naive relationship to economic concerns, republican political thought was not predatory; its passion for glory and grandeur was kept under control.

Never, however, did the humanists develop a theory of eco-nomics, and such little economic knowledge as they had at their disposal was automatically purged from consciousness as soon as they set about writing history. It is Dati and not Bruni, as Professor Baron admits,[52] who ferreted out the economic reasons for the failure of Giangaleazzo to vanquish Florence. A burgher must needs think about revenues and expenses, but a humanist is forced by the conventions of his historical art to neglect them. In humanistic historiography nothing mattered except those factors to which Livy had been attentive, and if economics was not one of them, so much the worse for economics. To battles he had been attentive, and to the glory or shame that accompanies them, hence military affairs and grandeur became the themes that preoccupied Florentine humanist historiography. It was these histories, moreover, of all the humanist writings of Bruni's period, that were cited time and again by the humanists of later generations, including Machiavelli.[53] Consequently, by the time we get to Machiavelli's *Florentine History*, the prevailing representation of the past had long evolved into something significantly Machiavellian. Fully a century earlier humanists had deleted the saving grace of economic calculation from historiography, leaving "greatness" with no other competitor than Bruni's feeling for all republics endangered by the Milanese tyrant. Machiavelli had only to rewrite the record of the Milano-Florentine conflict as a story of politics-as-usual in order to render history thoroughly Machiavellian. At last *gloria* stood alone, or rather it took as its companion the *forza* (force) which had always been its blood brother.

Perfectly consistent with Machiavelli's general viewpoint is one other revision he brought to bear upon the usual humanistic account of the wars of Florence with Milan. Unlike his predecessors, Machiavelli was eager to call attention to the importance of money in the struggle against the tyrant of Milan,[54] because the Florentine substitution of coins for citizen-soldiers was all the evidence he needed to contrast the heroic wars of ancient Rome with the disappointingly unheroic wars of modern Florence.

Possibly then the cinquecento "prophets of force" of whom

Felix Gilbert[55] speaks—the youthful generation of the wellborn among Machiavelli's contemporaries—are the natural and legitimate offspring of the rising generation of quattrocento idealists portrayed by Hans Baron. Separated by a hundred years, the two generations nevertheless shared the ideology of "civic humanism," with the difference that the latter group disdained the concessions their forebears had made to commerce in nonhistorical writings. It is not likely that this final and absolute deletion of the man of business[56] is unassociated with the emergence, in their thought, of the man of force.[57] When Professor Baron applauds the waning of a Florentine foreign policy based on "down-to-earth [economic] realism" and the upsurge of a policy rooted in the idealism of civic humanism,[58] he may be inadvertently applauding the rise of power politics.

Marxist historians of ideas, believing humanism has yet to exist, are not tempted to idealize the past, and obviously they are not about to pass lightly over economics. But they, too, have confused the issues. All too frequently Marx's notion of compulsive acquisitiveness, worked out to explain the competitive dynamics of mature capitalism, is read back into early modern Europe, where it quickly becomes the reason why this or that "advanced" intellectual living in a postfeudal age posited a *libido dominandi* (lust for power) as the driving force of human endeavor.[59] A more unhistorical view than this is difficult to imagine, for acquisitiveness was limited, glory unlimited in the conceptualizations of preindustrial Europe, and it was the anti-economic notion of glory espoused by the most advanced intellectuals, the humanists, that was responsible for the prevalence of a *libido dominandi* in Renaissance thought. Significantly, the rise of economic theory in a later era had as one of its goals the taming of what had always been insatiable, the heroic ethic championed by the humanists.[60]

Alfred von Martin is one scholar of a sometime Marxist persuasion who, for all his stress on the supposedly capitalistic aspect of the Renaissance, nevertheless recognizes Machiavelli's passion for glory; but only insofar as it provides an early example of a bourgeois civilization which, grown decadent, produced an ideologist calling for catharsis in the form of a "Third Reich."[61] Against this proto-fascist Machiavelli of the 1930s, Sheldon Wolin's discernment of an "economy of violence"[62] in the writings of the Florentine secretary is most welcome. Not violence for the sake of violence but violence as a means to an end, and the more economical the means the better, is Machiavelli's message, Wolin argues. Ironically Wolin's essay, while proper as a corrective, might better be applied to Villani, who quite literally believed that the economy placed limitations on violence.

Sir Herbert Butterfield is perhaps closer to the mark with his suggestion that the "swiftness and niceness" of Machiavelli's adjustment of means to end has about it "a sort of poetry and something like an aesthetic thrill."[63] Only we must add to Butterfield that the norm of beautiful action is itself derived from the ideal of glory, and in Castiglione no less than in his Florentine contemporary, but in Machiavelli alone do beauty and efficiency meet as one instead of being parceled out as values appropriate to the aristocracy and bourgeoisie, respectively. Even, or perhaps especially, on the field of battle the ideal courtier of Castiglione cares not for effectiveness.

> Whenever the courtier chances to be engaged in a skirmish or an action or a battle in the field, or the like, he should discreetly withdraw from the crowd, and do the outstanding and daring things that he has to do in as small a company as possible and in the sight of all the noblest and most respected men in the army, and especially in the presence of and, if possible, before the very eyes of his king.[64]

By contrast, the citizen-soldier of Machiavelli is part of a system of disciplined, organized fighting, and knows that to withdraw from his fellows in a search for individual glory is despicable vainglory, the kind that Roman leaders mercilessly punished.[65] True glory is collective, organized, effective, and in its fulfilment is a work of art and a thing of beauty.[66]

So far I have argued that the concept of "civic humanism," as formulated by contemporary scholars, errs in de-emphasizing or even expurgating the vital notions of *grandezza* and *gloria* from the republican tradition. These arguments must now be complemented by the claim that the political significance of speech and rhetoric has been overemphasized. Among political philosophers, Hannah Arendt has offered an exceptionally influential interpretation of classical ideals in which public speech figures as the essence of the *vita activa*.[67] For their part, contemporary historians in great and increasing numbers have insisted that the republican tradition is incomprehensible without rhetoric.[68] My contrary contention is that one of the essential meanings of republican thought will never be recovered unless speech and rhetoric first suffer a certain demotion in contemporary scholarship.

On a careful look it may well be less Livy or Machiavelli centuries ago than Hannah Arendt in our own day who sees in speech an end in itself or, better yet, an activity that abolishes the distinction between means and ends. As she views politics, the public realm was at the time of the polis and should be today the ultimate stage on which a human actor can appear and be applauded for a performance in gestures and words. Choices, decisions, and policies are consequently far less important to her than the formal debates preceding them. Power, violence, force— all these are merely the props holding the public stage together; they are pre- or extra-political. Significantly, at no point does Arendt make a serious effort to prove that her vision of the ancient city-state has about it anything of historical reality. Hers, rather, is the city-state as it should have been if it wanted to reject the modern world of men-as-animals who have traded in the *vita activa* for the creature comforts of a consumer's society.

Arendt's downgrading of power and upgrading of speech as

the defining characteristic of politics would have baffled Gian-michele Bruto, a Venetian humanist of the sixteenth century. "We are educated," he insisted, "not by the inactive and barren philosopher, but by Scipio in arms; not by the schools of Athens, but in the Spanish camps. We are educated not by speeches but by deeds and examples."[69] While Hannah Arendt sees great deeds as speeches, Gianmichele Bruto obviously feels cheated when action stops at words and does not proceed to military deeds. How could he feel otherwise? Speeches in Livy's history effectively dramatize the issues of domestic or foreign politics, but there is little to suggest that words have great value in and of themselves. The position of the Roman historians was well stated by Sallust, who proudly noted that in Rome "the best citizen preferred action to words, and thought that his own brave deeds should be lauded by others rather than that theirs should be recounted by him."[70]

It is of course true that speech had been cited by Stoic phi-losophers as evidence of a power to reason distinguishing humans from animals, and that the Stoic position stood in contradiction to the Epicurean belief that human speech was simply a higher development of the sounds natural to animals.[71] Machiavelli, however, shows not the slightest concern for this philosophical debate between the Stoics and the Epicureans. It is true too that Livy and the Roman historians owed something to Stoic thought. Yet Livy did not regard speech as the highest expression of po-litical manhood, and indeed thought the Greek addiction to words a proof of their lack of *virtus*. "This was the Athenians' war against Philip, a war of words, written or spoken; for that is where their only strength lies."[72] Typically, Machiavelli quotes with hearty approval the words Livy puts in the mouth of a Roman general, about to lead his troops into glorious battle: "My deeds, not my words, soldiers, I would have you follow."[73] There is in fact only one place in his writings where Machiavelli bothers to discuss oratory, and that is in the *Art of War* in a passage noting its usefulness to a general intent upon controlling the spirits of his men.[74] Speech is instrumental or, failing that, is mere words.

In Machiavelli's thought speech is, if anything, even less important than in Livy's. All the real decisions of politics, in his view, are made behind closed doors and with voice lowered lest the many should overhear the discussions of the few. For the great majority of the citizens, in fact for all but the "forty or fifty"[75] who hold positions of authority in republics, political education is military training and nothing more. Michael Walzer cannot be thinking of the republicanism of Machiavelli when he writes that "whispering is to royal courts what public speaking is to democratic assemblies";[76] for Machiavelli's ideal city, however much it belongs to the populace, is a republic of whispers.

Arendt's conclusions are the opposite of Machiavelli's because her starting point and his are radically different. She, sounding strangely like a Stoic arguing against Epicureans, is out to discover a realm unshared by man with animal, an activity distinctively human and therefore uniquely worthwhile. Labor, fabrication, and force being common to man and animal, they do not satisfy her quest—only public speech does. Contrariwise, exactly that which man shares with animals fascinates Machiavelli. Political animals are centaurs, half man, half beast, the human half characterized by law, the bestial by force.[77] Even without law, force can sometimes succeed, and with law force is still essential, so the bestial in man is primary, and its use, effective or ineffective, constitutes the criterion upon which fame should be allotted.

PARADOXICALLY, even though the republican commitments of Machiavelli have been stressed in recent research, *The Prince* is his best understood work. The interpretive literature on *The Prince* is as satisfying as that on the *Discourses* is unsatisfying, and provides a clue to the methodology needed to recover the meaning and significance of the republican Machiavelli.

Decades ago Allan Gilbert[78] broke with the usual treatment of *The Prince* in which an investigator troubled by a problem of recent history, be it fascism, the Soviet purge trials of the 1930s, or some other pressing concern, rifled through the pages of Machiavelli's classic, isolating passages praiseworthy for their seeming modernity. As atonement for the sins of unhistorical interpretation, Gilbert wrote a book proving *The Prince* had been written by a thousand authors before Machiavelli, beginning in the Hellenistic age, working through the Middle Ages, and moving on to the Renaissance and Machiavelli, whose pamphlet is simply the most famous example of treatises written in the venerable genre of works "on princely rule."

Gilbert's scholarship is impeccable and his contribution to Machiavelli studies undeniable. Were it not for his keen desire to save Machiavelli from his popular and pejorative reputation, Gilbert might have accomplished a great deal more, however. So eager is Gilbert to whitewash Machiavelli that he nearly loses him in a glut of continuity with the Christian Middle Ages. *The Prince* becomes, as the subtitle of Gilbert's book announces, "a typical book *de Regimine Principum*." In the closing pages of *Machiavelli's Prince and Its Forerunners*, Gilbert does acknowledge that Machiavelli used a traditional art form to say new things; yet it never occurs to him that Machiavelli might have written in an established Christian genre for purposes of subversion, and that such is his originality.

Felix Gilbert's "The Humanist Concept of the Prince and *The Prince* of Machiavelli"[79] is strong precisely where Allan Gilbert is weak. Not only does Felix Gilbert contrast the prince of the Italian humanists with the prince of medieval theologians, but he effectively plays off Machiavelli's prince against both of his predecessors, Christian and humanist. A Machiavelli who is appropriately shocking and novel is the result. The humanists prepared the way for Machiavelli, argues Gilbert, when they pictured a good prince whose reward was fame in this world rather than a blessed place of retirement in the world to come. Again, the humanistic "mirror of princes" made Machiavelli possible by proclaiming the utility, along with the goodness, of liberality, clemency, fidelity, and all the other virtues typically catalogued chapter by chapter in works of this kind. Such was enough to open the door to Machiavelli's claim that virtue is not always useful, evil sometimes is, so that the ideal prince must learn "how not to be good"[80]—his goodness is being good at politics, his *virtù* is virtuosity in the political arts. Thus in one fell swoop the extreme moralism of both the humanists and their theological predecessors was stood on its head by a self-conscious *provocateur*. From Allan Gilbert's book to Felix Gilbert's articles, we finally arrive at J. R. Hale's one-sentence summary: "Because of its formal resemblance to old manuals *Of Princely Government*, Machiavelli's *Prince* was like a bomb in a prayerbook."[81]

What has been done for *The Prince* must now be done for the republican writings of Machiavelli: these, too, must be restored to their intellectual context, which for the *Discourses, Art of War*, and *Florentine History* is classical political thought, Roman in particular. To some extent, of course, such an undertaking has been attempted in the secondary literature; but with results far less impressive than those secured for *The Prince*. Neither the continuity nor the discontinuity of Machiavelli's republican treatises with their classical forerunners has been adequately comprehended. For if, as we have argued, a Machiavellian potentiality always inhered in the republican tradition, the secondary literature errs in dwelling solely on the "idealism" of civic humanism and in contrasting it with the so-called "realism" of Machiavelli. Much of Machiavelli's work had necessarily been done for him by his predecessors because the values of grandeur, greatness, and glory had always implied a vision of interstate relations wherein restraint is anomalous and must be explained, while expansion is normal and may be taken for granted. This is Machiavelli's most significant link with those who preceded him, and about this the secondary literature is silent.

Likewise Machiavelli's break with his republican ancestors has been inadequately delineated. After thoroughly immersing Machiavelli in the tradition of civic humanism, Quentin Skinner[82] stops for a moment in his book on "the foundations of modern political thought" and asks what makes Machiavelli different. That he devalued Christianity and believed social conflict could be functional are Skinner's unobjectionable but less than decisive answers. Suddenly a mountain on the landscape of republican political theory has been reduced to a molehill, a slight protuberance on the plain of intellectual continuity. Yet all that is needed is a slight adjustment—the addition of the theme of empire—for Skinner's list to assume a totally different aspect, allowing Machiavelli the sayer of shocking and spectacular truths to come to the fore. Social conflict, to Machiavelli, is functional not merely because it sustains checks and balances assuring "liberty,"[83] but also because it fuels a machine of war, the Roman republic bent on "greatness."[84] No more effective way to buy off the populace could be found than for the senators to propose an unending succession of wars.[85] Republicanism is predatory, and especially so when untroubled by a Christian conscience—such is Machiavelli's striking claim.

That which is novel in Machiavelli and that which is old are one and the same: the empire demanded by the collective glory known as civic virtue. Forever calling out for more great deeds, glory had always been a thing insatiable; but before Machiavelli, republican theorists had settled for less than wars that would end all war as they eliminated every republic save their own. Bruni's imperialism quit after reaching the outer limits of Tuscany because he recalled the history of ancient Rome. That greatest of all republics had destroyed not just some, but all other republics, only to forfeit her own liberty to Caesar.[86] For Machiavelli, however, there was no turning back, no halfway measures were acceptable—it was all or nothing: "Since all human affairs are in motion and cannot remain fixed, they must needs rise up or sink down."[87] In his theory a republic was either rising or declining with the middle excluded, hence the Roman way of conquest was the only sensible course to follow.

Hans Baron repeatedly states that from the moment the study of the classics took a political turn, an "explosive"[88] force was planted in Western culture. The violence of that explosive charge has been consistently underrated by scholars, including Professor Baron, and equally underrated has been the shattering effect of the secondary explosion within the republican tradition triggered by Machiavelli. Because of its formal resemblance to the old moralistic writings "on republican rule," Machiavelli's *Discourses* was like a bomb in a moral treatise.

The interpretation of Machiavelli suggested in the present chapter and which will be further developed in the following chapters is not without its predecessors. Sir Herbert Butterfield once remarked that Machiavelli "did not admire ancient Rome because the Romans had a republic; he admired republican government because it was the form under which ancient Rome had achieved unexampled greatness and power."[89] Unfortunately, no other sentence in his book treats the subject of imperialism. More recently, J.G.A. Pocock has detected a "virtue . . . become cannibal" in the *Discourses*: "The truly subversive Machiavelli was not a counselor of tyrants, but a good citizen and patriot."[90] This is well but briefly said. The why and whither of republican empire are only hinted at, and soon all is forgotten and swallowed up in the sheer mass of Pocock's book, subtitled *Florentine Political Thought and the Atlantic Republican Tradition*. Neal Wood, after writing excellent essays demonstrating that for Machiavelli "the model of civic life is always military life,"[91] writes a culminating essay on "Machiavelli's Humanism of Action" which is an out-and-out return to the standard Machiavelli. Unthinkable thoughts on the meaning of Machiavelli, even when occasionally thought, yield all too readily to the powerful forces of scholarly revisionism.

The subversive message of Machiavelli is not hidden or mys-

terious.[92] Outspoken, irrepressible, and fearless, it is pagan to
the core and hinges on the recovery of the original meanings of
"glory"[93] and "virtue."[94] From the Italian words *virtù* and *gloria*,
Machiavelli worked his way back to the Latin *virtus* and *gloria*;
and he did so effortlessly, without steeping himself in the painstaking philological labors of the Renaissance. To him it was
intuitively obvious that *virtù* and *gloria* were not Christian, since
in his own Tuscan tongue *gloria* was synonymous with *grandezza*,
and *virtù* was coupled not with *vizio* (vice), as in the Italian of
today, itself a tribute to the victory of the Counter-Reformation,
but with *fortuna* (fortune), as in the ancient pagan authors.*

Machiavelli was equally adept at recovering the original meaning and full implications of *virtus*, taking as his unlikely ally in
this endeavor Cicero, the Stoic moralist from whom he normally
differed. Speech was the bond of society,[95] lust for war its nemesis[96]
in Cicero's fusion of republicanism with Stoicism. "Those who
say that one standard should be applied to fellow citizens but
another to foreigners, destroy the common society of the human
race,"[97] Cicero lamented. His conviction is the direct opposite
of that voiced in Machiavelli's idealized *Life of Castruccio Castracani*: "He was gracious to his friends, to his enemies terrible, just
with his subjects, not to be trusted by foreigners."[98] It is also
totally at odds with Machiavelli's understanding of the Roman
republic, a predator if ever there was one, and of republics in
general: "Of all hard slaveries, the hardest is that subjecting you
to a republic . . . because the purpose of a republic is to enfeeble
and weaken all other bodies in order to increase its own."[99] To
read Cicero, Roman foreign policy was the most just ever known;
to read Machiavelli, it was the most Machiavellian.

Yet on the meaning of *virtus* Machiavelli could, in effect, fling
back at Cicero the latter's own words, as stated in the *Tusculan*

* When, under Spanish auspices, the spirit of the Counter-Reformation took
hold in Italy shortly after Machiavelli's death, one of its representative acts was
the expurgation of the word *fortuna* from the text of Castiglione's *Book of the
Courtier*. Machiavelli's writings were placed on the Index of Forbidden Books.

Disputations: "It is from the word for man [*vir*] that the word *virtus* is derived."[100] By an exercise in simple logic, Machiavelli could arrive at virility and power as the defining qualities of the *vir virtutis*, the manly man. Shedding all traces of the Stoic domestication of *virtus* so as to revive its original connotations, Machiavelli consistently used "effeminate" as a pejorative adjective. Indecisive, fickle, and unarmed cities were "effeminate republics."[101] Nothing could be more unfortunate than the delicacy of modern warfare, and nothing was more sinful in the record of Christianity than its responsibility for turning men into women.

> Ancient religion . . . attributed blessedness only to men abounding in worldly glory, such as generals of armies and princes of states. Our religion has glorified humble and contemplative men rather than active ones. It has, then, set up as the greatest good humility, abjectness and contempt for human things; the other put it in grandeur of mind, in strength of body, and in all the other things apt to make men exceedingly vigorous.

In short, "the world has grown effeminate."[102]

Again and again, Machiavelli tells his reader he writes for and about young, aggressive men.[103] His attitude may be contrasted with Aristotle's, who believed youths should not be taught political science.[104] Not so asserts Machiavelli, for *fortuna* is a woman and yields to the audacious advances of young men willing to use force.[105]

The conquering prince is merely "human and ordinary":[106] to the conquering republic goes the glory, thanks to paganism, of bestial and extraordinary deeds.

> The pagans, greatly esteeming honor and believing it their greatest good, were fiercer [than the men of today] in their actions. This we infer from many of their institutions, beginning with the magnificence of their sacrifices, compared with the mildness of ours. . . . [Theirs were] full of blood

and ferocity in the slaughter of a multitude of animals; this terrible sight made the men resemble it. [107]

Without advantage of reading *Il Principe*, the pagan Romans knew they were centaurs, half man, half beast, and readily converted their bestiality into manliness and grandeur.

When Nietzsche restored *areté* and *virtus* to their original meanings, the result was exactly as he anticipated: a shock wave numbed and subsequently angered the humanitarian intellectuals of the nineteenth century. Much earlier, during the sixteenth century, Machiavelli had conducted a similar enterprise, salvaging the classical world from centuries of first Stoic and then Christian revisionism. Surely Machiavelli would not appreciate the efforts of twentieth-century intellectuals to redeem him through initiating a new round of revisionism and expurgation. It was as vital to him to shock the humanists of his day as it was to Nietzsche to shock the humanitarians of his day and ours.

Machiavelli, of course, was no Nietzschean, nor Nietzsche a Machiavellian. There is a distinction of the most profound significance between the will-to-power of the great community against other communities and the will-to-power of the great individual against the community. "How could there be a 'common good'! The term contradicts itself: whatever can be common always has little value."[108] Thus speaks Nietzsche, and it is unthinkable that the author of the *Discourses on Livy* should ever make a similar statement. Machiavelli incessantly speaks of the "common good,"[109] the well-being of the *patria*; and particularly admires heroic, uncommon acts performed in its behalf. Nietzsche looks backward to the Homeric hero and forward to the superman, each a law unto himself; Machiavelli looks backward to the Roman infantryman and forward to the Florentine infantryman, each a lover of the laws.[110]

—II—

THE REPUBLIC THAT WAS

HISTORY is the praise of Rome. With this statement Petrarch inaugurated the Italian Renaissance, and in Machiavelli's writings on the Roman republic, above all in his *Discourses on Livy*, that same intellectual "rebirth" came to a spectacular and shocking fulfilment. For Machiavelli was much more Machiavellian as a republican than as a monarchical author, and never more so than in his interpretation of republican Rome. When viewed through the lenses he ground, ancient Roman democracy was democracy on the march—its objective and achievement was world conquest. A democratic politics maximized Rome's power in that it allowed everyone to be armed; and since this enormous power was harnessed and led by the most astute and Machiavellian ruling class ever known, the Roman senators, it is apparent that Rome succeeded where others failed because she could hardly do otherwise. Truly the grandeur that was Rome shamed the moderns, and yet it beckoned, cajoled, and taunted them to imitation.

Wherever one turns in Machiavelli's writings, his remarkable Romans are present—present not only in the *Discourses on Livy*, but also in the *Art of War*, *The Prince*, the *Florentine History*, even in the familiar letters and poetry. Not for a moment could Machiavelli forget his Romans, who proclaimed themselves masters of the political and military arts and backed up their boasts by citing the grandeur and longevity of their empire, gloriously gained during the centuries of the republic and merely maintained during the subsequent centuries of inglorious court politics. All that was admirable in history was Roman and republican; all that remained of antique grandeur was the memory of the Roman republic and the hope that the study of Roman methods of governing and fighting might yet save the moderns from the misery of their histories. For the sake of the Florentines Machiavelli retold the story of the Romans, told so many times before, making it more edifying because more "Machiavellian," more instructive in the methods of power politics, of force and fraud, of the ways of the lion and the fox. Machiavelli's account of the Roman republic, particularly as given its most complete expression in the *Discourses on Livy*, is the foundation of all his thought.

REPUBLICS are superior to monarchies, and the people are superior to princes, Machiavelli maintains. Tested against the standard of longevity, republics are the unequivocal winners because it is impossible that a government is "going to last long if resting on the shoulders of only one man; but it is indeed lasting when it is left to the care of many, and when its maintenance rests on many."[1] No republic lasts forever,[2] but a well-constituted one will endure much longer than a monarchy, and for proof there is Sparta, which deferred the inevitable decline of all things human for the generous span of eight centuries.[3] The people, furthermore, have an ability to persevere in policies which is unknown among princes, as may be observed in the contrast of the Roman emperors with the populace of earlier Rome. While inconstancy was endemic and notorious in the behavior of the emperors, the populace, unbudging in its preferences, "was for four hundred years an enemy to the name of king, and a lover of the glory and the common good of its native city."[4]

Republics and peoples also have the advantage over monarchies and princes in matters of leadership. A good monarch is a rarity, two good monarchs in succession are almost unheard of, but "a succession of able rulers will always be present in every well-ordered republic":[5] meritorious versus hereditary succession making all the difference. Because "a people makes far better choices than a prince,"[6] the secondary positions of political leadership are likewise more ably filled in republics than in monarchies. How can a prince tolerate talented advisors and generals? "So natural to princes . . . is suspicious fear that they cannot defend themselves from it and cannot show gratitude to men who by victory have under princely banners made great gains."[7] Spirited and talented men are always viewed as a threat by the prince, even when they do his bidding, because there is room for only one sun in the heavens.

Envy and malice are not peculiar to princes; indeed, so basic to human nature are these vices that congratulations are all the more due "the people [who] are less ungrateful than princes."[8] Ingratitude is infrequent in republics, as opposed to monarchies, because the free city breeds many more men of stature than the unfree city, so that by their very numbers the ambitious men police themselves, leaving the great mass of the populace with little to fear from their betters and less reason to deny honors to the most deserving citizens. "There rose up in Rome in every age so many valiant men, famous for various victories, that the people had no reason for fearing any of them, since they were many, and one watched another."[9]

In republics, moreover, there is more liberty, more *virtù*, and more dedication to the public interest than in monarchies. "Without doubt the common good is thought important only in republics";[10] for in monarchies the concept of a public interest is either absent or is fatally confused with the private interest of the prince. How very different is the politics of republics where, even when the people go too far, they express their allegiance to a good transcending personal ends: "The cruelties of the multitude are directed against those who they fear will interfere with the common good; the cruelties of princes are against those they fear will interfere with their private interests."[11] As for freedom, more is to be found in republics than in monarchies for the reason that the republican way of life *is* freedom, just as its monarchical counterpart, by its very nature, is servility. To take part in political and military affairs, to act in the public realm, is to be a free man, and all properly constituted republics foster participation in politics. By contrast, monarchies, if they do not precisely constrict politics to the prince, do not permit it to wander far from court, and this contraction of the political sphere, its isolation from the everyday life of the many, entails the unfreedom of the city; for the only free society is a civic society. Finally, there is more *virtù* under republican than monarchical rule, more vigor, "more life,"[12] more greatness of spirit, since the free city produces many men who are manly, as opposed to the principality, in which the capacity for *virtù* is the monopoly of one man.[13]

Most of Machiavelli's arguments for republics and against monarchies were stated with as much attention to interstate as to domestic politics. If republics "of necessity have a series of able rulers," the most admirable consequence is that "therefore their gains and increases are great."

> Two successive reigns by able princes are enough to gain the world. Such were Philip of Macedon and Alexander the Great. For a republic this should be still more possible, since the method of choosing allows not merely two able rulers in succession but countless numbers to follow one another.[14]

Liberty, too, and the sense of the common good, are conducive to empire.

> Experience shows that cities never have increased in dominion . . . except while they have been at liberty. Truly it is a marvelous thing to consider to what greatness Athens came in the space of a hundred years after she freed herself from the tyranny of Pisistratus. But above all, it is very marvelous

to observe what greatness Rome came to after she freed herself from her kings. The reason is very easy to understand, because not individual good but common good is what makes cities great.[15]

Behind all Machiavelli's hopes for the glory of conquest stands the distinction "between an army that is satisfied and fights for its own glory and an army that is ill-disposed and fights for some leader's ambition,"[16] that is, the contrast of a citizens' militia with a mercenary or professional army. Otherwise stated, Machiavelli relies heavily on the advantages of a republican over a monarchical military. When Montaigne, some decades after the death of Machiavelli, remarked that "there is no other virtue that spreads so easily as military valor,"[17] he might as well have been quoting the *Discourses on Livy*, except that to the Frenchman such words were expressions of despair, whereas to Machiavelli they were the stuff dreams are made of. What is democracy, to Machiavelli, if not the capacity of the most common man to fight and die for his country?

Quite possibly the single greatest advantage of a republic over a monarchy is its unflinching willingness to "enslave," "enfeeble," and "weaken" its foreign prey.

This is not done by a prince who subjugates you, if that prince is not some barbarian prince, a destroyer of cities and a waster of all the civilization of men, as are the Oriental princes. But if he has in himself human and ordinary qualities, he usually loves equally the cities subject to him and leaves them . . . almost all their old institutions.[18]

Love, a feeling "human and ordinary," is, then, an obstacle to the monarchical will-to-power, since it prevents all but the most despotic rulers from thoroughly exploiting their conquered territories.

Conversely, fear makes it impossible for the tyrant, the "new" and illegitimate prince, to achieve the greatness of empire. In the first place, he can rarely conquer given that his domestic strategy, inspired by fear of his unwilling subjects, is divide-and-rule; in the second place, "if chance brings about the rise of a vigorous tyrant, who through courage and through force of arms increases his dominion, no advantage comes from it to that state, but only to himself, because he cannot honor any of those citizens he tyrannizes over who are strong and good, unless he is willing to fear them."

> Nor can he, moreover, subordinate or make tributary to that city where he is tyrant the cities he conquers, because making his city powerful does not benefit him, but it does benefit him to keep his state disunited and to have each city and each province acknowledge him. Hence he alone profits from his conquests—not his country.[19]

In brief, the tyrant can and must exploit his own city, but will not survive if he exploits those foreign, conquered, and yet necessarily well-treated cities that provide him with the allies he lacks at home.

Thus, neither the good prince nor the tyrant is likely to be able to conquer indefinitely, feeding on one victim as he pursues another. The glorious capacity to "enslave," "enfeeble," and "weaken" foreign prey is distinctively republican.

Only the well-regulated republic can take full advantage of the potential for conquest and grandeur that inheres in civic existence. Institutions, a way of life, and a ruling class, all properly constituted, are necessary if a republic is to be all that its monarchical competitor is not. A model of the best republic, best because historically tried and proven, not best in a utopian and illusionary sense, must be offered by a republican political theorist. For Machiavelli, as for virtually all the civic humanists before, during, and after his day until the French Revolution, the model republic was ancient Rome.

Institutionally, Rome evolved a system of mixed and balanced government, becoming in fact the kind of "polity" that Aristotle theorized about but never experienced in Greece. So Polybius, a thoroughly Romanized Greek,* had argued, and Machiavelli eagerly seconds his opinion.[20] After the early kings were expelled from Rome, a universal hatred of royalty soon was transformed into the mutual hatred of social classes, patricians against plebeians. Whatever comradeship among all Romans had once existed during the struggle against the tyrant was quickly dissipated by the insolence of the nobles. The people, seeing their former allies turn into their newly acquired enemies, struck back by withdrawing from Rome to the Sacred Mount, which brought the Roman senators to their senses. A democratic ingredient was added to the constitution through the creation of the Tribunes of the People and a popular assembly.[21]

Social conflict, in Roman history, led to institutional developments so perfect they might as well have been designed by a demigod working in a frictionless vacuum. Thanks to an uprising of the populace, aristocratic dictatorship was overthrown; and yet popular rebellion never went so far as to develop into a democratic dictatorship. Thus the Romans could enjoy all the benefits of democracy without having to endure the hardships or bitter legacy of revolution. Once the people entered the political system of Rome, everyone had a stake in the status quo, instability was no longer a threat, and the senators could not afford to fall into the internal bickering that so often is the downfall of a ruling class.

In Polybian terms, Roman political institutions were exceptional in that they drew upon all the three good forms of government, monarchy, aristocracy, democracy, and combined them in a fashion that created a fourth type of government far superior to any of the simple governmental forms. With powers inherited from the days of royalty, the consuls were the monarchical ele-

---

* During his seventeen years as a hostage of Rome, Polybius traveled in the highest social circles and grew much enamored of things Roman.

ment; the senate was the aristocratic ingredient; and the popular assembly the democratic. In itself, the democratic element was an inclusionary force; the democratic factor combined with and offset by the aristocratic factor provided the mutual vigilance of class checking class; and leadership was never wanting given the monarchical and aristocratic ingredients—the senators, the consuls, and the emergency powers of the dictator.[22] From social conflict a political structure of the most stable and durable kind emerged, shoring up Roman government with institutions born of party strife but thereafter elevated above particular interests in a convincing triumph of the public good.

A republic is as much the people who compose it as the institutions which assure regularity and order, and therefore a mature republican theory, such as Machiavelli's, must account for the way of life, the values and beliefs giving meaning to the daily lives of the citizenry—a meaning painstakingly passed on from generation to generation. It is the ideal of citizenship, of virtue as civic virtue, that holds the key to explaining the lives of the noble Romans. Equality, frugality, competition, glory, discipline, and freedom all figure integrally in the political and civic life, the *vita activa*.

Equality is an indispensable element in the reign of civic virtue.[23] Too keen a desire for equality is disruptive and undesirable,[24] but at the middle of society there must be a force of attraction pulling the more well-to-do citizens down and the less well-to-do up. One law—the Twelve Tables—for all citizens, nobles and commoners alike, a law applied rigorously to everyone regardless of personal reputation or past deeds,[25] and a graduated tax[26] go far toward fostering relative equality. A sense of comradeship does the rest. To say that all who reside within or just outside the city walls are citizens is to say that they partake in a common liberty ruling out the phenomenon of a parasitical few living off the misery of the many. A community of citizens means superiority not for the minority but for all, and a prejudiced view of others that has little to do with the supercilious disregard of one social class for another, but much to do with the supercilious disregard of one city-state for every other, and all the more so for foreign monarchies where citizenship is unknown and men are therefore hardly more than slaves. Projected outward into foreign affairs, haughtiness binds man to man, group to group, and class to class on the domestic front as it reminds them of what they equally share, unequal social status notwithstanding.

Equality and public-mindedness are both easily sustained when frugality is socially commended. Rome's riches increased even as the Romans remained poor but content: "To get honor from war was enough for them, and all the gain they left to the public."[27] So long as civic virtue was uncorrupted, the average citizen, finding his fulfilment in honors rather than riches, gladly abandoned his plow for military gear at the beckoning of the militia. Economically, a Roman's life was spent practicing the simple frugal virtues of the sturdy farmer, the free peasant, uncorrupted by temptations to grow rich through merchant trade. Since conspicuous consumption was condemned as a sin against civic virtue, an abstemious existence was more likely to win social approval than to become an object of social contempt: consequently, "four hundred years after Rome had been built, her people still lived in the utmost poverty."[28] Poor citizens are equal to one another, susceptible to the appeal of honors, and hence good citizens.

Because each citizen was a soldier, discipline was central in the life of a Roman. Always the people of Rome were kept occupied in the business of military preparedness and "at all times they made war."[29] During the aristocratic predominance, the noble in his chariot or on his horse was the chief combatant, but during the democratic ascendancy and predominance the focus shifted to the heavily armed foot soldier: "In early times wars were first made with cavalry, because there was as yet no discipline for the infantry, but when these were disciplined, at once it was realized how much more valuable they were than cavalry."[30]

Marching shoulder to shoulder, the Roman infantry was much more powerful than the sum total of the powers of its individual soldiers added together.[31] Precise and painstaking execution of military tactics was possible, however, only if the rules of discipline were inviolable. Machiavelli cites with wonder and approval the action of the consul Manlius Torquatus, who killed his son for defeating the enemy before the order to attack had been given.[32] Seemingly opposites, liberty and discipline were in fact friends because self-sacrifice and repression of one's private passions for the sake of the public good preserved the freedom of the city and its inhabitants. The opposite of discipline is not freedom but idleness, and idleness is debilitating. "The disunion of republics usually results from idleness and peace; the cause of union is fear and war."[33]

The competitive pursuit of excellence, expressed in a penchant for turning virtually all social activities into contests with winners, losers, prizes, and trophies, is another inescapable characteristic of civic *virtù*. Victory over other city-states time and again satisfied the thirst, common to all Roman citizens, for glory and greatness. But so unquenchable was the yearning for distinction that in the very act of conquering the enemy the Romans vied with their comrades for additional distinction. Consider the words of Sallust, one of Machiavelli's favorite authors.

> [The Romans'] hardest struggle for glory was with one another; each man strove to be first to strike down the foe, to scale a wall, to be seen of all while doing such a deed. This they considered riches, this fair fame and high nobility. It was praise they coveted . . . their aim was unbounded renown.[34]

And compare the words of Sallust with those of Castiglione:

> If the courtier happens to engage in arms in some public show—such as jousts, tourneys, . . . or in any other bodily

exercise—mindful of the place where he is and in whose presence, he will strive to be as elegant and handsome in the exercise of arms as he is adroit, and to feed his spectators' eyes with all those things that he thinks may give him added grace. . . . He will never be among the last to show himself, knowing that the crowd, and especially women, give more attention to the first than the last.[35]

True glory in all its wondrous bloody reality, versus false glory as a bloodless and empty show, marks the difference between republics and monarchies. Competition even unto death versus competition as a mere game marks the same difference.

One should not be surprised, therefore, that Machiavelli, like Guicciardini, refuses the hypocrisy of his fellow Florentines who, disturbed by Christian conscience, denounce ambition in the abstract while devoting themselves to its service in their everyday lives. *Ambizione* (ambition) occurs as frequently as virtually any other word in Machiavelli's writings, and his advice is not to rid the republic of the passion for advancement and fame, but rather to channel it constructively. In a well-ordered republic, ambition is asserted publicly and for the cause of the common good, as in acts of political counsel; in a poorly-ordered republic, ambition assumes private forms—providing citizens with protection from the magistrates and other acts designed to build up a personal following, even if by circumventing the law. The very life of the republic hangs in the balance when the difference between ambition properly or improperly regulated is in question.

I say that a republic without citizens of reputation cannot last and cannot in any way be governed well. On the other hand, reputation gained by citizens is the cause of tyranny in republics. . . . A well-ordered republic, therefore, opens the ways . . . to those who seek support by public ways, as Rome did.[36]

Civic in its ethos, a polity in its institutional arrangements, Rome also possessed a ruling class so distinguished as to enable her to live up to her magnificent promise. Usually a ruling class is closed, hostile to fresh talent, self-satisfied, and prone to incestuous quarrels that eventually lead to its demise, not from without but from within, from a failure to perform its political duties effectively or from an outright abuse of its privileges leaving the governed with little choice but to rise up in rebellion, at which time they meet small resistance to their upward thrusts. Uncannily adept and adaptive, the Roman elite effectively countered the corrosive forces that spelled the doom of virtually all previous and subsequent ruling classes.

Machiavelli's interpretation of the Roman ruling class was as old as Polybius and as new as the Renaissance debate over whether nobility is based on birth or merit. Although an aristocratic factor is a necessary part of mixed and balanced government, an aristocracy that succeeds in transforming itself into a hereditary nobility has signed its own death certificate: before long it will be corrupt, senile, and vulnerable.[37] In the absence of an aristocracy, the ship of state is without a rudder or overtaken by mutineers; but aristocracy is only good if truly composed of the best men— which means the elite must always be open and its members constantly on the lookout for new talent to co-opt. At this juncture the frugality of the Romans came to their rescue; it prevented the nobility from cutting itself off from the people and enabled a gifted plebeian to join the ranks of the patricians: "Poverty did not close the road to any rank or honor, and *virtù* was sought in whatever house was her home."[38] The Roman elite was also saved from corruption by its tenacious adherence to the maxim, Aristotelian in origin, that citizenship is "ruling and being ruled."[39] Knowing how to govern, the most able Romans likewise knew how to step down and be governed:

Observe the noble minds of those citizens. When they were put at the head of an army, the greatness of their spirits raised them above every prince . . . yet on returning to private stations, they became economical, humble, careful of their little properties, obedient to the magistrates.[40]

At Rome's call Cincinnatus left his plow to serve as dictator; his term of office over, he willingly returned to his farm.

By way of summary, the Roman elite was open to recruits from all social ranks; the elite rotated; and finally, Machiavelli adds, it never made the mistake of wasting the abilities of a brilliant young man for years on end while waiting for him to grow old and senile before securing his promotion: "There never was any requirement as to age in Rome but always she went looking for *virtù*, whether in a young man or an old one."[41] To many republican theorists, the Roman elite signified the rule of elders and hence of wisdom, but not to Machiavelli, for whom the better part of wisdom was to combine the advantages of youth and age.

One of the most prominent features of Machiavelli's works is that he wrote for the leaders, constantly offered them advice, and frequently slipped into direct address—you should, you ought. As he saw matters, everything depended on the rulers, both the good and the bad of the world, and thus his praise of the people and condemnation of their princes loses much of its democratic glow. If "the sins of the people are caused by their princes,"[42] it is because the common run of citizens, under whatever type of regime, are incapable of sinning politically—they haven't the capacity for a political version of that drama of the soul's choice whereof theological thinkers speak. Friedrich Meinecke was right to insist that Machiavelli's writings contain a distinction between original and derivative *virtù*.[43] Those Roman nobles worth their family names were originals of *virtù*, whereas the members of the populace were great only insofar as they were faithful copies. Most people in most times and most places, Machiavelli assures us, "walk in the paths beaten by others"[44] and act by imitating their social superiors. When the nobles are truly noble, high-

spirited, and valorous, the mimicking people are thereby enno-
bled. Likewise a corrupt nobility will eventually corrupt the
people whose actions are reactions, whose glory is borrowed, and
who cannot even claim their shame as their own doing. Nevertheless, that an entire society should be valorous despite the poor
stuff human nature[45] is made of, was to Machiavelli no mean
achievement.

A deferential democracy was the government best fitted for a
city with a sizeable popular party. Since the Roman plebeians
continued to choose patricians to fill public offices long after
gaining the concession that members from their own undistinguished ranks were eligible, Rome won Machiavelli's praise.[46]
Indeed, the Roman populace in mind, he could urge that "not
without reason is the voice of a people likened to that of God";[47]
yet the reverse side of his democratic rhetoric was the conviction,
never doubted for a moment, that "a multitude without a head
is helpless."[48] Despite occasional eulogies of the people and hits
at the nobility, the not-so-wellborn Machiavelli conjures up a
vision of politics that focuses on the aristocracy. The nobles wish
to oppress, the people wish only to avoid oppression, the democratic Machiavelli had repeatedly said;[49] the aristocratic Machiavelli counters with the assertion that the desire to dominate
stems from the *virtù* of the nobles, their drive for glory, greatness,
grandeur, and fame. Take away from the nobles their will-to-
power and you have taken it away from the people as well.

Machiavelli's imagery and symbols effectively convey his political vision. Throughout his works the Aristotelian pairing of
"matter" with "form" incessantly recurs,[50] and whenever this
leitmotif appears the message is the same: that the people, an
undifferentiated mass of matter, are nothing without the form
"stamped" upon them by the elite, the ruling class. Symbolically,
Machiavelli drives home the same point with images of the builder,
the sculptor, and the architect working with their materials.
Between "the builder and . . . what he builds" the relationship

is that "the latter is more or less astonishing according as he is more or less able who has been its cause."[51] Between the sculptor[52] and his materials the relationship is that while they are passive and lack intrinsic value, he is active and in conferring form upon them creates such value as they have—or, in the event of a poorly conceived or improperly executed form, he ruins his materials beyond hope of repair. Whether the sculptor is a prince, as in *Il Principe*, or a ruling class, as in the *Discorsi*, the people—save for the gifted few welcomed into the ranks of the political artists— are creations.[53]

The most creative of all ruling elites was that of ancient Rome, and its most outstanding creation was pagan religion. Unlike the militaristic ethos of *virtus*, passed unintentionally from the nobles to the commoners, Roman religion was planned and even invented by the rulers, who thereafter deliberately imposed it upon the populace from above. To Numa goes everlasting fame for fabricating religion, to Roman generals honor for using oaths to get the most from their troops, and to the senators credit for making the auspices say whatever political prudence dictated they ought to say, regardless of what the unruly plebeians wished to hear. "Never was there so much fear of God as in that republic; this facilitated whatever undertaking the Senate or those great men of Rome planned to carry on."[54] Thus both of the noteworthy items in the faith of the people, their passionate adherence to *virtù* and to pagan religion, were derived from the nobles; but Roman religious belief was unique in being self-consciously constructed by the elite for popular consumption, and is possibly the greatest single tribute to the creative powers of leadership.[55]

No one, therefore, should be surprised that Machiavelli, although ostensibly a democrat, writes about the average citizen, but for the general and the politician. For if *virtù* is military deeds, which all can perform, it is also, and even more so, the ability to rule, which only a few can do; moreover, even among military deeds, the highest are those performed by the general who rules his troops.

With the addition of an astute ruling class to a mixed government and a civic ethos, one has a city-state bound for glory. In the Machiavellian reading of ancient history, the triumph of one city over all others must have been planned and could not have been accidental. "Rome had as her end empire and glory, not tranquillity,"[56] he maintains. And even when he understands Plutarch and Livy as attributing the Roman conquest of the world to *fortuna*,[57] Machiavelli counters them with the claim that "if no republic ever produced such results as Rome, there has never been another republic so organized that she could gain as Rome did."[58] To move from the first book of the *Discorsi*, on internal Roman affairs, to the second, on Roman foreign policy, is not to lose the Machiavelli who cannot speak too warmly of freedom, but it is to put his admiration of freedom in a new light.

A city living in freedom has two ends: the first, to make gains; the second, to keep herself free.[59]

All cities and provinces that live in freedom anywhere in the world . . . make very great gains.[60]

Doubtless freedom is praiseworthy for the grandeur it grants human lives; grandeur, however, is unachievable without conquest.

Throughout the first book of the *Discorsi*, Machiavelli is anxious to discover in the Roman republic the Aristotelian polity that Polybius had imagined was the essence of internal Rome; throughout the second book Machiavelli argues his view, also Polybian in origin, that the internal strength of Rome, her mixed and balanced government, was the reason why that republic achieved universal domination. Polybius, present with Scipio at the final siege of Carthage, was dazzled by Rome's march in a mere fifty-three years to world empire, "a thing the like of which had never happened before,"[61] and he was certain that in discovering a

Roman realization of the Aristotelian idea of polity he had explained why Rome attained unexampled success. Previous governments, in contrast, had all been unmixed, hence weak, vulnerable to foreign powers, and incapable of sustaining a successful imperialism. In Romanizing the concept of polity, Polybius made Aristotle advocate from the grave and against his will the urge to conquer from which the living Aristotle had attempted to dissuade Alexander. What more did Machiavelli need to conclude that Polybius was a pre-Machiavellian? Barely has Machiavelli finished telling us that conflict between social classes in Rome, regulated by the give and take of a polity, was conducive to liberty, than he adds that it promoted "power" and "grandeur."[62]

> If the Roman state had become quieter, this difficulty would
> have followed, namely, that it would also have been weaker,
> because the way to come to the greatness it reached would
> have been cut off from it. Hence, if Rome had planned to
> take away the causes of riot, it would also have taken away
> the causes of growth.[63]

Comparison of Rome with other great city-states, ancient and modern, is the only certain way to underscore its brilliance and singularity. Other cities might be virtuous, as Athens was; they might even be virtuous and long-lasting, as Sparta and Venice were; and all three republics, the Athenian, Spartan, and Venetian, were able to achieve empire for a moment—but Rome alone, masterful Rome, had combined virtue, durable institutions, and permanent empire.

Athenian democracy, which lit up the skies with glory for a tragically brief moment, was a magnificent failure and a warning to Florentine democracy. A popular regime, Athens could arm the people and boast formidable military might; a popular regime, Athens had destroyed her nobility, and in her egalitarian excesses did not permit the rise of a new ruling class. Hence hers was a politics of passion unconstrained, undirected, and uneducated by an experienced ruling elite, the incarnation of political reason; and from a leaderless and irrational politics nothing lasting can ever be fashioned. Although the passions of the demos are the raw materials of greatness, they were never properly molded by the Athenians, whose empire was therefore a necessarily brief affair. Similarly, the Florentine empire, insofar as it existed, weakened the city on the Arno,[64] because Florence, too, as the pathetic republican resurgence from 1494 to 1512 attested, was a democracy devoid of leadership. However much a Florence that was the reincarnation of Rome might be Machiavelli's aspiration, a Florence that was the reincarnation of Athens was his reality.

Sparta exceeded Athens and every other republic in civic virtue, lived to the ripe old age of eight hundred years, and enjoyed the benefits of a splendidly disciplined ruling class. Nevertheless no sooner had she won the Peloponnesian War than she lost her empire. Lycurgus, the great lawgiver of the Lacedaemonians, had failed to allow for empire in the blueprint he drew up for the construction of an ideal community, and eventually a price had to be paid for his nearsightedness. Thrust into a magnificent conflict of superpowers, militaristic Sparta could not have been better prepared for war, or worse prepared for the aftermath of victory. Conquered peoples cannot be held in subjection by the naked force that inadvertently urges its victims to rebellion. "Love" is far more subtle than "force" as a method of subjugation,[65] and the imperialistic expression of love is the incorporation of foreign peoples into the conquering city through conferring upon them titles of citizenship. Rome understood this method so well that wherever her aggression took her, new Romans, formerly her enemies and now her friends, were sure to follow. Sadly, it never entered the minds of the Spartans to try this method. Exclusionary with a vengeance,[66] just as Lycurgus intended them to be, they wanted none of their citizens to travel abroad, nor any citizens of foreign cities to visit Spartan soil, much less to call it their own; for the splendors of civic virtue make such strong demands on human nature, and the unity of a people is so easily disrupted, that collective isolation, Lycurgus believed, is the best policy. The absence of walls surrounding Sparta signified not that everyone was invited in, but that everyone was all the more obstinately held out, because valorous men living in fraternity do not need walls to unite with one another or to divide themselves from the rest of mankind. "This is the reason why a Spartan, asked by an Athenian if the walls of Athens seemed to him splendid, answered: 'Yes, if they sheltered women.' "[67]

Sparta's mistakes as an imperialistic power began long before the moment of her triumph over Athens. In the case of the Lacedaemonians, the acquisition of empire must have been less their doing than fortune's, since their power was limited from the beginning by the nature of their political arrangements. As an aristocracy Sparta could not arm her own people for fear of revolution; hence her supremely militaristic mode of existence was as quantitatively deficient as it was qualitatively beautiful. Manly men, organized, disciplined, and massed in huge numbers are the makings of empire, and that means Rome rather than Sparta is the most Machiavellian of city-states. Whereas Rome at her peak could arm two hundred and eighty thousand men, Sparta could manage a mere twenty thousand.[68]

The Venetians "imagined they were going to form a monarchy like the Roman";[69] Machiavelli holds it against them that they did not succeed. Idolization of Venice was a commonplace of Florentine political thought, particularly in aristocratic circles, and although Machiavelli wrote his *Discourses* for the aristocratic and pro-Venetian audience of the Orti Oricellari,[70] his comments on the republic of St. Mark are a challenge to aristocratic ideology.*

* The gardens of the Rucellai family, the Orti Oricellari, were a favorite meeting place for aristocrats and humanists, and an ideal setting for the exchange of ideas.

He begins by conceding that the Venetian republic shared with the Spartan the honor of living longer than republican Rome;[71] he concedes also that the Venetian ruling class was exceptionally accomplished. But it was not without grave faults. "In Venice," unlike ancient Rome, "there is still the bad practice that a citizen, after holding a high rank, is ashamed to accept a lower one, and the city allows him to reject it."[72] Ruling but never ruled is apparently the misreading of Aristotle resorted to by selfish Venetian rulers. Moreover, the Venetian ruling class is closed, admitting none but sons of gentlemen.[73] Thus it ignores the Polybian warning that transmission of public office by hereditary succession is the major cause of the breakdown of political regimes.[74] Worst of all, Venetian advances in Lombardy left her as enfeebled as Florence was after her Tuscan gains.

> The whole comes from having wished to make gains and not having known how to take the means. These cities deserve blame the more in so far as they have the less excuse, because they have seen the means the Romans used and could have followed their example. . . .[75]

Venice's maritime empire of trade was considerable and durable, but her empire on the land was so fragile that one great battle was enough to shatter it.[76] Antidemocratic, the Venetians were no more capable than the Spartans of assimilating foreigners or of arming their native populace. Compounding their mistakes, the Venetians resorted to mercenaries and mistakenly tried to buy an empire with the kind of soldiers who specialize in never shedding blood, especially their own. "This was that ill-fated decision that cut off from them their legs for climbing to the sky and becoming great."[77]

Clearly the Roman model constituted a category of one—the one city-state that achieved and sustained grandeur because she was uniquely outfitted from the beginning to be the talk of antiquity and the nostalgia of all subsequent ages. In Roman

political experience the aristocratic and democratic elements were
so effectively absorbed, balanced, and utilized in the constitutional structure—the people having the assembly, the nobles the
senate, and the elite being open to all talented men—that here
was the only city of all history to pass the Aristotelian and Polybian test for determining whether a polity truly existed, namely,
that not even a native should be able to say for certain whether
he lived under an aristocratic or a democratic government.[78] Each
class, moreover, gained from the other: the people were elevated
to grandeur and heroism when they imitated the nobles, and the
nobles, constantly menaced by the people, were forced to channel
their ambition and greatness of spirit into planning the creative
destruction of other city-states rather than in plotting to destroy
one another. The Roman republic was not vulnerable, as other
republics were, to overthrow by a foreign enemy profiting from
the internal weakness of its prey.[79] Conversely, the internal strength
of Rome made her exceptionally powerful in external affairs,
always the victimizer, never the victim. Of all cities Rome alone
knew how to combine virtue and empire, virtue and glory.

Yet, despite all its awesome potential, Rome would not have
achieved world conquest and the undying fame that is its reward
had the senators lacked the nerve to utilize every means, fair and
foul, by which foreign powers may be subjugated. By turns lions
and foxes, sometimes using force, sometimes fraud, according to
the nature of the occasion, the Romans in fact—Machiavelli would
have us believe—dared be the resolute and uncompromising
Machiavellians who otherwise would figure in his works merely
as theoretical beings. Virtually all the wars of the Romans, he
maintains, were made "by attacking others and not by defending
themselves";[80] indeed, in the largest sense, the eventual Roman
empire was the fulfilment of the preconceived design of the senators, whose powers to wage and oversee war survived the democratization of Roman politics. Surely anyone who deciphers
the tactics, strategies, and masterplan the senators employed in

subduing every republic and monarchy of the ancient world will have acquainted himself with the most profound power politics ever known.

What were the Machiavellian strategies and tactics of the Romans? In the first place, wars had to be won, and for this the massive and highly disciplined Roman infantry, directed in the field by able generals, was most effective, particularly since the Romans fought and won a given war so rapidly that the threatened city hardly had time to prepare its defense. "On observing all the wars they fought from the founding of Rome to the siege of Veii, we see that they finished them all, some in six, some in ten, some in twenty days."[81] In the wake of Rome's amazing succession of victories, each so brilliant in design and swift in execution, the image conjured up by Thucydides, Plato, and Aristotle of democracy as a government internally divided, fickle, at once volatile and lethargic, has to be reconsidered. Democracy need not be the leaderless and inglorious regime Athenian democracy had been; not at all, for democratic Rome was the most ably led and glorious republic imaginable.

In the second place, victories won had to lead to the permanent subjection of the losers, and to this end Rome was so discriminating that she forged one set of chains fit for republics and another for monarchies. By their unrelenting devotion to self-rule, republics posed considerable difficulties and provoked at once the most violent and the most subtle Roman stratagems. With monarchies, on the other hand, the Roman lion did not need to use his jaws nor the Roman fox his trickery. In a city that had long submitted to a prince, neither much bloodletting nor much astuteness was needed in order to assure Roman domination; a simple massacre of the princely family sufficed to render the inhabitants helpless, since they had never learned how to act collectively, politically, or, what amounts to the same thing, how to be free. Besides, a servile people has no reason to care what the name of its master happens to be. "But in republics there is

THE REPUBLIC THAT WAS   53

more life, more hate, greater longing for revenge; they are not
permitted to rest—nor can they be—by the recollection of their
ancient liberty; so the surest way is to wipe them out or to live
among them."[82] Such were the bloody triumphs of the Roman
lion.

Actually the alternatives, as a further reading of Machiavelli
discloses, are not so either/or. Between the extremes of laying
waste a republic or residing in it, the Romans often adopted the
intermediary course of erecting colonies on newly conquered soil.
"The Romans, in the regions they conquered, . . . sent colonies,
showed favor to those not very powerful without increasing their
power, [and] humbled the powerful."[83] Divide and rule, in short,
was the mission each Roman colony was charged with; the mutual
animosities of city-states in a given region provided the opportunity Rome needed to rob those republics stealthily of their
freedom. Moreover, that Roman colonists should have ample
occasion to exploit the pre-existing suspicions of local enemies
was only to be expected considering that the initial appearance
of Rome in a region was always at the invitation of a local power
threatened by a neighbor. The Romans "always tried to have in
a new province some friends who would be a ladder or a gate for
them to climb there or go in there, or a means by which to hold
it."[84] Once Rome answered the plea of a city in distress it was
only a matter of time before there were Roman colonies, and soon
thereafter every power in the region was on its way to absorption
in the Roman empire. Such were the relatively bloodless triumphs
of the Roman fox.

What prevents men from acting like lions is not incapacity for
violent deeds, of which there is never a shortage, but an unwillingness to do evil without regret, without excuses, and in
full recognition of the grandeur and heroism of some forms of
wrongdoing.[85] Caught in the middle, weak, irresolute—of such
men and such peoples histories are full, and the incidence of acts
of wanton bestiality on the part of such feeble humans is appal-

lingly high, because they haven't the courage to destroy the requisite number of lives and be done with it. Hence they must kill again and again, and usually end by being killed.[86] Machiavelli seemingly cannot say too often that the middle is to be avoided,[87] halfway measures rejected, and irresolution spurned, nor can he hit upon a better way to shame us than by citing the example of "the Romans [who] never used indecisive measures." When a conquered city rebelled, the Romans always were willing to destroy it if there was no more effective way of securing their empire. Any state worthy of grandeur will follow "the method of expansion used by the Romans, who in punishments of state always avoided half-way measures and turned to complete ones."[88]

What prevents men from acting like foxes is not unwillingness but skill, the skill that is ordinarily learned from a qualified teacher. Now the Romans, Machiavelli assures us, not only were skilled in fraud, cunning, and deceit, and thus eminently qualified as teachers of those arts, but they themselves were untaught—they were the originals of dissimulation,[89] the first foxes and the most successful. Therefore, their tricks and ploys merit special attention.

Fraud was not an occasional tool of the Romans; nor were Roman acts of deception frequent but unrelated to one another; nor, finally, was the record of Roman dissimulation separable from the grandeur and glory of that greatest of all cities. For the incredible span of four hundred fifty years,[90] Rome wore down the resistance of its neighbors by constant small-scale wars and a scheme of treaties and alliances which was surely the most devious diplomacy imaginable. With the kind of admiration that only one Machiavellian can feel for another, Machiavelli reconstructed the Roman masterplan.

> Throughout Italy she obtained many associates, who in most respects lived in equality with her; and yet . . . she always reserved for herself the seat of authority and the reputation of command; hence these associates of hers found that with-

out realizing it they had subjected themselves with their own labors and their own blood. For Rome sent armies [of Romans and associates] outside Italy and turned kingdoms into provinces and made subjects of peoples who, accustomed to living under kings, did not mind being subjects; then these people . . . did not recognize any other superior than Rome. Hence these associates of Rome who were in Italy found themselves at once encircled by Roman subjects and kept down by such a very great city as Rome. When they realized the deception under which they had been living, they were not in time to remedy it. . . .

Rome's erstwhile allies were then reduced from free associates to unfree subjects. "This method of proceeding . . . has been observed only by the Romans; a republic that wishes to expand cannot use any other method."[91]

Here, in Rome's foreign policy, was power politics in its purest form.

Because Rome used . . . all the methods she needed for attaining to greatness, she did not fail to use [fraud]. Nor could she have adopted in the beginning a more important deception than her method . . . of making herself associates, because under this name she made them slaves, as were the Latins and other peoples round about.

From humble beginnings to grandiose finale, the Roman republic single-mindedly applied every sinister device that passed into the hands or into the fertile imagination of the senators, ever ready to test the latest in Machiavellian means.

So it is plain that the Romans too in their early growth were also not lacking in fraud, which it has always been necessary for those to use who from little beginnings wish to climb to high places—something which is the less to be censured the more it is concealed, as was this of the Romans.[92]

The grandeur that was Rome was the greatness of a people completely powerful and completely in control of its powers. Originally a rude people, the Romans shed the savagery and bestiality of their beginnings when the yokes of law[93] and religion were imposed upon them. Yet these restraints were aimed not at breaking their animal spirits but at channeling them and making them manageable. Under pagan direction religious sacrifices and rites both inflame the people and render them obedient. Terrible and terrifying, just as the violent spectacles of their religion had made them,[94] each young Roman was willing and eager to prove he was a *vir virtutis*, and together they constituted the unstoppable collective reality known as *virtus Romana* (Roman virtue). Men were never before or since lifted so far above the beasts in grandeur of soul as were the Romans when they undertook a program of systematic destruction and acted the part of beasts abroad.

The power politics of *The Prince*[95] was grounded in the necessity to face up to the *verità effettuale della cosa*;* the power politics of the *Discourses*, by contrast, goes beyond a mere recognition of the factual truths of monarchical power politics to a glorification of republican power politics. The factual truths of Roman power are exciting, ideological truths when comprehended by moderns, and a model for making their politics as heroic as those of their ancestors.

ON OCCASION, Machiavelli himself was troubled by his deliberately troubling political vision. Not that there was enough of the Christian in his psyche to bother him with belief in a moral standard over and above Rome, outside history. Rather, the problem was internal to pagan values, particularly to the notions of grandeur and greatness; and the problem was inescapable: for if

---

* The Gilbert translation reads, "the truth of the matter as facts show it." What Machiavelli advocates in this celebrated passage is a politics based on a frank recognition of the brute facts of power.

destroying republican peoples is especially glorious, it is also especially iniquitous. Achilles is nothing if Hector, his victim, is not great; Rome, a collective hero, is not great if it rests content with victories over monarchical, and therefore servile, cities. Only the destruction of republican, free, and great peoples, peoples unconquerable save by Rome,[96] could make the Romans great. Shades hovering above a mound of decaying republican corpses, each one once vibrant with civic virtue, might at any moment haunt Machiavelli.[97]

Now and then in his poetry Machiavelli recognizes the darker side of the heroic ethic. His verses on *Ambizione* are a brief but definite bemoaning of carnage, and in *L'Asino* he interrupts the narrative to gaze nostalgically at the German republics where "at the present day each city lives secure through having less than six miles round about." Yearning for empire, he continues, is to risk repeating the fate of Icarus, who destroyed himself by flying too near the sun.[98]

Still, Machiavelli's occasional self-questioning, carefully set aside for minor writings and answered to his satisfaction in his major works, should not receive undue attention. In the *Discorsi* he dismisses the significance of the nonaggressive German republics on the grounds that they, residing within the not completely meaningless jurisdiction of the Holy Roman Emperor, were subject to a minimal rule of law in their relations to one another. Thus they were exempted from the usual pattern of interstate violence, but did not constitute a model on the basis of which other city-states might escape the same.[99] Likewise he uses his discourses on Livy, as we have already seen, as a platform for praising ambition as the lifeblood of a healthy republic.[100] Obviously, therefore, his swearing off of ambition and empire in *L'Asino* is no more his characteristic mood than is the argument, with which that poem ends, for pigs and against men. Closer to nature than man will ever be, the pig and other animals are untroubled by the woes of politicking and womanizing, the two activities that, the human-hating pig would not be surprised to learn, encompass the greater part of Machiavelli's correspondence. For a moment and as a change of pace, Machiavelli has assumed the un-Machiavellian voice of works *de contemptu mundi*. He has not, however, changed his mind, nor has he given evidence of being of two minds. It is well to remember that the heroic tradition itself had always sanctioned moments of concern for its victims, as when the rage of Achilles abated just long enough for him to share emotionally with dead Hector the dreadful fact of mortality.[101] For all that, to forgo the grandeur of carnage is unthinkable. Machiavelli was not about to join the ranks of those he despised, stranded in the middle, too weak to be totally good or totally bad.

What uneasiness Rome's destruction of non-Roman freedom and *virtù* caused Machiavelli was easily alleviated in incidental writings. Rome's subsequent loss of her own freedom and *virtù*[102] troubled him much more deeply. Just offstage throughout Machiavelli's entire performance in the *Discourses* were the annoying presences of Plato and Aristotle whose condemnation of imperialism[103] was not moralistic, Stoical, or Christian, and had nothing to do with easily dismissed notions of the oneness of mankind. Theirs, rather, was the claim that imperialism is necessarily fatal for its republican perpetrator, because a city-state expanded is no longer a city-state: it may live on after its conquests but only by forfeiting its civic virtue and republican politics. Machiavelli's response is evasive. At various points in the *Discourses* he expresses his awareness of almost every factor needed to demonstrate that between Roman imperialism and Roman corruption a causal relationship obtained. Growth of personal riches; decline of frugality, simplicity, and repression; a loss of interest in public affairs; the ravages of class struggles; an infusion of foreign mores into the city; and soldiers more attentive to their general than to Rome definitely figure in Machiavelli's account of ancient Rome.[104] Nowhere, however, does he bother to integrate them by citing their common denominator, the corruption that necessarily followed from Rome's determination to annex the world.[105]

Refusal to make a causal argument was, then, one way by which Machiavelli sidestepped the inconveniences of his position. Making a weak causal argument served the same end of evasion. Of necessity Rome had to conquer the world or be conquered, he argued in the opening pages of the *Discourses*, because all physical bodies move up or down and cannot remain balanced in between.[106] A mere metaphor was Machiavelli's substitute for the hard work of determining when, if ever, a state must play the aggressor to survive, how far its aggression need reach, and at what point aggression becomes self-defeating. Soon he forgets himself and says Rome's drive for empire was the upshot of ambition, not of necessity;[107] and he constantly asserts that the Romans were seekers of grandeur, glory, and greatness.[108] But in the meantime, the word "necessity" has allowed him to pretend there is no human choice involved when wars, conquests, and empires are in question and the life and death of entire peoples hang in the balance. Machiavelli's analogy of political with physical bodies is the language of self-deception.

A choice, a very difficult choice, had to be made, he insisted, between a republic for "preservation" or for "increase," between Sparta and Rome, between a durable civic virtue without empire, and half as durable a civic virtue with empire, between the eight hundred years of stationary Sparta and the four hundred years of mobile Rome.[109] Rather than accept the harsh alternatives, Machiavelli clouded the issues and sought refuge in spurious arguments suggesting the Roman way had to be followed. Only by deceiving himself into believing there was no middle way was Machiavelli able to avoid it and to be totally bad.

Machiavelli's irresponsibility, his unwillingness to face up to the full implications of his thought, does not detract from the intellectual significance of his work; it does, however, rob his

outlook of tragic grandeur.[110] Anyone who follows directly in his
path will not be found struggling to learn how to live with the
furies, nor again shall we encounter an heir to Machiavelli compulsively washing his hands in a vain effort to remove a permanent
stain. More likely, a descendant of Machiavelli will deny there
has ever been blood on his hands, or will claim that it can easily
be washed away. Rubashov, the old Bolshevik in Arthur Koest-
ler's *Darkness at Noon* who buries the significance of his past violent
acts under a natural law of historical necessity, is, to Machiavelli's
discredit, much more the descendant of the opening pages of the
Discourses on Livy than is Maurice Merleau-Ponty, who argues that
the terrible dialectic of humanism and terror is unnecessary in a
scientific sense, but very necessary in a moral sense, and signals
a modern rebirth of Greek tragedy in all its majesty, pain, and
horror.[111]

TRAGIC OR NOT, Machiavelli's Romans accompany him everywhere his thought leads him. Yet they are never his only com-
panions. Beside his Romans we always find his Florentines, jux-
taposed for purposes of dramatic and instructive comparison.
Whatever begins in Machiavelli's writings as a depiction of the
Roman republic that once was, soon becomes a commentary on
the Florentine republic still alive in his day. Within his thought
there is an internal necessity to complete the praise of the republic
that was with a critique of the republic that is.

–III–

THE REPUBLIC THAT IS

MEASURED against the Roman republic, proud Florence, convinced its sophistication, culture, and economic prowess were unparalleled, was a puny thing, indeed. Rome had been a glorious success, Florence was an abject failure; Rome had been powerful, Florence was weak; Rome had been noble, Florence was ignoble; Rome had been virtuous, Florence was corrupt. Comparative analysis, as conducted by Machiavelli, was an exercise in deflation. The reverse side of Machiavelli's eulogy of Rome was a vigorous critique of Florence.

It is particularly in the *Discourses* and *Florentine History* that Machiavelli sets forth his views on the republic of Florence. In two senses the *Florentine History*, Machiavelli's last major work, is the fulfilment of what the *Discourses* had said about Florence. That earlier work, burdened with the task of expounding the principles of Roman government, had time to discuss only those Florentine and Italian events that, for Machiavelli and his audience, were recent history, the events of their period. The *Florentine History* complements the *Discourses* by extending the discussion of Florentine affairs found in that earlier volume backwards in time to the very beginnings of the republic of Machiavelli's birth. Secondly, the *Florentine History* complements the *Discourses* by completing the process of demonstrating that the republic of Florence was the republic of Rome turned upside down. After reading the *Florentine History*, we know in much greater depth what the *Discourses* had already taught, that if Rome's history lighted the way to the greatest republican and democratic treasures, Florence's republican and democratic history showed the pitfalls along the road to greatness and fame. To the *Discourses*, which is a how-to-do-it manual for republics, Machiavelli added a how-not-to-do-it manual in his *Florentine History*. Writing a history of Florence, as envisioned by Machiavelli, was an experiment in a kind of negative policy science that left little doubt as to what constituted inferior politics.

The *Discourses* and *Florentine History* are also doubly linked by the personal experience they draw upon and by the project they share of doing more than merely recording the symptoms of the disease that afflicted Florence. Each book posits an underlying cause accounting for Florentine ineptitude: in the *Discourses* (and the *Art of War*) Christianity is the culprit; in the *Florentine History* it is the triumph of the commercial classes and demise of the nobility that accounts for the absence of *virtù* in the modern era. Both books, moreover, emerge from Machiavelli's personal experience, first as an observer, then as a servant, of the republic that proved to be merely an interregnum so far as the Medici were concerned, the republic of 1494 to 1512. The endpoint of Machiavelli's investigations into Florentine history is the discovery of explanatory causes; the starting point of Machiavelli's historical writings is his outlook on the events of his lifetime. For what his *Discourses, Florentine History*, and all his other comments on his native city in his various writings amount to is his primary political experience written large, read back into the past, and placed within a theoretical framework.

WEAK, VACILLATING, indecisive leadership had marked, so Machiavelli believed, the Florentine republic of 1494 to 1512. For four years Florentine affairs were dominated by the religious zealot Savonarola, whose enthusiasm and prophecy had not the same effect on Machiavelli as on the Florentine populace. Although eventually able to see more in Savonarola than a charlatan,[1]

Machiavelli could never accept a state of affairs in which religion dictated to politics rather than politics to religion. Prophets, admittedly, have their uses, for religion is the foundation of society, but it was hardly acceptable that the modern Numa should be a dupe of his own message. It was all the worse that the prophet was unarmed,[2] and inevitable that such a saint should fall victim to the worldlings, in this case the Florentine aristocrats, disgruntled by Savonarola's democratic reforms, and to a pope who was more worldly than the men of the world and unforgiving of saintliness that dared leave the monastery and seize the world.

After the demise of Savonarola, the Florentine republic lasted for an additional fourteen years but did not solve the problem of leadership. However much the worst democratic excesses were curbed, an able ruling class did not emerge. Instead, in 1502, hopes for stability, once various compromises had been struck, were placed in the creation of the office of Gonfalonier for life and in the person of Piero Soderini, whom Machiavelli the politician faithfully served, but on whose deeds, and lack of deeds, Machiavelli the writer heaped constant scorn. At the risk of denunciation as a traitor to his class, Soderini ruled by befriending the common people—a strategy Machiavelli had no reason to censure;[3] but he could never forgive his political boss for following the many rather than leading them.[4] Nor could he forgive him for sharing with the populace its weakness. Surrounded by envious aristocrats, Soderini did not have the courage to eliminate them. Foolishly, he believed that "with time, with goodness, . . . and by benefiting others he could extinguish envy."[5] Hence he, like Savonarola, fell victim to envy, and his failure is all the less deserving of absolution in that he, as a politician and not a prophet, should have realized that "his works and his intention would be judged by their outcome."[6] In Soderini's case as in so many others, Machiavelli clinches an argument demonstrating the ineptitude of Florentine events and personalities by a comparison drawn from ancient Rome.

Those who read ancient history will always observe that after a change of government, either from republic into tyranny or tyranny into republic, the enemies of present conditions must suffer some striking prosecution.

Brutus slew his sons to maintain newly acquired liberty; Soderini petted them and thus reared the enemies who eventually overthrew his regime.[7]

Unable to be decisive and violent in its internal politics, the Florentine republic Machiavelli served was equally wavering in its willingness to inflict full-scale violence upon foreign cities falling within the ambit of its imperialist designs. While still a political insider, Machiavelli wrote the *Discourse on the Pisan War*, describing the methods available for taking Pisa.[8] Later, in his major writings, Pisa figures repeatedly, usually as an example of the failure of nerve that caused Florence to waste numerous opportunities. Continuous efforts both before and during Machiavelli's day to subjugate Pisa, a city whose port was valuable to Florentine traders, were taken by him as symbolic of the bellicose and yet indecisive intentions of Florence.[9] Forever taking and then losing Pisa, Florentine merchants never had the courage of their own imperialistic convictions—or, more accurately stated, theirs was the wrong kind of imperialistic creed. True grandeur and glory, the kind Rome had known and which could not be counted in florins, was beyond their ken.

It was also during his years in office that Machiavelli witnessed Florence's half-hearted suppression of the rebellion in the Valdichiana. Twice in his writings Machiavelli used a Roman counterexample to condemn this prominent example of Florentine squeamishness, once in his paper *On the Method of Dealing with the People of Rebellious Valdichiana*[10] and again in the *Discourses*, where the incident in the Valdichiana received noteworthy attention. A gentle treatment of the rural people of the Valdichiana met with Machiavelli's approval, but he blamed his fellow Florentines for stopping short of a ruthless destruction of Arezzo and its citizens. This was not how the Roman senate had dealt with the rebellious peoples of Latium. Citing the example of the ancient Romans who abjured halfway measures and did whatever was necessary to maintain their empire, was Machiavelli's tactic for expressing the contempt he felt for the rulers of Florence. Had his countrymen followed the example of the Romans, he maintains, "they would have made the city of Florence great. . . . But they used a half-way policy."[11] The Florentines, it seems, not only failed to imitate the Romans; they might as well have been consciously striving to make themselves the opposite of their illustrious ancestors.

Machiavelli's politics of grandeur was constantly frustrated by the businessmen,[12] whose attitudes, he believed, were so small-mindedly calculating and fearful of risk as to outlaw the quest for glory and fame. In office Machiavelli was the opponent of all businessmen who carried their mentality into the inner circles of politics;[13] out of office Machiavelli used his writings to substitute counterslogans for the politically debilitating proverbial wisdom of timid Florentine businessmen. Only if we realize that the "middle way" was a favorite expression in Florentine political debates can we appreciate Machiavelli's untiring insistence upon choosing one dramatic course of action or another, either an unequivocal "either" or an unequivocal "or," in situations calling for political decision. Likewise Machiavelli's repeated insistence on immediate and forceful action must be understood in the context of a customary recourse in the political life of his city to a strategy of "enjoying the benefit of time."[14]

Least of all could Machiavelli ever forget that the businessmen were largely responsible, in his opinion, for disbanding the citizens' militia, leaving Florence in a state of military incompetence and degradation.[15] That a prophet should be unarmed is understandable but that a republic should be unarmed is disgusting and despicable. Much better than ignoring the adages of dull businessmen was the substitution of counteradages; better still was the substitution of humanists, especially humanists of political experience and Machiavellian persuasion, for businessmen in ruling circles.

Given the circumstances to which Florence had been reduced, the best Machiavelli could do for the businessmen of his city was to mitigate their guilt by placing part of it on the shoulders of the priests. Clergymen shared with businessmen the distinction of being the bane of Florentine political life, in Machiavelli's view. His anticlericalism, acknowledged by all his friends and shared by many, his disdain for a corrupt clergy and papacy, marks only the first layer of his condemnation of Christianity. In the *Art of War*, in the *Discourses*, and even in his poetry Machiavelli generalized his disdain for the prelates to the point of naming Christianity in general, the Christianity that is true to its values no less than the overtly corrupt Christianity of the papacy, as a general cause underlying the phenomenon of Italian corruption.

When Machiavelli ended his poem the *First Deccenale*, which described the political events of 1494 to 1504—the invasion of Italy, her great sufferings, and near collapse at the hands of the "barbarians"—with a plea to "reopen the temple of Mars,"[16] one consideration that may have weighed heavily on his mind was that the Florentine church of Saint John the Baptist stood, according to tradition, on the ruins of what was once a temple erected in honor of Mars. Speculation as to Machiavelli's meaning in his other writings is unnecessary. Near the end of the second book of the *Art of War* Machiavelli stated in the most graphic terms the guilt of Christianity in softening conflict between states to the point of making wars as worthless in modern times as they were worthwhile in antiquity. Not the corrupt Pope Alexander VI but Christianity in its pristine state was responsible for the flight of greatness from Europe. Christianity's effect on "our way of living today," he remarks, has been to banish *virtù*, to ostracize it from Italy, the very country that had been its home in classical times.[17] The conclusion seems clear: Christian virtue is not *virtù*; it is the very opposite, it is corruption.

The *Discourses* is even more insistent on placing the blame for the woes of Florence on Christianity. Each of the three books of this work begins with a denunciation of Christianity; every such denunciation is uncompromising and pertains to that faith even when reformed. At the outset of the volume Machiavelli asks why the moderns have hesitated to adopt the ways of Roman *virtus*, and answers his own question. "This I believe comes from the weakness into which the present religion has brought the world."[18] Equally remarkable is the treatment of Christianity found in the famous first chapter of the third book, devoted to the need to restore institutions and ways of life, every so often, to their corruption-free origins. Here Machiavelli discusses, among other things, the Franciscans and Dominicans, the reforming orders established for the purpose of restoring Christianity to the original, simple teaching of Christ. His refusal is total. These reforming orders, he asserts, "having great influence with the people . . . give them to understand that it is evil to speak evil of what is evil, and that it is good to live under the prelates' control and, if prelates make errors, to leave them to God for punishment. So the prelates do the worst they can, because they do not fear that punishment which they do not see and do not believe in."[19] Reformed Christianity delivers the world into the hands of the worst elements of the human kind, the corrupt clergy.

Reformed and corrupt Christianity, in Machiavelli's view, are inseparable—inseparable because every gain of the reformer, an anti-worldling, is transferred to the regular and very worldly clergyman. That is the lesson of *Discourses* III, 1; and the same lesson may be found near the beginning of the second book but in a much more radical form. The distinction between reformed and corrupt Christianity is nowhere present in *Discourses* II, 2, where Christian values per se are attacked as corrupt and contrasted with the virtuous values enshrined by pagan religion. Rarely has Christianity been more savagely attacked than in this passage. Arrayed on one side are the pagan virtues, *virtus*, glory, grandeur, magnificence, ferocity, exuberance, action, health, and manliness; on the other side are the Christian virtues, humility, abjectness, contempt for human things, withdrawal, inaction, suffering, and disease—and the upshot of these Christian "virtues," he concludes, is the womanish mankind of postclassical times, whose histories are as ignoble as Rome's was noble. Christianity, the religion corrupt and despicable by its very nature, is one major cause accounting for what plagues Florence.

THE OTHER major cause of Florentine degradation, accounted for systematically and historically in the *Florentine History*, is the triumph of the commercial oligarchy, a class unskilled in the art of rule, internally divided, and lacking in *virtù*. An aesthete such as Burckhardt could run away from the bourgeois nineteenth century he despised and enjoy hours of solace contemplating the artistic beauties of Renaissance Italy. Machiavelli, however, has almost nothing to say about the masterpieces of sculpture and painting produced in his day. For him beauty, along with everything else worthwhile, was primarily political, and he never doubted for a moment that in his bourgeois republic he was surrounded by the horror of philistinism. In the absence of political artists—molders and shapers of men—a history of Florence could not be other than a tale of sadness and regret, of desirable might-have-beens that never were and disasters that frequently were.

Ousted from power and commissioned by his erstwhile enemies, the Medici, to write a history of Florence, Machiavelli occupied his enforced leisure in an endeavor to prove that the political disabilities of his contemporaries were not the handiwork of *fortuna*—that they were, rather, merely the latest disturbing manifestation of the purge, centuries earlier, of the *virtù*-bearing nobility from his city-state. What was wrong with Florence was wrong systematically and a product several centuries in the making.

Machiavelli's *Florentine History*, full of invented speeches, weighty generalizations at the beginning of each book, and elaborate attention to battles and wars, is obviously written in the genre of humanist historiography,[20] but with a series of special twists. Unlike previous histories of cities written by humanists, Machiavelli's history of Florence cannot assume the tone of eulogy; rather, irony, mockery, and disdain, mixed occasionally with outright contempt, are his literary resources, and together they constitute an impressive repertoire of denunciation. Humanistic, too, but also with a difference is the manner in which he insists on using the past for the sake of the present; here again he turns the tables on Bruni, Poggio, and all previous authors who, writing the history of Florence in accordance with classical canons, had derived moral inspiration from the Florentine past. In Machiavelli's contrary estimation, Florence had no positive message to offer posterity—only Rome can fulfil that role—and yet the bungling and wasteful history of Florence need not be any less educational than the record of ancient Roman splendor. With unfailing eloquence Machiavelli spelled out his reasons for reviving the memory of what he regarded as a disappointing past.

> If in describing the things that happened in this wasted world, I do not tell of the bravery of soldiers or the efficiency of generals or the love of citizens for their country, I do show with what deceptions, with what tricks and schemes, the princes, the soldiers, the heads of the republics, in order to keep that reputation which they did not deserve, carried on their affairs. It is perhaps as useful to observe these things as to learn ancient history, because if the latter kindles free

spirits to imitation, the former will kindle such spirits to avoid and get rid of present abuses.[21]

Not that Florentine history was one of unmitigated disaster and unrelenting failure. Stating, as Machiavelli does, that his was a "wasted [*guasto*][22] world" may and does imply that it was not for want of opportunity that the Florentine record was relatively undistinguished. A man proclaiming "I love my native city more than my soul,"[23] even though he knows the scandalous past of his beloved mistress, must see in her some evidence of a charm recklessly spent but not irretrievably lost. A wasted world was composed of something worthwhile that had been squandered with great profligacy. From 1250 to 1260, at the end of the thirteenth century, and again between 1381 and 1434, Florence had reached great heights in Italian politics, adding numerous formerly free cities to the list of the peoples she held in subjection. "It is not possible to imagine how much authority and power Florence in a short time gained" during the decade following the midpoint of the thirteenth century.

> Not merely did she become head of Tuscany but took her place among the first cities of Italy. . . . The Florentines lived under this government for ten years, and in that time they compelled the Pistolese, the Aretines, and the Sienese to make alliances with them; and returning from Siena with their army, they took Volterra.[24]

Such were the fruits harvested by the government known as the *Primo Popolo*. Equally admirable was the state of Florentine affairs several decades later, when the century drew to a close:

> Never was our city in a higher or more prosperous state than at that time, for she abounded in men, in riches, and in reputation. The citizens fit for arms amounted to thirty thousand, and the inhabitants fit for arms in the surrounding

district to seventy thousand. All Tuscany, partly as subject, partly as ally, obeyed her.[25]

Moreover, "from 1381 to 1434 [Florence] . . . carried on with such glory so many wars that it added to the Florentine dominion Arezzo, Pisa, Cortona, Livorno, and Monte Pulciano; and it would have done greater things if the city had kept united."[26] The general proposition may be put forward that Florence "would have risen to almost any greatness if frequent and new internal dissensions had not tormented her."[27] Nevertheless, in spite of "dissensions which had might enough to destroy the greatest and most powerful of cities," Florence "seemed always to grow stronger. . . . And beyond doubt if Florence had had the good fortune, when she freed herself from the Empire, to take a form of government that would have kept her united, I do not know what republic, modern or ancient, would have been superior to her."[28]

Constantly hinting of but never realizing glorious aspirations, the history of Florentine politics, one can well imagine, must have tantalized and annoyed Machiavelli in the extreme. Even as Florence underwent a profound change from patrician and aristocratic to plebeian and democratic rule, the one thing that remained constant was imperialistic lust, an urge of the spirit to which Machiavelli's forebears had never been immune.[29] By combating neighboring feudal nobles and a sometimes not so distant Holy Roman Emperor, Florence, like many another Italian city, had won her municipal freedom; later, by combating and incorporating other cities in her empire, Florence achieved the status of a great Italian power, one of several regional states. But never did she come close to, or even dream of, a universal empire reminiscent of ancient Rome's.

The contrast Machiavelli draws between Rome and Florence is not the distinction between a Machiavellian and a non-Machiavellian republic, but rather the emotionally and aesthetically more provocative contrast of constantly magnificent versus chron-

ically pathetic. Machiavellism. On a second look at the passage
in which Machiavelli designates Florentine experience as educational because it teaches how not to conduct great enterprises, it
is worth noting that the politics of his city, by his account, was
not lacking its fair share of "deceptions, . . . tricks, and schemes."[30]
But to the same degree that an intelligent, hidden, and grand
Machiavellism is admirable, so also is an unintelligent, obvious,
and petty Machiavellism despicable.[31] Bearing this in mind, it
is immediately clear why Machiavelli was as contemptuous of
Florentine politics as he was enamored of ancient Roman politics.
Greatness, to repeat the lesson of the *Discourses*, is impossible
without fraud, and fraud "is the less to be censured the more it
is concealed, as was that of the Romans."[32] By contrast, Florentine
fraud, and that of Italian cities in general, was transparent, in-
famous, ineffectual, and cut off from that dream of universal
conquest that was the glory of Rome. If fraud, deceit, and dissimulation are praiseworthy in direct proportion to the grandeur
and in inverse proportion to the meanness of the ends they serve,
then Florentine Machiavellism, so limited in vision, so unworthy
even in its puny successes, was every bit as damnable as Rome's
was redemptive.

Amoralism abounded in Florentine foreign policy, as in that
of every Italian city-state, but it was an amoralism rarely reminiscent of a fox, hardly ever of a lion, and never of a lion and
fox combined. Dependent on mercenaries, Florence could not be
a lion; cunning in particulars but devoid of a masterplan of
deception, Florence was far from a first-rate fox. If an animal,
Florence, it seems, was a stupid beast venting its mindless anger
or pursuing its latest passing fancy. If a human, Florence, with
its limited span of attention, was a child: puerile outpourings of
enthusiasm for newly proposed projects were matched by an equally
childish want of perseverance at the first sign of trouble. Roman
democracy always acted with determination, Florentine democ-

racy never so; actions of Roman democracy were always preceded by careful calculation, actions of Florentine democracy rarely so.

The other great flaw of Florentine politics, and the sad refrain of Machiavelli's historical tract, was that "when wars outside are finished, those inside begin."[33] The glory that was Rome's rested on the unshakeable foundation of internal stability; the glory that might have been Florence's perpetually eluded her and did so because of her internal defects. Factional strife and class conflict, common sights everywhere in Italy, were exceptionally early arrivals in Florentine history, and as occurrences chronic and unusually severe, they had soon become intolerably destructive. In Roman history class conflict and the consequent democratization of politics had given birth to an excellent political structure, an Aristotelian polity, whereas in Florentine history the regrettable outcome of similar circumstances, carried to an extreme, was interminable instability, the escalation of hostilities within the city walls to the breaking point, and political decay in its most virulent form. A stranger to the blessings of stability, Florence could never know the joy of a lasting glory in foreign affairs. Ancient Rome was twice blessed (internally and externally); medieval and Renaissance Florence was twice cursed.

If there was one essential element that was present in the Roman but missing in the Florentine political context—one factor of exceptional fecundity in explaining the stark contrast of Rome with Florence—that singular missing link was a Machiavellian ruling class. A democrat in the *Florentine History* as in the *Discourses*, Machiavelli was convinced that the historical ills of Florentine democracy could have been remedied had she not been denied a ruling class of Machiavellian stamp—had she not lacked, that is, a latter-day counterpart to the Roman senators. Denied an astute ruling class, Florence was denied internal stability, rational political calculation, and noble examples for the populace to reproduce through the psychology of imitation. Denied stability, calculation, and noble examples, she was denied external glory. Hers was a history of deprivation.

Dissatisfied with simply calling attention to the political void left by the absence of a ruling class, Machiavelli probed for a possible but frustrated Florentine analogue to the Roman senators. Finally he came across the object of his aspirations, finding it in the most unlikely of places—unlikely, that is, to anyone who has read the *Discourses*. From a class marked for slaughter in the *Discourses* on the grounds of its incompatibility with republicanism, the erstwhile feudal nobility, transformed into an urban patriciate, was elevated in the *Florentine History* to the stature of cornerstone in the structure of hopes for republican greatness.

Previously, in the *Discourses*, Machiavelli had unmercifully castigated the feudal nobility.

> They are called gentlemen who without working live in luxury on the returns from their landed possessions, without paying any attention either to agriculture or to any other occupation necessary for making a living. Such men as these are dangerous in every republic . . . , but still more dangerous are they who, besides the aforesaid fortunes, command castles and have subjects who obey them. These two kinds of men crowd the Kingdom of Naples, the city of Rome, the Romagna, and Lombardy. From this it comes that in those lands there never has arisen any republic or well-ordered government, because men of these types are altogether hostile to all free government.

Without hesitation or mincing of words, Machiavelli suggested a remedy. "He who attempts to set up a republic in a place where there are many gentlemen cannot do so unless he first wipes them all out."[34]

Whereas a nobility born of the city, such as ancient Rome's, was a source of civic well-being, the feudal nobilities of Europe, standing for inequality, personal followings, and an anarchical drive to subdue every other noble family, had no proper place within the city and belonged to monarchical governments where a prince and his officialdom—for example, the French king and the *parlements*—could hold them in check.[35] No city-state could afford to have a feudal nobility relocate from the countryside to the urban center, unless it was a city tired of being a republic and longing for princely rule.

As opposed to a feudal nobility, continues Machiavelli, a commercial aristocracy such as that of Venice is all to the good.

> I am aware that my opinion that where there are gentlemen a republic cannot be organized appears contrary to the practice of the Venetian republic, in which no position can be held except by those who are gentlemen. To this I answer that this instance does not oppose my belief, because the gentlemen in that republic are so rather in name than in fact; they do not have great incomes from landed possessions, but their great riches are based on trade and movable property; moreover, none of them holds castles or has any jurisdiction over men.[36]

An aristocracy of the Venetian variety knew how to live in peace within the walls of the city, how to act as a unified and corporate body, how to refrain from all-out contravention of republican egalitarianism. But when the feudal nobles took up residence in the city of Florence, they brought feudal anarchy along with them.[37] Noble family slashed the throat of noble family; the lawlessness of vendetta was continuously practiced; the overweening pride of each noble made discipline, concerted action, and equality impossible. Each class within the city suffered at the instigation of the nobility.

Still, in the revised estimate of the *Florentine History*, that was not too high a price to pay, considering that under the aegis of the nobility the military virtues and a contagious noble demeanor accompanied unwanted feudal anarchy as it entered the city.

Caught within the severely circumscribed confines of the city's walls, feudal passion—always militaristic, hungry for glory, and contemptuously arrogant—would be more concentrated, potent, and explosive than it had been in the wide-open agrarian hinterland. Potentially, the nobility could have furnished the city with excellence in arms, and its grandeur of soul could have been transmitted downward by way of the imitative impulse. No peasant in the countryside dared mimic the actions of a nobleman, but within the city each citizen, however humble, could aspire to live nobly if he so pleased.

Sadly, Florentine history had unobligingly followed another course. Having called for the heads of the nobles in the *Discourses*, Machiavelli was eventually driven to the strange position of belittling the democrats of Florence in the *Florentine History* for subduing their noble oppressors. Once the nobility was eliminated, he now feared, there was no source from which the democracy could be infused with grandeur, and soon the democratic spirit was manifest as a vile lowest-common-denominator equality, dragging the great down and forcing them to forsake their noble sentiments if they wished to survive.

> Through the people's victories the city of Rome became more excellent [*più virtuosa*], because, along with nobles, men from the people could be appointed to administer the magistracies, the armies, and the high offices; thus, the latter acquired the same *virtù* the former had, and that city, as she increased in *virtù*, increased in power. But in Florence, since the people won, the nobles continued to be deprived of high offices, and if they wished to get them again, they were forced in their conduct, their spirit, and their way of living . . . to be like the men of the people.

When the nobles suffered this debasement, "the *virtù* in arms and the boldness of spirit possessed by the nobility were destroyed, and these qualities could not be rekindled in the people, where they did not exist, so that Florence grew always weaker and more despicable."[38] Grandeur and nobility of soul gave way to humble behavior not just for the nobility but for all Florence, including the triumphant upper middle class which was so eager to be regarded as a new aristocracy.

If, as we have seen, the fate of the nobility was the central drama of all Florentine history and a tragedy in one act as well, yet in another sense it was only a single episode in a miserable tale of all too many scenes and acts. For the history of all hitherto existing Florentine politics had been the history of class struggles and factional intrigues. Noble and citizen, patrician and plebeian, major and minor guild, guild master and journeyman, citizen and proletarian, in a word, oppressor and oppressed, stood in constant opposition to one another, carrying on an uninterrupted, now hidden, now open fight, a fight that each time ended in a reconstitution of the political structure or in the common ruin of the contending classes. From this perspective the scarred bodies of the nobility, mutilated in internecine intracity quarrels instead of in the glory of intercity combat, were only a few of the downtrodden in a much larger and thoroughly agonizing pattern of mean-spirited politics. This depressing story must be retold, thought Machiavelli, so that men will never again repeat such foolish and self-destructive politics.

The most promising place to initiate an examination of Florentine domestic strife is with the nobility, the class most hated and most loved by Machiavelli. Eventually every class comes under fire for violating Machiavelli's most cherished political maxims, but the nobility is singled out for especially harsh censure, so harsh that it initially seems we are back in the nobility-hating *Discourses*.

Historically, the nobility of Florence was the first offender, the first group to place personal and party interests above dedication to civic virtue. In Roman history the coming of democracy was accompanied by the promulgation of a body of laws, the

Twelve Tables, copied from Greek democracy, and to these laws everyone paid homage, the nobility included. As always, Florence reversed the Roman pattern. The nobility refused to submit; even after taking up residence in the city, it continued to direct violence against the classes below it and practiced vendetta, blood-feud, and kinship vengeance against its own kind, all of which brazenly transgressed the framework of municipal legality.[39]

As if that were not bad enough, the wayward nobles were also responsible for initiating the divisions that fragmented all of Florence into hostile factions. The quarrel of Blacks and Whites was originally the exclusive affair of noble families but with time it contaminated the whole of society.[40] Much worse was the long-lived split into Guelphs and Ghibellines, supporters of the papacy and the Holy Roman Empire respectively. From rival claimants to dominion over all Christendom during medieval times, papacy and empire had been reduced to one power among several contending Italian powers in the former case and in the latter to weak and disjointed sham. Under the names "Guelph" and "Ghibelline," neither papacy nor empire was really to be found, but only the ambition of rival noble factions in Florence and their common sin against civic virtue in looking for allies outside the city who could help them settle a domestic conflict.[41] Civic virtue suffered such repeated molestations by the nobility that it could never attain full strength of character.

Before long the insolence of the nobility was so intolerable that it united everyone situated below them on the social ladder. The particular animosities felt by various groups for one another were temporarily set aside and replaced by the common animosity of all to the nobility. For a change, greater and lesser guilds were in agreement, and even the peasants outside the city were anxious to support measures designed to break the power of the nobility. Finally, in Giano della Bella, the populace was given an enlightened leader, willing to act against the nobility into which he had been born, so that a better and more stable republic might be secured.[42] On the initiative of this exceptional man, the political structure of Florence was remade so as to deprive the nobility of prominence in governmental affairs. Under the new arrangement, known as the Ordinances of Justice, the guilds were all-powerful and the old nobility was degraded socially as well as politically by being forced to enter the guilds.[43] Hence emerged the humble nobility Machiavelli abhorred, a nobility that could not ennoble the populace now that it had to live in accordance with pedestrian bourgeois mores if it hoped to survive.

After the nobility was domesticated, the battles within the city did not subside but rekindled time and again: ever a new factional alignment, ever a renewed class struggle. Although the *virtù* of the nobility was not allowed to flow downward to the middle class, one thing did follow such a route of social diffusion, namely, feudal anarchy:

> The pride and ambition of our nobles were not destroyed but were taken . . . by our people, who now . . . strive to gain first rank in the republic. Since they have no other way to gain it than through dissensions, they have divided the city once more. . . .[44]

Unheroic bourgeois values moved upwards, enveloping the nobles, but the ghost of the nobility lived on in innumerable acts of petty self-esteem and a pattern of ridiculous factionalism.

Had feudal valor been maintained intact, had it been segregated from feudal anarchy and passed down the social scale until universalized in the social psychology of the Florentines—had all these conditions been met, heroic civic virtue could have flowered. As it was, feudal valor was uprooted, and when the dreaded fruits of feudal anarchy ripened, chaos was multiplied a hundredfold by the intensification of anarchistic feudal passions trapped within the city's walls. Discipline, so essential to Rome's and to any civic virtue, was impossible to maintain. Personal and dynastic quarrels shook the entire society, a reality inimical to the col-

lectivism of civic virtue. Crossbreeding democratic and aristocratic strains gave Rome everything and Florence nothing, neither
a Machiavellian ruling class, nor a democracy worth having, nor
even simple stability.

Far from infusing Florentine democracy with greatness, the
nobility dragged it into a political abyss. Given this scathing
indictment drawn up by Machiavelli, it is incredible that he then
went on to blame the democracy for manhandling the nobles.
All the Florentine democrats had done was to fulfil in their day
what the Machiavelli of the *Discourses* hoped other city-states
would accomplish in his: the destruction of the nobility. One
can only reconcile Machiavelli's inconsistency by saying that if
he could not have a heroic democracy, then it was not always
certain whether he wanted democracy at all.

With the demise of the old nobility, a new aristocracy stepped
forward, the "nobles of the people." Recruited from the great
merchants and the leaders of the guilds, these leading members
of the bourgeoisie were noble only by virtue of falsely assumed
airs. For a while they managed to stay on top by a game of what
in anachronistic retrospect looks very much like the divide-and-
rule strategy of nineteenth-century Whiggery. Just as "their fathers made use of the masses to destroy the haughtiness of the
nobles, [so] now that the nobility had become humble and the
masses haughty, the haughtiness of the lowest classes could well
be checked with the aid of the nobles."[45] There was democracy,
but only among the well-to-do; the democracy was their democracy and too much democracy was bad for government.

Sometimes events spun out of control, and after an expensive
war they instigated failed, the fat burghers had to submit to a
graduated levy of taxation. Not a magnanimous leadership sworn
to abide by republican egalitarianism, but a frightened and pu-
sillanimous leadership was responsible for passage of this reno-
vated system of taxation.[46] In general the new aristocracy—really
nothing more than an oligarchy with aristocratic pretensions—

was vulnerable for two familiar reasons. First, after consolidating its power, the new upper stratum began to take its primacy for granted and was soon unbearable; second, having thus severed itself from everyone below its station, the new elite added to its weakness by intraclass quarrels, conflicts, and feuds. In short the new "nobility," learning nothing from the demise of the old, went about repeating those mistakes that always mark a ruling class for insurrection. Before long the pattern of post-aristocratic politics was apparent; the new nobles were the "promoters of slavery" and the people were the "promoters of license."[47] Ill deeds of a ruling class are always evil compounded: a vile ruling class brings the worst out in everyone. Whether extraordinarily noble, as in Rome, or extraordinarily despicable, as in Florence, a ruling class is never a thing indifferent.

The political evils begotten by class hostilities were sometimes unqualified. Three episodes in particular stand out in Machiavelli's history as illustrations of how far he believed the degradation of Florentine politics could go. One was Florence's early encounter with a despot, the Duke of Athens, in 1343; a second was the speech Machiavelli put in the mouth of a disillusioned Florentine patriot in 1372; and the third was the revolt of the Ciompi in 1378. Each of these episodes recapitulated the wasteful past or was pregnant with the self-destructive future.

Holding what was meant to be a temporary position in the Florentine republic, the Duke of Athens capitalized on the widespread frustration and renewal of class antagonisms that followed in the wake of a lost war. The nobles, not yet completely abject, encouraged the Duke to declare himself prince, and their suggestion was seconded by several noteworthy upper middle-class families who, "burdened by debts they could not pay from their own property, wished to pay them from that of others, and with the slavery of their city to free themselves from slavery to their creditors."[48] Seizing his opportunity, the Duke won immediate popularity by executing the leaders of the ill-fated war against

Lucca. Nobles and lower classes applauded enthusiastically and the middle classes were too immobilized by fear to respond at all. Next, with the assistance of the old nobility and the lowest classes, the Duke's office was changed from a one year grant to a position held for life. And when the Duke undertook the dismantling of the constitutional structure, so long the shield and weapon of the middle class, it became perfectly evident that the premonitions of the bourgeoisie were well-founded.

Faithful to classical models in his techniques of historical writing, Machiavelli constructs from his own imagination a speech by a Florentine who hopes to dissuade the Duke from his transparent designs.

> You seek to make a slave of a city that has always lived free.
> . . . Have you considered how important and how strong in a city like this is the name of liberty, which no force crushes, no time wears away, and no gain counterbalances? Consider, my lord, what great forces are needed to hold as a slave so great a city.

Not even the winning of a great Italian empire could possibly compensate the Florentines for the loss of their liberty.

> What actions do you intend yours shall be that can counterpoise the sweetness of free government . . . ? Not if you should join to this state all of Tuscany, and if every day you should return into this city triumphant over your enemies; because all that glory would be not hers but yours, and the citizens would gain not subjects but fellow slaves.

The Duke is further informed that the political absolutism he craves cannot be bolstered by a solid social foundation. As soon as the nobles have wreaked vengeance on the middle class, they will withdraw their support, and the fickle plebeians who form the other pillar of the Duke's power are apt to change their minds at a moment's notice. Abandoned and isolated, the Duke could not be a prince but only a tyrant, and, like all tyrants, his hands would soon be soiled by the blood of innocents, and his own person would be in constant danger. So the patriotic Florentine informs the Duke in truly prophetic words. But until the time when the fulfilment of prophecy is at hand, the Duke has the last word. To all charges that he is robbing Florence of her liberty he has one trenchant reply: "He said it was not his purpose to take away the city's liberty, but to give it back again, because only disunited cities were slaves and united ones free."[49]

Both accuser and accused, the patriotic Florentine and the Duke, were correct. A city excessively disunited is not free, but neither can unity be had from the absolute power of a single person. Initially the darling of large segments of Florentine society, the Duke, in his lust for unlimited power, alienated classes in a steady progression until at last he stood alone, completely powerful and completely weak. Hardly had tenure for life been offered him than he turned against the nobles as well as the middle class, crushing both indiscriminately under an immense burden of taxation. If the Duke had his way, no one in the entire city would be noble, wealthy, or secure except himself. To this end he forged an alliance of support consisting, from within, of the lowest classes, the unenfranchised and noncitizens, and, from without, of the peoples of cities long held in subjection to Florence. Other unpleasant consequences of his reign included an influx of Frenchmen into the city who flaunted their alien ways, much to the annoyance of the natives; worse still, and a blunder Machiavelli rated as particularly egregious, stupid, and inflammatory, the Duke and his henchmen violated Florentine women repeatedly.[50] Of the Duke's reign it might be said that the "severity and kindness he had pretended were transformed into pride and cruelty, so that many citizens . . . were fined or put to death or tortured in strange ways," and the only ones saved from oppression were those whom Florence had overcome in battle—those whose oppression was essential to the grandeur of Florence.[51]

So erratic and unjust was the Duke's government that conspiracies were brewing against him at every level of the social scale, top to bottom; indeed, the history of the Duke's reign, in one sense, reads as a case study of the principles articulated in *Discourses* III, 6, "On Conspiracy," and might be placed under a subheading worded "How to provoke conspiracies." At last Florence rid herself of a tyrant. Yet, for all the satisfaction he took in relating the overthrow of the Duke, Machiavelli refused to construe this event as a vindication of the city's free and democratic spirit. Rather it was but one more event confirming his picture of the Florentines as a people "who cannot keep their liberty and yet cannot endure servitude"[52]—a phrase borrowed from the *Histories* of Tacitus,[53] where it was used to characterize the degraded Romans of the early Empire, who could not be citizens but would not be subjects.

To read between the lines, the entire history of the Duke's brief rule may be viewed as a premonition of Florence's later submission to the Medici, whose political longevity was due to two considerations. More devious than the Duke, the Medici observed republican rituals and forms even as they circumvented republican substance.[54] The second source of the strength of the Medici was derived, ironically, from the strength of their opponents. Never absolute rulers, the Medici and their circle were too involved in placating the populace to permit serious dissension to break out among their own numbers.[55] Florence could discard the Duke of Athens, but all she gained was a breathing space, and not a permanent exemption from the coming of the prince. When the Medici prince entered the city at a later date, inaugurating a period of counterfeit republicanism, liberty[56] and glory departed, impostors taking their place.

In truth the Medici prince, rather than entering the city from the outside, as did the Duke of Athens at an earlier date, was an entirely homegrown product, and exemplified Machiavelli's rule that ambition expressed through private means, notably by building a personal and ostensibly nonpolitical following, signaled the presence of an ill-regulated, corruptible republic ready to decline into tyranny.[57] Hardly the worst of tyrants, usually able to hide their tyranny, the Medici nevertheless revealed what they were by their understanding of the process of "renewal." Every so often, it is true, the Florence of the Medici did return to its pristine first principles—not, however, to the first principles of the republic, but to the first principles of the Medici.

> Those who managed the government of Florence from 1434 to 1494 commonly said that every five years they needed to revise the government. . . . By revising the government they meant inspiring such terror and such fear in the people as they had inspired on first taking charge. . . .[58]

Under the Medici, the violence that almost always accompanies renewal meant a rededication to corruption rather than a recovery of virtue.

A brief period of turbulence followed on the heels of the expulsion of the Duke of Athens in 1343. Externally, the rise of the Florentines against their individual tyrant was the signal for a rise of foreign subjects against their collective master—the city of Florence.[59] Internally, a compromise divided the government between nobles and burghers, but proved to be short-lived.

> The city would have been quiet if the nobles had been content to live with the modesty demanded by life as citizens, but they did the opposite, because in private life they tolerated no equals, and in the magistracies they were determined to be lords, and every day there was some instance of their arrogance and pride. This offended the people, who lamented that for one tyrant who had been removed a thousand had sprung up.[60]

From the ensuing confusion there emerged a new constitution, more democratic than any preceding it, which lasted from 1343 to 1382. Into the established governmental pattern the lesser guilds were absorbed, which is another way of saying that this was a democracy not only of great merchants and guildmasters but of shopkeepers and artisans, a petty-bourgeois paradise. Inclusion of the artisans was matched by the definitive exclusion of the nobility from Florentine politics, so it is not surprising that Machiavelli shows not the slightest trace of that enthusiasm for the coming of democracy that was written large in his treatise on Roman politics. He could not believe that anything noble could ever come from the democracy of the humble, the pecuniary, the economically preoccupied.

How very degraded Florence had become is the theme of a speech supposedly delivered in 1372 by a lover of his country. In this speech, one of many that dramatize the most important events depicted in the *Florentine History*, Machiavelli's imaginary protagonist recites with revulsion the litany of his native city's woes. It is an exercise in rhetoric well worth re-creating because in it Machiavelli's wounded republican pride is transformed into the anger of a terse indictment of the overall pattern of Florentine politics.

Liberty, equality, and fraternity, forever the words emblazoned on the emblems of republics, have in Florence been perverted beyond recognition, or so we are informed in this remarkable speech. Instead of liberty, there are personal followings, factionalism, and license. Instead of equality among great men, there is the vile equality of corruption. Instead of fraternity as the brotherhood of free men, there is the fraternity of wrongdoing: "There is among the citizens," the Florentine patriot bitterly complains, "neither union nor friendship except among those who are sharers in some wickedness undertaken either against their city or against individuals."[61] Chronicling the history of Greek corruption, Thucydides had noted that words changed their meaning, new and perverted definitions taking the place of old and virtuous meanings;[62] the same theme later occurs in Sallust,[63] historian of Roman corruption; and now Machiavelli appears to have made an identical observation about Florentine corruption.

One of the principal sources of Rome's unity was the power of religious belief and the extraordinary efficacy of oaths in binding together the populace.[64] In Florence, on the contrary, "because religion and the fear of God have been extinguished in all men, an oath and a pledge are valuable as far as they are profitable, for men employ them not with the purpose of observing them, but to use them as means for deceiving more easily,"[65] sighs Machiavelli's patriotic speaker. From Machiavelli's viewpoint, religion does and should deceive, since its deceptions, when correctly used, forge communal solidarity; but in Florence, always the antithesis of Rome, religion had become a weapon wielded by one faction against another.

Factionalism, unrepentant factionalism, was the sin of Florence and it dragged everyone into the mire, even the best: "The wicked adhere to factions through avarice . . . , the good through necessity." A man alone in a factious society is a man extremely vulnerable. By a political version of Gresham's law, the good are either driven out or devalued until they reach the level of the bad. "The good, trusting in their innocence, do not seek, like the wicked, for those who will unlawfully defend and honor them; hence they fall undefended and unhonored." Young and old alike, men of every class and station, are debased and stricken by a common malady in a city "sustaining herself by means of factions rather than laws."[66]

Corruption of such magnitude was bound to affect the ability of Florence to assert herself against other states. Though corruption is a disease of the inner parts of the body politic, its effects are visible in the external actions of that body, its foreign policy. The winners in factional struggles, generalizes the spokesman of Florentine patriotism, "make laws and statutes not for the public benefit but for their own; hence wars, truces, alliances are decided not for the common glory but for the pleasure of a few."[67] In ancient Rome the wars proposed by the ruling class to divert the people were always fought with the common glory of Rome constantly in mind, and fought successfully. In Florence the wars advocated by the rulers were fought for the glory of the few, fought unsuccessfully, and eventually the many saw through the sham.[68]

Repeatedly in the *Florentine History* Machiavelli makes the statement that "the whole city was under arms."[69] Virtually the same statement may be found in the *Discourses*, where we read that "the whole city, both the noble and the ignoble, were employed in war."[70] Perhaps nothing so well summarizes the difference between Florence and Rome as these two nearly identical assertions, because in the Roman case they describe an entire city armed for glorious deeds in battle against other cities, while in the Florentine case they describe a city ingloriously at war with itself.

Like every government preceding it, the regime of 1343 to 1382 was a volatile and unstable compound, always in danger of explosion or more gradual decomposition. The outbreak of hostilities in 1378 between major and minor guilds, traders and artisans, was, then, nothing out of the ordinary, and even the involvement of the urban plebes was not in itself a novel phenomenon. Many times before the plebeians had been mobilized, answering the summons of one or another party, only to be victimized by their erstwhile ally once the victory was assured. Yet the plebeian politics of 1378 did have its unique side. This time the poor and miserable wretches were out to secure their own good and by whatever measures were necessary. Scum of the earth, these vulgar refugees from the countryside had not found liberty awaiting them within the city's walls, but rather a wool industry ready and eager to grind and waste their bodies and spirits. Denied permission to organize as a guild, so essential if they were to gain access to the politics of peaceful group bargaining, they now formed an illegal and inevitably revolutionary association. Their wrath was implacable and their capacity for violence immense. The insiders were not to ride roughshod over them this time.

Unsympathetic first to the democracy of merchants and traders and later to the democracy of artisans and shopkeepers, Machiavelli now expresses his distaste for "the stench of the lower class."[71] Consistent to the end, he turns his back on commercial republicanism in all its variations of regimes, from the most oligarchical to the most plebeian and including everything in between. Be that as it may, Machiavelli, who was as eager to accentuate the Ciompi episode as Bruni[72] had been to downplay it, paid the plebeians an eccentric compliment while reconstructing the history of its brief upsurge. With several careful strokes of the pen, the dregs of society are transformed into masters of Machiavellian politics. Puzzling over a series of events during which the plebeians acted in concert, Machiavelli does not seek the explanation of their awakening class consciousness, as Marx would, in the conditions of social production, but rather centers, as was his wont, on the success of their leaders in instilling a common awareness. What is most fascinating about the speech he puts in the mouth of a plebeian leader is its vivid exposition of Machiavellian maxims, maxims not the property of the ruling class, as in ancient Rome, but of the wretched of the earth.

Political radicalism in the modern sense has nothing to do with Machiavelli's striking account of the plebeian cause. His, rather, is a remake and politicization of a rhetorical convention which, in nonpolitical form, was frequently found in Latin literature: the formula of "the world upside down." The topsy-turvy image of the ox harnessed behind the cart, the lamb hunting the wolf, the natural order of things overturned and changed into its opposite is a theme frequently found in Latin letters.[73] For plebeians to be Machiavellians is as unnatural as a dog fleeing a hare and hence a perfect insult when directed against the pathetically inept leaders of Florence.*

* Ironically, "the world turned upside down" later became a stock phrase in the rhetoric of revolutionary politics.

The plebeian leader's speech merits a close look. Illusions of every variety, he argues, are to be torn away, the naked facts of power exposed, and rational calculations of the utility of violence weighed. "We must . . . if we expect to be pardoned for our transgressions, commit new ones, doubling our offense and multiplying our arson and robbery"—the counterpart to which is Machiavelli's demand in *The Prince* that a new ruler commit decisive acts of violence. Anything less is ineffectual violence, leaving the perpetrator of wrongs vulnerable to vengeance.[74]

Of all their illusions, the one the plebeians need most desperately to free themselves from is the belief that some men are their superiors by birth—the counterpart to which is Machiavelli's demand in the *Discourses* that the ruling elite not be based on hereditary succession.

> Do not be frightened [argues the plebeian leader] by their antiquity of blood which they shame us with, for all men, since they had one and the same beginning, are equally ancient; by nature they are all made in one way. Strip us all naked; you will see us all alike; dress us then in their clothes and they in ours; without doubt we shall seem noble and they ignoble, for only poverty and riches make us unequal.

In order to be unfettered in their actions, the plebeians must first be unfettered in their psyches by the chains of remorse—their enervating qualms about good and evil.

> I am very sorry to hear that many of you, for reasons of conscience, repent of the things you have done and wish to refrain from anything more; if it is true, you certainly are not the men I believed you were. Neither conscience nor ill fame ought to frighten you. . . . Of conscience we need take no account, for when people fear hunger and prison, as we do, they cannot and should not have any fear of Hell.[75]

All previous conquerors, he informs and exhorts his comrades, were maligned as inhuman until their victory, when suddenly they were eulogized as the stuff heroes are made of: "Those who conquer, in whatever way they conquer, never because of it come to disgrace." Without knowing it the plebeian is virtually quoting from *The Prince*: "Truly it is very natural and normal to wish to conquer, and when men do it who can, they will always be praised, or not blamed. But when they cannot and try to do so all the same, herein lies their error and their blame."[76]

If, continues the plebeian, the greatness of the rich and powerful has always rested on "either fraud or force"—another famous phrase borrowed from *The Prince*[77]—why should not the humble, now that the blinders are off, apply the same methods to their own ends? And indeed they must, like it or not, because "when necessity pushes, rashness is judged prudence." So says the plebeian agitator, whose invocation of "necessity" brings to mind one of the most quoted passages of *The Prince*:

> A prince, in order to hold his position, must learn how not to be good, and understand when to use it and when not to use it, in accord with necessity.[78]

In the *Florentine History* the person best versed in the lessons of *The Prince* is anything but a prince.

As to providing for their well-being, continues the rebel leader, the plebeians can live off confiscated goods. Fortunes have always been owing more "to stealing than to labor, and to bad rather than good arts." A policy of confiscation does not pretend to end the pattern of exploitation that has always been the rule; it proposes nothing more than to give the exploited an opportunity to exploit. Machiavelli had propounded a similar doctrine of riches gained through pillage instead of economy in his *Art of War*, when he congratulated Rome on its parasitical withdrawal of resources from conquered foes and blamed Florence for failure to follow Roman precedent.[79] In Florentine politics, one city-state did not devour others—a policy Machiavelli approved; rather one part of his beloved city threatened to devour the rest—a catastrophe pure and simple.

Here, as Machiavelli conceived it, was one of the greatest ironies of Florentine history. An apology for Machiavellism and an articulation of its uses is not delivered by a prince or by a representative of a ruling class but by the wretched of the earth. Neither the glory of conquest, nor a return to the first principles of civic virtue, nor even simple stability was the object of this Machiavellism. Instead, its object was the undoing of Florence itself, a declaration of war on the citizenry coming from the dispossessed within the gates of the city. That a self-conscious Machiavellism should emerge at last but in this form—as the ultimate exacerbation of Florence's destructive internal struggles—underscored the pitiful futility of that city's history as nothing else could.

Presumably the Machiavellism of the Ciompi bore the same relationship to a proper Machiavellism as a battle fought by mercenary armies in 1424 bore to the wars fought by citizens' militias: "In so great a defeat, reported everywhere in Italy, nobody died except Lodovico degli Obizzi with two of his followers; these three, falling from their horses, were drowned in the mud."[80] So much is Florentine history a monument to futility that it must be told as a mock-heroic epic.

"TRULY A GREAT and miserable city":[81] such was Florence in Machiavelli's judgment. Great and miserable, she is both the stuff dreams are made of and the disappointment that follows dreaming. Machiavelli does not say his city was unpromising; he says she failed to live up to her promise. He does not say opportunity is wanting; he says she had a penchant for wasting opportunity. While other historians of Florence adopted the conventional humanist tone of eulogy, Machiavelli writes history in the unconventional tone of irony. Frustration is his most deeply felt experience when examining the deeds of his city, and his bitter irony is this frustration put into words.

Despair, however, is not his tone. What once was can be again because human nature is no different now than it was in ancient times.[82] From the apparent pessimism of a cyclical view of history springs the optimistic note that defeat is never final: after winter comes spring and renewed hope, after corruption virtue—and especially so when there are those who know how to learn from the past and who strive by their lessons learned consciously to redeem the present.[83] If the glory of Rome is the shame of Florence, it is equally true that the glory that was Rome can be revived, whether in whole or in part, by moderns willing to learn from the ancients.

Machiavelli said of the Florentines what Tacitus had said of the corrupt Romans: that they were men who could tolerate neither servitude nor liberty. Yet Machiavelli, however much he used Tacitus to chide his fellow Florentines, did not believe, as Tacitus did, that the era of republicanism was irrevocably past. Far from it, Machiavelli was convinced the times were quite compatible with a revival of virtue.

> To honor and reward excellence, not to despise poverty, to esteem the methods and regulations of military discipline, to oblige the citizens to love one another, to live without factions, to esteem private less than public good . . . are things that could easily fit in with our times.[84]

He was particularly convinced that the citizens' militia of the Florentine past could be revived and greatly improved upon, if modeled along the lines set forth in his *Art of War*, a handbook on how to retrieve Roman military methods.

Under a prince blessed with enough political vision to build his own army, mercenary troops and the comic wars they wage will become a thing of the past, Machiavelli argues at the end of the *Art of War*. Even better than a prince with his own army, of course, is a republic with soldiers who are citizens; and Florence can be such a republic if the Medici will relinquish their princely ambitions. Machiavelli gives the Medici good reasons for accepting the status of powerful citizens, rather than princely rulers, in his *Discourse on Remodeling the Government of Florence*, a paper presented to the Medici and applying the lessons of the *Discourses on Livy* to their circumstances.

Recapitulating *Discourses* I, 55, Machiavelli argues in the essay on *Remodeling* that, although Florence has historically wavered between monarchy and republic and has never truly been one or the other, her social situation—her "matter"—is unambiguously of the sort calling for a republican "form." Where feudal hierarchy holds sway, as in the social structure of Milan or Naples, a monarchical government is called for; where, on the contrary, a relative equality of social conditions prevails, as in Florence, republican government is natural, monarchical unnatural. Doomed to fight perpetually against the natural order of things, a Medici prince can only be a hated tyrant, subject to "a thousand dangers" and condemned to infamy; whereas (an adaptation of *Discourses* I, 10) a Medicean ruler who reconstitutes Savonarola's Great Council, giving everyone a stake in a republican status quo, and then becomes in fact what the Medici have traditionally claimed to be, merely the leading citizens of a republican government, will enjoy the "everlasting fame" that has always been the reward of "those men who have with laws and with institutions remodeled republics and kingdoms."[85]

Should rational argumentation fail, there is a second method of ridding Florence of the prince, the method of conspiracy—one of Machiavelli's favorite topics in all his writings and the subject of discussion in the longest chapter of the *Discourses*, chapter six of the third book. Machiavelli begins by commending Tacitus's resigned and despairing advice to accept whoever is prince, simply because he is the prince.[86] By the time he has finished his discourse on conspiracy, Machiavelli has, however, given excellent lessons on the method of conducting a successful conspiracy; and we must not forget that the *Discourses* were written for the republican audience of the Oricellari Gardens, some of whose members did conspire against the Medici in 1522.[87]

Greatness could still be Florence's. The first modern ruler to revive Roman military methods was destined to possess one of the most magnificent empires this side of antiquity.

> [Of the rulers] who today have states in Italy, he . . . will
> be lord of this country who first sets out on this road. And
> it will happen to his state as to the kingdom of the Mace-
> donians when ruled by Philip. . . . While the rest of Greece
> sat idle . . . Philip by means of this organization and these
> [military] exercises became so powerful that in a few years
> he could entirely conquer her, and could leave his son such
> a foundation that he made himself ruler of all the world.[88]

Thus does Machiavelli conclude the *Art of War*, and it need hardly be added that he wishes Florence to be this new Rome, conqueror of Italy and then the world.

The conquest of Italy is an occasional but recurring theme in Machiavelli's writings. Now and then in the *Florentine History* he pauses to note that a given city, at a certain moment, found itself in circumstances favorable to the acquisition of a great empire, far beyond anything seen in postclassical Italy.[89] In the *Discourses* he observes that "no region is ever united or happy if all of it is not under the sway of one republic or one prince."[90] Later, in that same work, he caps a discussion of the imperialistic methods of ancient Rome with the statement that "since we are in this ignorance [of Roman ways], we are the prey of whoever has wished to overrun this land."[91] Machiavelli was not the Italian nationalist that nineteenth-century historians, the final chapter of *The Prince* in mind, made him out to be;[92] twentieth-century historians are surely correct in stressing that for Machiavelli, as for all Italians, his native city was his *patria* and Italy merely the *provincia* (province).[93] But what the historians of today have missed is the constant theme of imperialism in Machiavelli's writings, his hopes for a revival of ancient Roman conquest by modern Florence, which, besides the glory that attends all aggrandizement, could win additional fame if it resulted in "root[ing] out these frightful [foreign] beasts, which beyond the appearance and the voice have nothing human [in their makeup]."[94]

Francesco Guicciardini did not overlook the brief comments in the *Discourses on Livy* on the possibility of a modern Italian empire. Coming upon the passage in which Machiavelli's admiration for Roman conquest blossomed into the hope that the Florentine republic, if rearmed, dangerous, and imitative of the ancient Romans, might subject all of Italy to a single rule, Guicciardini did not balk at the thought of the violence Machiavelli's scheme would entail. Nevertheless, he did reject Machiavelli's proposal.

> I really do not know whether its not becoming united under one rule has been this country's luck or misfortune. For, if as a republic, unity could have brought glory to the name of Italy and happiness to the ruling city, it would have meant disaster for all the others, for under the shadow of that city they could not attain any greatness.[95]

Forced to choose either the grandeur of a republic uniting Italy by enslaving all other republics, or the grandeur of multiple republics, each enjoying freedom and independence, Guicciardini opted for the second alternative. Machiavelli unhesitatingly opted for the first alternative because the grandeur he most cherished was aggrandizing in the first place, and did not need—any more than ancient Rome did—the goal of an Italy cleansed of foreigners to justify its liberty to end all liberty save its own.

How very bold Machiavelli's political position was may be discerned by a contrast with the politics of his republican friends,

advocates of aristocratic rule. Nostalgically, the Florentine aristocrats of Machiavelli's day looked back to the fifteenth century
and the reign of Lorenzo de'Medici, the *Magnifico*, congratulating
him on a policy—possibly less consciously intended by him than
attributed to him after the fact—of balancing power between the
several Italian regional states, Milan, Venice, Florence, the Papal
States, and Naples.[96] Insofar as they dealt at all with the problem
of foreign invasions in and after 1494, the Florentine aristocrats
of the early cinquecento did so through the hope that the major
Italian powers might overcome their mutual rivalries long enough
to forge a common alliance against the Oltramontani,* instead
of pursuing their various individual designs by siding with one
or another of the "barbarians" against neighboring and competing
Italian states.[97]

To the aristocratic dream of an alliance overriding regional
differences Machiavelli responded with a crisp "You make me
laugh."[98] To the aristocratic discussion of a period when power
in Italy "was in a certain way balanced"[99] Machiavelli responded,
in *The Prince*, simply by using the past tense.[100] A superior appreciation of the *verità effettuale della cosa* is not, however, what
separates Machiavelli from the likes of Francesco Guicciardini and
Francesco Vettori, his equals in a frank recognition of the primacy
of force in politics.[101] What makes Machiavelli different is that
he cared not in the least for the fifteenth century, in which there
was an Italian balance of power. Obliged to narrate the events of
the last century in his *Florentine History*, Machiavelli does so; but
he seems downright bored when dealing with the quattrocento,
during which "the chief care of those princes was to watch one
another and to make themselves secure against one another with
marriages, new friendships, and alliances."[102] What had this to
do with grandeur and glory?

Different, too, is Machiavelli's preference for a democratic rather

---

* Italians referred to Frenchmen, Germans, and all peoples living beyond (north
of) the Alps as Oltramontani—and as barbarians.

than an aristocratic republic. Here again Machiavelli's arguments supporting his choice initially invite us to conclude that his is a superior "realism": the many, as a matter of fact, enjoyed power during Savonarola's recent reign; the many, as a matter of theory, ought to enjoy power according to the Aristotelian and Polybian concept of polity; and therefore a return to democracy is a stabilizing, whereas a return to aristocracy is a destabilizing, strategy. But upon closer inspection it is once again ideological fervor, not a facing up to the factual truths of things, that dictates Machiavelli's choice: Rome would never have achieved the greatness of world domination had she followed the Spartan example of withholding arms from the hands of the people, nor can Florence achieve greatness if she follows the example of oligarchical Venice, model state of Florentine aristocrats. Democracy reopens the road to ancient greatness, provided it be a heroic, not a priestly or commercial, democracy; and heroism is still possible, if only the rulers will take their classical education more seriously.

"The real muse of Machiavelli," commented Francesco de Sanctis, "is not enthusiasm but irony."[103] Unquestionably irony is Machiavelli's device when he discusses modern history; but it is equally true that Machiavelli discusses ancient history with an enthusiasm that never wanes and is especially vigorous because he believes the present can recapture the past. Irony and enthusiasm are ordinarily not conjoined; Machiavelli, however, was far from ordinary. As opposed to the aristocrats, who looked back nostalgically to the fifteenth century, Machiavelli looked back much further, to classical times, and yet was convinced his politics were far from nostalgic. What he stood for was grounded in a comprehension of history and politics that transcended, so he believed, both the temporal barrier separating past from present and the conceptual barrier separating power politics from ideological politics. To the very end of his life, he remained convinced Florentine regeneration and greatness were possible, given a new ruling class of the kind he championed.

–IV–

A DAY AND A NIGHT IN THE
LIFE OF A CITIZEN

VIRTUE and corruption in politics, the methods of effective and
ineffective internal rule, the strategy and tactics of empire-building, the organization of a citizens' army—all these matters dealing
with public affairs were Machiavelli's concerns in *The Prince*, the
Discourses on Livy, the *Art of War*, and the *Florentine History*. In
none of these works is private life discussed, other than for a few
scattered, incidental comments. And, indeed, it is not my contention that Machiavelli ever sat down and wrote something even
remotely approaching a treatise on the nature of private existence
within a properly regulated republic. Yet I do wish to argue that
Machiavelli's comedies and familiar letters have a theoretical significance in their constant readiness to sanction seduction and
sexual play, whenever such activities are well done and do not
threaten the stability of the family. The sexual puritanism of civic
humanism, so spartan in its ideals, so intent on repressing sex-
uality, was overturned by Machiavelli, who encouraged politicians
to be serious by day but frivolous at night. Machiavelli's laughter,
voiced in his comedies and familiar letters, is theory-laden.

MACHIAVELLI wrote a play that has frequently been hailed as
the best comedy of the Italian Renaissance. The question which
inevitably arises is whether there is a connection between the
serious and the comic works of Machiavelli, whether the *Man-*

dragola* stands alone, a tribute pure and simple to the versatility of Machiavelli's mind, or whether the themes of the *Mandragola* are an extension of the themes found in the bulk of his writings. Is there, in short, a political message, cleverly disguised, in the *Mandragola*? Some of Machiavelli's commentators think so, but they flatly contradict one another. Alessandro Parronchi regards the *Mandragola* as an "allegory on the return of the Medici to Florence," while Theodore Sumberg interprets the play as a call to overthrow the Medici.[1] Not surprisingly, then, the literary critic is apt to insist that students of politics should mind their own business: literary studies should be left to literary critics, political studies to political critics.[2]

---

* The plot of *Mandragola* may be briefly summarized. After living abroad most of his life, Callimaco decides to return to his native Florence. Love is his motive—he has heard that Madonna Lucrezia, wife of the aged Messer Nicia Calfucci, is the most beautiful woman in the world. No sooner does he lay eyes on Lucrezia, moreover, than he knows he must have her, for all the superlatives he has heard spoken in her behalf hardly do her justice. Unfortunately, her exceptional virtue, above all her fidelity, stands in his way, and he is too lovesick to know how to exploit the three openings he sees in the door barring him from her bedroom: the stupidity of her husband, the frustrated hope of the couple for children, and the easily compromised virtue of Sostrata, mother of Lucrezia.

In contrast to Callimaco, the trickster Ligurio does not suffer from the excesses of love; he knows perfectly well how to get an ill deed done, and is more than willing to engineer the seduction of Lucrezia when he learns that a permanent place at another man's table will be his reward. Following Ligurio's directions, Callimaco poses as a renowned physician. A doctor with a cure for every malady, Callimaco offers to concoct a potion which will induce fertility from a mandrake plant. But since the first man to have intercourse with Lucrezia after she has drunk the potion runs the risk of death, Nicia agrees he will not be that man. A young vagabond—Callimaco in disguise—is kidnapped and forced to bed down for the night with Lucrezia, whose scruples have been worn down, though not entirely eliminated, by the urgent pleas of her mother and the expert casuistry of Friar Timoteo. As the play ends, everyone is happy: Callimaco has won his prize, Lucrezia has enjoyed the feel of youthful male flesh, Ligurio has gained the meal ticket he covets, Nicia and his mother-in-law await an heir, and the confessor has enriched either his church or his purse by three hundred ducats.

When the political commentator invades the realm of literature, the literary critic adds, foolishness is the all too predictable
result. The politically-minded put forth their interpretations of
the *Mandragola* through allegorical reasoning—the seduction of
Lucrezia, they maintain, is an allegory of conspiracy—and by
such arguments any and all assertions can be proven; hence the
diametrically opposed opinions of Parronchi and Sumberg. Moreover, the interpreter who reads politics into the *Mandragola* is
guilty of overlooking what is most obvious—that the play is a
genuine comedy arousing volleys of laughter, a lighthearted,
indeed a frivolous work, serious as art but resolutely opposed to
seriousness of content. The *Mandragola* is for fun, and fun is
spoiled when the conveyance of a message is at stake.

The claims of the literary purist are partly well-founded, partly
ill-founded. It is true that the *Mandragola* cannot, except by an
arbitrary move, be directly connected with politics; it is not true,
however, that the play stands in isolation from the general corpus
of Machiavelli's writings. Fully as "Machiavellian" as any of his
works, Machiavelli's comedy centers on the topics of immorality,
intrigue, dissimulation, strategem, and the relationship of means
to ends. There clearly is an area of significant overlap between
Mandragola and the rest of Machiavelli's major works.

Again, the literary critic is wrong if he regards the *Mandragola*
as pure art, having nothing to do with civic life and indifferent
to didactic concern. We need only realize that Machiavelli's drama
is in the classical mold to disprove this view. In every way the
Mandragola is cut from the cloth of ancient Roman comedy, the
comedy of Plautus and Terence: the action takes place within
twenty-four hours, the order of the drama proceeds from protasis
to epitasis to catastrophe, and all scenes are confined to a single
street. Being the author of a classical drama, Machiavelli simply
took for granted the intimate tie of art to the life of the city.
Drama, he believed, as did Plato, Aristotle, and Cicero, was a
mimetic form; it imitated and it amplified life, the life of the

city. And it taught lessons on how to live in the city. Like his
classical forebears, Machiavelli could never have begun to understand the modern notion of art for art's sake. For him, as for
the ancient dramatists, the purpose of art was civic education as
well as entertainment. Thus, given the classical lineage of *Mandragola*, we should be thoroughly prepared for the claim stated
in the *Discorso o dialogo intorno alla nostra lingua*, a work many
scholars attribute to Machiavelli, that a "useful lesson" is "the
aim of comedy."[3] At the beginning of *Clizia*, Machiavelli's other
noteworthy play, it is definitely Machiavelli who calls attention
to the didactic function of comedy.[4]

Far from severed from civic concern, the *Mandragola* immerses
us in the life of the republic and distils lessons on how citizens
should act. Nevertheless, the *Mandragola* is no more about politics
than were the comedies of Plautus and Terence, or at least it is
not about politics understood as an activity pertaining to the
public realm. Rather, the purpose of comedy, as understood by
Machiavelli and the Renaissance in general, was exactly as Cicero
had defined it: to hold up a mirror to domestic life.[5] Comic
preoccupation is with the hours a citizen spends off the battlefield
and outside the political assembly; the focus of the comic author
is on private, domestic, and familial concerns. Whenever a citizen
is not fighting or politicking, he is likely to be found at home
or on a street corner, and never have the whereabouts and behavior
of the private citizen been more delightfully portrayed than by
Machiavelli and his Roman forebears, Plautus and Terence. What
comedy offers is a dramatization of twenty-four hours, a day and
a night, in the private life of a citizen.

Another look at the political interpretation of the *Mandragola*
is in order. There is, to be sure, an affinity in Machiavelli's
thought, as Parronchi and Sumberg claim, between seduction
and conspiracy. Where they go wrong is in assuming that Machiavelli's tale of seduction is an allegory of conspiracy in politics.
They are wrong because seduction is seduction to Machiavelli,

and not a symbol for conspiracy. The true link between seduction and conspiracy, as understood by Machiavelli, is that they are in many respects interchangeable phenomena, to be conducted according to identical rules. No more than five persons should be involved in a conspiracy, Machiavelli wrote when discussing politics; some five persons, Callimaco, his servant Siro, Ligurio, Friar Timoteo, and Sostrata are involved in the seduction of Lucrezia. The chief conspirator should wait till the last moment to divulge the details of his plot to his fellow conspirators, wrote the political Machiavelli; the comic Machiavelli has Callimaco, the chief seducer, speak similar words to Siro.[6] Seduction and conspiracy are similar phenomena and the same maxims apply to each. One is distinguishable from the other simply in that seduction pertains to the private sphere, conspiracy to the public.

Both in his statecraft and in his stagecraft Machiavelli addresses himself to the theme of deceit, trickery, and immoralism. Under the sponsorship of the *Mandragola*, we encounter a new variety of Machiavellism, the Machiavellism of domestic life, the Machiavellism of the household, a topic that would have shocked Aristotle. Otherwise stated, *The Prince*, the *Discourses*, and the *Florentine History* give us the Machiavellism of public life, the *Mandragola* the Machiavellism of private life.

There is one sense, and one sense only, in which the *Mandragola* is political. When Machiavelli carried the problem of conspiracy into the private sphere in the *Mandragola*, redefining it as seduction, he rendered privacy political. Politics was everywhere, everything was political. Those who follow Benedetto Croce's lead in crediting Machiavelli with positing "the autonomy of politics" should therefore reconsider their findings. Had he labeled his doctrine, Machiavelli might have preferred to term it "the ubiquity of politics." Politics has its own rules, which is what is meant by "the autonomy of politics"; but these rules pertain to the private sphere as well as to the public: therefore, "the ubiquity of politics."

If every human relationship is political and politics is immoral, has Machiavelli destroyed morality? Time and again Machiavelli's interpreters have argued that he accepted conventional morality, only to discover its sad irrelevance in matters of state. All states lie, cheat, steal, and murder, and necessarily so, because any state that does not will fall prey to those that do. In privacy, on the other hand, good faith and human decency can and should be upheld—so, we are told, Machiavelli believed. This familiar notion of two moralities in Machiavelli's thought, an immoral or amoral one for public affairs, a moral one for private affairs, must be reconsidered now that we are aware of his penchant for spying politics everywhere. True, he said in the *Discourses* that those of us who cannot abide the evil of politics have the option of withdrawing to private life.[7] The *Mandragola*, however, implies that private life, rather than an alternative to power politics, is a continuation of such politics. So how can we salvage the view that Machiavelli accepted conventional notions of good and evil?

By taking another look at *Mandragola* and *Clizia*. Those comedies, however immoral in certain respects, were moral, even moralistic, in other respects, and their morality was conventional morality. On the comic stage of Machiavelli, as on that of Plautus or Terence, we rarely if ever see genuine individuals; instead we see general types, the father, the mother, the servant. The roles of comedy, in short, are those of society written large; dramatic roles recapitulate social roles. This in itself advances us far along the road to a Machiavelli committed to conventional morality, since an acceptance of society's roles is an acceptance of conventional morality as well. Anyone, for instance, who accepts the role of father accepts the attendant notion of what constitutes a good or bad father.[8]

At times the moral side of Machiavelli's comedy is downright moralistic, as when Siro holds forth on the duties of his station in *Mandragola*:

I'm your servant, and servants ought never to ask their masters questions about anything or pry into their business, but when the masters themselves tell them, they ought to serve faithfully; and so I've done and so I'm going to do.[9]

In *Clizia*, Machiavelli presents an image of the good father, husband, and master:

He dined pleasantly with his family, and after he had dined, he talked with his son, advised him, taught him to understand men, and by means of various examples, ancient and modern, showed him how to live. . . . This ordering of his life was an example to all the others in the house, and everybody was ashamed not to imitate him.[10]

Other exhortations to live up to one's role are to be found in Plautus and Terence, whose comedies were, for that reason, used by sixteenth-century schoolteachers when giving lessons in moral conduct.[11]

Not every servant on Machiavelli's stage is a good servant, not every father a good father. But that does not mean his comedy has rejected conventional morality. Quite the contrary, when the aged Nicomaco sets out to seduce the youthful Clizia—an aspiration that violates his role of elder—he is laughed into submission. Laughter implies shared values; it is a reaffirmation of shared norms, a punishment inflicted upon those who defy convention, an exercise in social conformity.[12] Every laugh that Machiavelli evoked against those who act contrary to the expectations implied by their social roles is further evidence of his acceptance of conventional morality.

Machiavelli's comedy, we may conclude, always contains an implicit morality of social roles, and occasionally that morality becomes explicit, as when he urges us to abide by a role or warns us against failure to do so. Whenever he was not asserting his allegiance to conventional morality by taking it for granted, Machiavelli was actively promulgating or enforcing that morality.

One qualification must be added, however. In the *Mandragola*, Machiavelli does more than uphold the accepted definitions of social roles and obligations; he also takes positive delight in the ways of immorality, and communicates that delight to his audience with great artistry. But even here, as he shows how enticing immorality can be, he does so without attacking conventional morality. When we read Gide's *L'immoraliste* or Camus's *L'étranger*, we are dealing with protagonists who have rejected society and all its conventions, protagonists living beyond good and evil. When we attend a performance of *Mandragola*, we see that the immoralist is neither estranged nor a stranger; he is the neighbor next door, a citizen and fully aware of his citizenship. He belongs. We also see that the role of the immoralist is, like the other roles of comedy, a dramatization of a *social* role. Machiavelli's immoralist is a social being who despite his wrongdoing never questions the validity of society's standards and would be lost if the signposts of conventional morality disappeared.

The nature of Machiavelli's ethics may be further clarified by a brief comparison with Kant's. "What if everyone did it?" is the question that Kant insists we ask ourselves. Promises must be kept and lies avoided, for if everyone broke promises and no one told the truth, life would be impossible. "Everyone will not do it," would likely be Machiavelli's reply; therefore those of us who desire to be immoralists have a license to do so.

Since, moreover, most citizens are heedful of morality, no citizen is forced into immorality. Society is not at all like Hobbes's state of nature in which all must be aggressive because some are.[13] Everything is up for grabs in a Hobbesian world because no one knows his place; little is up for grabs in a Machiavellian world because everyone knows his place, his role.

Interpretations of Machiavelli based on the assumption that he substituted a modern emphasis on individualism and dynamic natural movement for a medieval accent on corporatism and static natural order[14] err insofar as they neglect his affiliation with classical thought. As a devotee of classical concepts and norms, he might well portray an exceptional individual, Cesare Borgia for example; but Machiavelli's world was always composed of collectivities, most of all the city-state and the family, two groups that were as permanent, to him, as the sun and the stars, and the very permanence of which made limited forms of deviation unthreatening. Machiavelli the seducer, the apparently uncivic Machiavelli, is still citizen Machiavelli; his adulterous misdeeds are very sociable and definitely the handiwork of someone dedicated to the "active life." Deep down in his psyche, so deep that it was never expressly articulated, Machiavelli knew what the comic spirit has always known, that the integrity, the cohesion, of society depends upon permitting its members to forget their integrity now and then.

Worth noting, too, are the limits to the parallel Machiavelli draws between the politics of private life and the politics of public life, and the manner in which the end of the parallel marks the onset of boundaries hedging in the practice of private immorality. Callimaco's plaintive cry that he must have Lucrezia or die[15] is sincere but mistaken; life and death do not hang in the balance. Survival is at stake in affairs of state but not in affairs of the heart. As defenders of the state against other states we are frequently immoralists out of necessity, but as private citizens we are immoralists out of choice. And most of us, to be sure, will not choose to be immoralists, if only because we are too weak.

In public affairs, all are called and all chosen for the life of civic virtue; all are called but few chosen for the additional life of Machiavellian conniver. The ruling elite is open, but only a handful of citizens will ever master the deceitful skills of statecraft. In private affairs, similarly, all are called and all are chosen for the conventional morality of their primary social roles; all are called but few chosen for the secondary role of immoralist.

That the Machiavelli of the *Mandragola* is truly Machiavelli and not just a literary persona, a mask, is proven by his private letters and by what we know of his personal life. He traveled around Italy with his mistress Barbera and devoted much of his correspondence to the delights of womanizing. In his familiar letters Machiavelli was free to speak of whatever he pleased, and it was adulterous love that was one of his two favorite topics, the other being politics. A good family man attentive to his children and relatives, and not totally indifferent to his wife, is also revealed in his letters. Quite obviously Machiavelli believed marriage was an institution whose continuing collective life did not depend on the undying sexual fidelity of its individual members.[16]

Everyone is familiar with the letter to Francesco Vettori in which Machiavelli describes a typical day in his life, ending with an evening spent in "the ancient courts of ancient men, where, received by them with affection, I feed on that food which only is mine and which I was born for." Less noted, in this same letter, is a passage that places the reading of the love poetry of Dante, Petrarch, Tibullus, and Ovid on the agenda of his normal day. "I read of their tender passions and their loves, remember mine, enjoy myself a while in that sort of dreaming."[17] Two points may be inferred from the preceding quotations: one is that an interest in love is a high point of everyday life, a second is that it is not the highest point. An evening spent with Livy studying the art of war is worth more than an afternoon spent with Ovid studying the art of love. An implicit rank ordering of values may be discerned in Machiavelli's letter, politics being ranked higher than love. Typical of Machiavelli is the opening of the *Art of War* where he says Cosimo Rucellai wrote love poetry because he lacked opportunity to devote himself to "higher activities."[18]

Further confirmation of Machiavelli's subordination of love, an activity of the private sphere, to politics, an activity of the public sphere, may be discovered in the manner whereby he deals with the two topics. Politics is treated in his letters as a matter of utmost importance, treated gravely, and—faced with the dismal prospect of Italy forced to her knees by "barbarians"—he can even suggest, in the closing of one of his letters, that he is a writer of tragedies.[19] His letters on love, conversely, are predominantly comical and necessarily so, because affairs of the heart have not the same significance as affairs of state.[20] Ovid's joke in the *Art of Love*, which his original Roman audience appreciated, lay in his treatment of the art of seduction exactly as other Roman authors had treated the arts of politicking and fighting. Later the medieval poets, for the sake of their ethos of chivalry, misread Ovid, taking seriously what was unserious and especially funny when spoken of with tongue-in-cheek seriousness. In the poetry of chivalry, adulterous love—adulterous because marriages were arranged and had nothing to do with love—was praised as the most worthy of human pursuits; it was made into a second religion, and Ovid was misunderstood as its spokesman.[21] Since he was a classical thinker, Machiavelli had no trouble recovering Ovid's true meaning, and when he retrieved Ovid he simultaneously demoted love to a pastime.

Machiavelli was as familiar with Boccaccio's bawdy *Decameron* as with Plautus's comedies, so much so that the *Mandragola* is in reality a novella wrapped inside the form of ancient comedy. But no matter how much Machiavelli enjoyed the *Decameron*, he rejected or misunderstood a great deal of Boccaccio. To the author of the *Decameron*, love is all-important: it can suppress the beast and awaken the human in a man; it is a law unto itself; it sits in judgment over society, condemning those institutions that obstruct the course of true love. Thus the marital bond may be rejected when not sealed by love.[22] Love's final accomplishment, in Boccaccio's estimation, is that she confers cleverness and cunning upon those who worship at her altar. A wife, for example, who must go outside marriage to find love always finds the means to dupe her husband. Indeed, the entire seventh day of the *De-*

cameron is devoted to a study of "the tricks . . . women have played on their husbands." Consequently one modern commentator characterizes the *Decameron*'s implicit doctrine as "a sort of Machiavellism where love replaces the 'reason of state.' "[23]

Doubtless the very first person to detect Machiavellism in Boccaccio was Machiavelli himself. Yet, Machiavelli's position is, in many respects, the polar opposite of Boccaccio's. Never does Machiavelli suggest that adultery is innocent, nor does he ever pit love against marriage in what, for all its Boccaccian lightheartedness, threatens one day to develop into a battle to the finish. He simply believes that marriage, an institution whose validity he never questioned, can survive a well-executed, though definitely immoral, adultery. Furthermore, for Boccaccio love is a matter of life and death, sometimes literally so,[24] whereas for Machiavelli love is a mere diversion. When Callimaco proclaims that he must have Lucrezia or die, he echoes the words of many a lover in Plautus or Terence, but none of these comic lovers ever dies of love. Love belongs to the order of "empty things [*cose vane*],"[25] Machiavelli tells Francesco Vettori, and no doubt that was why he, like the audiences attending comedies in ancient Rome, laughed at the all-or-nothing frenzy of a lovesick youth. In a day or two, he would come to his senses.

War, not love, is a life-or-death matter. One can always forget a woman but can never forget the republic, the first and last love of a citizen. At last we understand why Machiavelli singles out young men as those for whom he writes both his sublime works, which discuss politics and war,[26] and his comic works, which discuss love.[27] He can admire the excesses of a young man in love because tomorrow that same youth will vent those same passions on the battlefield. After all, loving and fighting are activities so similar that the lover and the soldier have much in common. Ligurio declares himself the captain of an army going into battle in a scene of the *Mandragola*.[28] He sends out scouts, utters a battle cry, establishes a rear guard and reinforces losing squadrons—all for the purpose of assisting Callimaco in his efforts to seduce Lucrezia. Obviously Ligurio recognizes the affinity of making love and making war. Similarly, Cleander in *Clizia* recognizes that "the man who said that the lover and the soldier are alike told the truth."

> The general wants his soldiers to be young; women don't want their lovers to be old. . . . Soldiers fear their commander's anger; lovers fear no less that of their ladies. . . . Soldiers pursue their enemies to the death; lovers, their rivals. Soldiers on the darkest nights in the death of winter go through the mud, exposed to rain and wind, to carry out some undertaking that will bring them victory; lovers attempt in similar ways and with similar and greater sufferings to gain those they love. Equally in war and in love, secrecy is needed, and fidelity and courage. The dangers are alike, and most of the time the results are alike.[29]

He who is good at war should therefore be good at love and vice versa, or so this passage stolen from Ovid[30] and reworked by Machiavelli, suggests. Machiavelli wrote a book entitled the *Art of War*, and in his comedies he came close to rewriting Ovid's *Art of Love*. Those hours that are not devoted to the conquest of enemies are naturally spent on the conquest of women, because a spirited citizen must always find outlets for his predatory instincts.

During the Renaissance, comic dramatists frequently used the stage to disseminate a sentimental, serious, and romantic idea of love.[31] Chivalrous notions of love had long before passed, via Boccaccio, from feudal courts to the Florentine city-state, and when Boccaccian plots were adapted to the comic stage of Renaissance times, the ideal of romantic love received a fresh stimulus. But Machiavelli senses none of this. Pagan through and through, he understood love as did the ancients. Flesh touching flesh, love is sex and sex is primal. Yet, for all its primacy, love is trivial.

Neither that exaltation of woman which is characteristic of chivalry nor the desexualization of Eros characteristic of Renaissance
Platonism figures in Machiavelli's attitudes. For him the only
way sexual desire can be transformed into something more than
a biological urge is by treating it as play, as an activity of *homo
ludens*.

Several playful potentialities are fully realized when we engage
in the game of seduction. Play, writes Johan Huizinga, "loves
to surround itself with an air of secrecy";[32] Machiavelli said the
same of seduction.[33] "All play has its rules,"[34] Huizinga tells us;
the rules of seduction were stated in Ovid's *Art of Love* and were
well known to Machiavelli. Furthermore, play is amoral, asserts
Huizinga, and yet it sets standards by which our prowess, courage, and tenacity are measured.[35] Exactly the same was said, in
effect, by Machiavelli of seduction, with the single revision that
he regarded adultery as immoral, not amoral. Huizinga adds that
play is freedom.[36] If that is so, seduction and adultery are expressions of freedom; apparently, then, Aristotle was wrong when he
limited freedom to the public sphere. The household, to Aristotle
a realm of necessity, was presumably to Machiavelli a realm of
freedom for every wife who unlocked the back door as soon as
her husband walked out the front door to attend to his public
"affairs."[37]

Regarded as a game, seduction was not only playful—it was
agonistic as well, allowing a man to compete with his fellows.
Whenever Machiavelli receives a letter from a friend boasting of
a sexual conquest, he tops it with a better story of an amorous
adventure of his own. And since love, unlike politics, is only a
game, winning is not always essential; sometimes, indeed, victory
can come in the form of an ostensible defeat when love, rather
than politics, is the topic of discussion. To Luigi Guicciardini's
letter describing a sexual success, Machiavelli responds with a
letter describing a personal sexual defeat that is so uproariously

comical and grotesque that it proves he is unbeatable as a teller
of tall tales.

Curse you Luigi: see how fortuna brings men different results
in the same affairs. You, when you have had her once, you
want to go back and do it again. As for me!—When I had
been here a few days, blinded by enforced abstinence, I came
across an old woman who washes my shirts. . . . I was
passing there the other day and she recognized me and made
a great to-do of me, and said that if I liked to come in for
a moment she wanted to show me some fine shirts. . . . I
believed her and once inside I saw in the half-light a woman
hiding in a corner. . . . The old hag took my hand and
leading me over to her, said "This is the shirt I want to
sell". . . . Shy as always, I shook in my shoes, all the same,
. . . I wanted a woman so badly that I went ahead. And
when it was over, since I had a fancy to see the merchandise,
I took a burning piece of wood from a stove that was there
and lit a lamp which was over it—and hardly was it alight
when it nearly fell from my hand. Ugh! . . . The first thing
I saw was a tuft of hair, half white, half black; piebald, that
is, with age, and although the crown of her head was bald—
which baldness enabled one to see a louse or two taking a
stroll—still, a few sparse hairs mingled with the whiskers
sprouting round her face; and on top of her meagre and
wrinkled head was a fiery scar which made her look as if
she had been branded in the market. There were colonies
of nits in each eyebrow; one eye looked up, the other down,
and one was larger than the other; the tear ducts were full
of rheum, the rims hairless. Her nose was screwed into her
face at an angle, the nostrils full of snot, and one of them
half missing. . . .

As I stood there staggered and bemused by the sight of
this monster, she noticed and tried to say "What is the

matter, sir?" but could not because she had an impediment, and as she opened her mouth such a stinking breath came out that my eyes and nose—the gateways to the two most vulnerable senses—were so upset by the stench that my stomach, unable to stand the strain, revolted and heaved so much that I vomited. . . .[38]

Machiavelli feigns a defeat in his exchange of letters with Luigi Guicciardini, but it is he who has won: he has proven himself the more spirited of the two men.

As an immoral, free, and agonistic activity, seduction promised Machiavelli much of what he valued. Just one essential element is missing, namely, the opportunity for achieving true greatness. Within Machiavelli's world the lover's heroism will never be more than mock heroism—the stuff fit for comedy.

It may be objected that Machiavelli sometimes speaks of love as an activity that is more satisfying than politics, his letter of August 3, 1514 to Francesco Vettori being a case in point.

I have abandoned, then, thoughts of affairs that are great and serious; I do not any more take delight in reading ancient things or in discussing modern ones; they are all turned into soft conversations, for which I thank Venus. . . . [O]f the other things talk with those who estimate them higher and understand them better, because I never have found in them anything but harm, and in these of love always good and pleasure.[39]

So be it. But Machiavelli never for a moment worried that Vettori, a kindred spirit devoting his life to politics, first, and womanizing, second, would be foolish enough to take him seriously. When the language of the sublime is occasionally applied to love in the letters of Vettori and Machiavelli, the intent of the writer, if not comic incongruity, is to strike a self-conscious and momentary pose. Quickly Machiavelli's letters return to political subjects, as is only to be expected given that even in the letter of August 3, 1514, in which love is praised and public life is criticized, it is political activity that is designated "great and serious."

Politics and love do mix. During the years of his service to the republic of 1494 to 1512, Machiavelli's letters are those of a lover as well as a politician.[40] Moreover, it bothered Machiavelli not in the least that Francesco Vettori, ambassador of Medicean Florence to the pope, filled his letters with accounts of amorous encounters and boasted "I know nothing more pleasing to think about and to do than fucking."[41] Far from censuring Vettori for behavior unbecoming to a public official, Machiavelli suggests that "an ambassador . . . , being obligated to countless serious doings, must necessarily have some recreations and pleasures." A more general argument is then put forward by Machiavelli.

> He who is thought a man of substance, and effective, whatever he does to refresh his spirit and live happily will bring him honor and not blame; and instead of being called a bugger or a whoremaster, it will be said that he is tolerant, ready, and a good companion.

Machiavelli clinches his defense of the politician's adulterous private life with the assertion "he who is thought wise by day will never be held crazy by night"[42]—a formula he found so felicitous that he used it again in his *Life of Castruccio Castracani*.[43]

To read his familiar letters is to understand that the genre of ancient Roman comedy was bound to entice Machiavelli, who possessed a keen sense of the comic, enjoyed its sexual content to the utmost, and could hardly fail to perceive that seduction, a favorite theme of comedies, was thoroughly "Machiavellian" insofar as it was a secretive and conniving activity, judged in terms of success or failure. Obviously, then, the classical comedy of Plautus and Terence was a perfect vehicle for the expression of Machiavelli's interests. The spirit of Plautus and the spirit of

Machiavelli were like the twins who appear in *The Brothers Me-naechmus* and whose identical visages lead to the confusions, the mistaken identities, that energize the dramatic action. Machiavelli was a comedian and comedy was Machiavellian. Few Roman comedies lack the themes of deception and trickery, and in many these are the main substance of the play.[44] Usually the schemer par excellence is a slave, but a parasite, a husband, a wife—most anyone—can assume the role of domestic Machiavellian. Sixteenth-century schoolteachers did not realize that in using Roman comedy for ethical instruction they were giving their pupils ample opportunity to learn the ways of Machiavellism.

When he used Boccaccio to pour Florentine content into the form of Roman comedy, Machiavelli again came face to face with a seemingly Machiavellian reality. The *beffa*, the trick, repeatedly appears in the *Decameron* and never fails to entertain. For both Plautus and Boccaccio, moreover, love usually provides the motivation for the Machiavellian tricks, schemes, and disguises which they relate with boundless zest.

Comedy was Machiavellian in another way as well. It allowed Machiavelli to illustrate his constantly reiterated doctrine of a less than splendid human nature. Attending a comic performance, we observe, he noted, "all men's unreliability."[45] These words, taken from *Clizia*, can be bolstered by quoting from the *Mandragola*. Consider Nicia's words: "I'm so eager to have children that I'm ready to do anything."[46] Callimaco's inclinations are equally mischievous: "I've got to try something, even if it's strange, risky, injurious, disgraceful."[47] For his part, Siro is willing to go along with most anything "if I thought it wouldn't be found out."[48] According to Aristotle, the characters of comic drama are worse than the characters of everyday life;[49] presumably Machiavelli would disagree: the characters on the stage reveal a universal tendency of human nature, the disposition to do wrong, to transgress.

All are inclined to transgress, but some transgress better than others. Although it is easy to be evil, it is not easy to be evil systematically, methodically. The serious Machiavelli never tires of saying that most of us are too weak to embrace evil without flinching; the comic Machiavelli says the same. To observe the characters of the *Mandragola* on stage is to grade them in terms of their capacity for transforming evil inclinations into self-conscious Machiavellism.

Callimaco signals great potential for virtuosity in evil when he asserts his willingness to endure damnation if that is the consequence: "The worst you can get from it is that you'll die and go to Hell. But how many others have died! And in Hell how many worthy men there are! Are you ashamed to go there?"[50] He is, furthermore, singularly adept at playing his part in a sinister plot. Nevertheless, Callimaco is a very imperfect Machiavellian since someone else, namely Ligurio, must concoct the deceitful masterplan. On another day, when his passions are less directly involved, he might well be able to plot evil. Today he cannot.

There are no obvious flaws in Sostrata's Machiavellian credentials. She is highly successful in her job, which is to water the seeds of evil present in the souls of Nicia and Lucrezia. "I've always heard that it's the part of a prudent man to take the best among bad choices. If for having children you don't know any other way, then you'll have to accept this one, if it doesn't burden your conscience."[51] Thus does she address Nicia in order to make certain he will not waver in his decision to have Lucrezia sleep with another man. It is Sostrata, moreover, who convinces Lucrezia that the casuistry of Friar Timoteo is worth a listen: "If Friar Timoteo tells you it isn't a thing to burden your conscience, you should do it without thinking about it."[52] Were Sostrata, a woman with a checkered past, permitted to play a larger part, she might display a total mastery of the art of doing evil. On the basis of the available evidence, we cannot know for certain.

Ligurio is the perfect Machiavellian. Exceptionally clever, he tests Friar Timoteo before recruiting him for the service of Callimaco. Ligurio pretends that a relative of Nicia's, a young woman living in a convent, is pregnant. If money can induce the priest to participate in an abortion, then money can induce him to participate in the seduction of Lucrezia. Should the Friar respond to the proposed abortion with indignation, Ligurio can reveal the fictitious nature of his request and treat the whole matter as a joke.

From the moment we overhear Ligurio practice casuistry on Friar Timoteo, and with a vigor that the monk himself cannot hope to excel, we know that Callimaco has hired the ideal man.

> See how much good will result from doing this. You keep up the reputation of the nunnery, the girl, her relatives. . . . And on the other side you injure only a piece of flesh not yet born, without sense . . . ; and I believe that good is what does good to the largest number and with which the largest number are pleased.[53]

Obviously a professional in the conduct of evil, Ligurio masterminds the overthrow of Lucrezia's virtue. And his efforts are crowned by success, one of the ultimate signs of prowess in a Machiavellian world.

"These friars," remarks Ligurio, "are knavish, crafty, and it's not strange, because they know our sins and their own."[54] We therefore expect Friar Timoteo to know a thing or two about the technique of confounding good and evil, and it cannot be said that he fails to live up to advance billing. With considerable dexterity, he pulls the wool, or the bedsheets, over Lucrezia's eyes.

> You must, as to conscience, accept this rule: where a good is certain and an evil uncertain, you ought never to give up the good for fear of the evil. Here you have a certain good,

that you will become pregnant, gain a soul for the Lord. The uncertain evil is that the man who lies with you after you take the medicine may die. . . . As to the action, the notion that it's a sin is a fairy story, because the will is what sins, not the body. . . . Besides this, one's purpose must be considered in everything; your purpose is to fill a seat in paradise, to please your husband. The Bible says that Lot's daughters, thinking they alone were left in the world, had to do with their father, and because their intention was good, they did not sin.

I swear to you, madonna, by this consecrated breast, that submitting to your husband in this affair is as much a matter of conscience as eating meat on fastday, which is a sin that goes away with holy water.[55]

Still, there are disappointing clauses in the Friar's pact with the devil. Initially he had embraced evil courageously: "However things go, I don't repent of it."[56] But before the play can end he is already issuing disclaimers.

Many times one comes to harm by being too accommodating and too good, as well as by being too bad. God knows I wasn't thinking of harming anybody; I was staying in my cell, saying my offices, dealing with my penitents. Then all at once this devil of a Ligurio turned up; he made me put my finger in a sin, then I have put in my arm and my whole body. . . .[57]

Truly, Friar Timoteo's words underscore Machiavelli's familiar complaint that most men are too weak to be either totally good or totally bad. And the Friar's indecision also tells us a great deal about priests regarded as a social type: as casuists they initially resemble Machiavellians, but soon their Christian consciences get in the way and compromise them.

Of all the dramatis personae, Lucrezia is originally the most virtuous and the least possessed of Machiavellian *virtù*. Before the last curtain, she nevertheless makes great advances toward self-conscious immorality. Her intention is to enjoy Callimaco on many another occasion.

> Your cleverness, my husband's stupidity, my mother's folly, and my confessor's rascality have brought me to do what I never would have done myself. So I'm forced to judge that it comes from Heaven's wish . . . , and I'm not strong enough to refuse what Heaven wills me to accept. I take you then for lord, master, guide; you are my father, you are my defender; I want you as my chief good. . . .[58]

Sad to say, she feels compelled to dream up a providential excuse for her immoral actions and leans excessively on the shoulder of Callimaco. But these defects can be forgiven, perhaps, considering she is a novice in Machiavellism.

Nicia, of course, is an utter failure as a Machiavellian. "I am not used to being made to take fireflies for lanterns,"[59] he says; in reality, however, he is living proof of Machiavelli's oft-stated contention that appearances satisfy the many all too well. Willing to do evil but completely gullible, Nicia does everything in his power to turn himself into a cuckold.

The *Mandragola* does more than grade characters according to their prowess in Machiavellism; it also conjures up a veritable Machiavellian dream world. "Pleasant indeed is the trick carried on to the dear conclusion that has been dreamed of,"[60] wrote the comic Machiavelli. If so, *Mandragola* is the most pleasant of comedies. A strategy of conquest by fraud, deception, and entrapment is conceived and carried to its conclusion without a hitch. Not a single move is wasted, not a single unexpected obstacle encountered; everything smacks of speed, dispatch, and efficiency.[61]

Callimaco is "afraid something'll come up to spoil my plan."[62] He need not have worried. Machiavelli had set out to create a

Machiavellian paradise in the *Mandragola*, an idyllic world wherein all well-planned, well-executed plots meet with the success they deserve, and he would allow nothing to stand in his way. In many an ancient comedy, by contrast, the Machiavellian schemer loses control of events, as in *The Ghost* of Plautus, a play that derives its humor from showing how a slave's successive tricks, one necessitating another, lead him into an ever more hopeless situation. "Oh! . . . my beautiful scheme blown to smithereens!"[63] he exclaims. Usually it takes a stroke of good fortune to salvage the happy ending that is mandatory in comedy. Somehow, for example, the discovery is made that the woman owned by a pimp and loved by a young man of respectable family is, perhaps to her own dismay, of free birth and gentle parentage; hence the course of true love is finally free of obstacles. It is Fortuna who upsets the best laid schemes of mice and men in comedy as in real life; and it is Fortuna again who extricates connivers from the shambles of their schemes. Machiavelli, however, drove Fortuna, the goddess of comedy, off the stage in the *Mandragola*.[64] *Virtù* wins by default.

"Chance," wrote Melanchthon, "prevails more often than reason [in comedies]. Fortune generally rules affairs."[65] Although this generalization is well taken, it is inapplicable to *Mandragola*. An artist can tamper with reality, should he so desire, and Machiavelli tampered with it by withholding *fortuna* while accentuating Machiavellism. His implicit reason for doing so may be ferreted out of his serious works. On various occasions in his political writings Machiavelli refused to abide by what many thinkers today regard as an essential term in "the problem of dirty hands," namely, that only success can vindicate immoral means, so that a failed Machiavellian, no matter how moral his reasons for adopting immoral techniques, no matter how brilliant his calculations of the uses of immoral means, can never be excused when his schemes backfire. Directly opposed to this modern version of the dilemma of means and ends is Machiavelli's habit of siding with the Machiavellian who deserved to win but lost, and of siding against the common run of men who, he suggests, only know how to judge by consequences.[66] Because *Mandragola* was fictional, because it was art rather than political art, his comedy was the one *occasione* when Machiavelli could assure a Machiavellian of receiving his just deserts in spite of the irrationality of *fortuna*, and he was not about to let this unique opportunity slip away.

As the translator of Terence's *Andria*, Machiavelli could do no more than strive to recapture the flavor of that ancient comedy. As the author who in *Clizia* adapted Plautus's *Casina* to Florentine conditions, Machiavelli could begin to come into his own as a comic writer. But it was not until he wrote *Mandragola*, a completely original play, that he could do whatever he wanted with Roman comedy. What he wanted was a literary representation of an ideal immoralist, a being who at a moment's notice could transfigure evil inclinations into self-conscious and exquisite calculations of evil, calculations guaranteed success by an expurgation of *fortuna* from the comic script.

IT REMAINS to refute other interpretations of the *Mandragola* and to underscore the full significance of my findings.

Shot through with immoralism, the *Mandragola* is plausibly a commentary on the corruption of Florence,[67] its fall from virtue to hedonism. Possibly so, but such an interpretation quickly runs into unbudging obstacles. To begin with, it is at variance with the temperament of the play, which is anything but dark and foreboding. Nor can it be said that the adulterous subject matter of the play, apparently so much at odds with the repressive and spartan emphasis of civic virtue, is an indication that Machiavelli had civic decline on his mind when he wrote his comedy. Adultery is so morally unimportant to Machiavelli that it hardly figures as a topic in the *Discourses*, his most systematic republican treatise.[68] Only when sexual laxity assumes a form that threatens the family is Machiavelli concerned. Nicomaco's lust for Clizia must be thwarted because, as one character puts it, "Nothing is being ruined by it—except a family!"[69] Everyone knows what Nicomaco is up to, so that the relationships of husband to wife, father to son, and master to servant are thrown into disarray. Lucrezia's adultery is altogether different. Because secrecy remains unbroken, the Calfucci family is not ruined. Far from it, Nicia stands to gain an heir thanks to the infidelity of his wife.

There is another way in which it can be argued that the *Mandragola* presents a picture of civic corruption. In this second version of the corruption thesis, one can readily admit that the play is a gay work and then go on to suggest that its gaiety swims in a current of disenchantment: when civic virtue is dead and the Medici prince alive, nothing is left for a citizen except frivolous endeavors. However credible it sounds, this interpretation is directly contradicted by Machiavelli's own words. The decisive passage appears in a letter of January 31, 1515 to Francesco Vettori, half of which discusses love, half politics.

> Anybody who saw our letters, honored friend, and saw their diversity, would wonder greatly, because he would suppose now that we were grave men, wholly concerned with important matters [*cose grandi*], and that into our breasts no thought could fall that did not have in itself honor and greatness. But then, turning the page, he would judge that we, the very same persons, were light-minded, inconstant, lascivious, concerned with empty things [*cose vane*]. And this way of proceeding, if to some it may appear censurable, to me seems praiseworthy, because we are imitating Nature, who is variable; and he who imitates her cannot be blamed.[70]

Instead of specifying that amorous pursuits are appropriate in times of corruption and political pursuits appropriate in times of virtue, he binds them together for all times by placing both under the rubric of Nature.

One other interpretation of comedy that runs counter to our understanding of *Mandragola* should be considered. This is the view that argues that classical comedy, owing its origins to festive occasions, is permeated with the flavor of carnival. The day depicted on the stage is therefore a holiday, a day completely unlike a normal day. It is a day during which all normal relations are suspended and inverted. On a normal Roman day all is order and moderation, on a Roman holiday all is anarchy and excess. For one day, and one day only, slaves triumph over masters, wives over husbands, sons over fathers, the pleasure principle over the reality principle. In short, a comic world is the normal world turned upside down.[71] Now, if the *Mandragola* is an escape from reality, as this interpretation implies, we are wrong to make so much of its Machiavellism. If it describes a holiday, then tomorrow will be different. Tomorrow puritanism will return to the private sphere, immoralism will leave it.

Whatever the merits of the foregoing theory of comedy, it was not the Renaissance theory. Supposedly comedy imitated reality. It held up a mirror to nature, to custom, to domestic affairs: so said all Renaissance theorists of comedy, repeating the opinions of various ancient writers. Or if comedy differed from reality, it did so, sixteenth-century comic theorists believed, through offering an idealization of what exists.[72] Against the backdrop of this highly moralistic outlook, one might say that comedy was understood to mirror the private lives of citizens in the same way the literature "on princely rule" reflected the public lives of monarchs—by prescribing what ought to be. Machiavelli could not have thought of comedy as the world turned upside down, a theory of our age;* he could, however, have thought of comedy as a mirror of reality, a theory of his age. Thus understood, his

* The notion of "the world turned upside down" was present in Latin literature but it was not applied to comic drama.

comedy of expertly conducted immorality diverged from Renaissance theories of comedy exactly as *The Prince* diverged from all previous books of its genre. *The Prince* teaches us "how not to be good"[73] and so does *Mandragola*.

Those critics of our day who regard comedy as an inversion of reality call our attention to the final moments of various Roman plays. A reminder that tomorrow the slave will return to his slavery frequently appears at the close of a comedy of Plautus: tomorrow will not be a holiday.[74] By contrast, as the *Mandragola* closes we learn that the transgressions of the past twenty-four hours will continue indefinitely: "What my husband has asked for one night, I intend him to have always,"[75] says Lucrezia. "I'm going," adds Nicia, "to give [Callimaco and Ligurio] the key of the room on the ground floor in the loggia, so they can come there when it's convenient."[76] He also tells Callimaco to take his wife's hand. As if that were not enough, the adulterous couple marches off to church, thereby gaining the sanction of eternity. Since the today presented on Machiavelli's stage is everyday, tomorrow will not be different. Only in the perfection of their immorality have the last twenty-four hours been extraordinary.

It may be added that we know perfectly well what Machiavelli believes a citizen should be doing on a holiday. According to the *Art of War* it is on festivals that the young man should undergo military exercises, maneuvers, training, and discipline. On festivals and only on festivals, he argues, youths should be subjected to the spartan ways of his proposed citizens' militia.[77] He also states that he prefers a city composed of "men who, when it is time to make war, gladly . . . go into it, and when peace comes more gladly return home,"[78] because an army that does not wish to return home is a mercenary army, not an army of citizens. What the most Machiavellian of his citizens do when home from the wars, on ordinary days when free from the obligation of holidays to prepare for war, and as a change of pace from their political activities, is revealed in his private letters and his comedies.

Machiavelli's thoughts on love are republican; possibly they are even Roman republican, whether by way of inspiration or merely jusification. The Romans, remarks Fabrizio, Machiavelli's mouthpiece in the *Art of War*, did not permit women in their armies. "This prohibition was not very difficult because so many were the exercises in which the soldiers every day . . . were employed, that no time was left them for thinking of . . . Venus."[79] It readily follows that Machiavelli believed Roman manhood did think of Venus when not serving in the army, and what was good enough for the republican Romans was always good enough for Machiavelli.

The republican flavor of Machiavelli's writings on love is further underscored when set beside Castiglione's discussion of love in *The Book of the Courtier*. Located at court, the eros of Castiglione was monarchical, and so Platonic was its philosophical rationale[80] that it would surely have reminded Machiavelli of the doctrine of love expounded by the Florentine school of neo-Platonism, which the more princely than civic Medici sponsored: apparently, then, monarchy and a philosophy of Platonic love went hand in hand. But they were not, to a republican mind, a particularly impressive pair. When Castiglione treated monarchical love in the desexualized, disembodied manner of Plato, he falsified its political significance at the same time that he idealized eros. Abstracted into a Platonic "idea," Castiglione's theorized courtly love lost all connection with the notorious practices of courts. In truth, it was normal in the courts of monarchs that politics should be reduced to sexual politics, and that power, influence, and policy should be decided in the bedroom.[81] From the standpoint of republican thought, this monarchical confounding of the private with the public realm, this willingness of monarchists to attribute public significance to private "affairs," was corruption pure and simple. So any good republican would assert, to which any classically educated republican theorist, but Machiavelli most of all, would add a denunciation of Castiglione's attempt—based on the Trojan War—to interpret ancient warfare as an exercise in chivalry, glorious because the masculine combatants fought all the more nobly knowing their feminine lovers were watching them from the windows of the castle.[82] For such politics the only possible defense was Castiglione's falsification by idealization.

On matters pertaining to eros as on most everything else, Machiavelli was not content with siding for a republican position and against a monarchical one. Here as elsewhere his thought is equally remarkable for standing republican thought on its head. As we have already seen, his comic sensibility is directly opposed to the Renaissance penchant for moralizing Plautus and Terence by way of turning them into schoolmarms, preachers of lessons in moral conduct. Against such an idealistic reading of comedy, he responded with an accentuation of the immoral themes of Roman comedy, the trickery, deception, and double-dealing that readily furnished him with the materials he needed to set comic practice so glaringly at odds with comic theory as to call out for a new comic theory, far less idealistic, far more Machiavellian, in tone.

Still more evidence of what is subversive of established republican doctrine in Machiavelli's amorous letters and comedies may be attained by a brief look at Alberti's *Book on the Family*, a noteworthy effort by a civic humanist of the quattrocento to rewrite the first book of Aristotle's *Politics*, on the theory of the household. Admonitions to shun adultery,[83] to "avoid love," to "flee from this fury of love,"[84] to prefer friendship and fatherly affection to erotic love,[85] abound in Alberti's treatise; and his polemic against romance is an essential part of his sense of civic mission. Romantic love is unworthy, Alberti contends, because it diverts us from the struggle for the fame and glory of public affairs.[86]

Machiavelli agrees that love is a diversion but regards that as

its charm, and recommends it to ambassador Francesco Vettori
(who hardly needed encouragement) as a welcome alternative by
night to the serious affairs of the day. As Machiavelli viewed the
world, there is so little danger that a man of *virtù* will sacrifice
politics to love that the politician is free to be a lover.

BY DEMANDING puritanical behavior in the public sphere but
not in private, Machiavelli drastically altered what has been called
"the Spartan tradition in European thought."[87] A strand of classical thought, derived from ancient Roman sources and highly
Spartan in its values, was reincarnated at the time of the Renaissance. Destined to a second life of several centuries, this intellectual tradition was no sooner reborn than Machiavelli revised
it. He substituted a two-faced vision of civic life for the single-
minded Spartanism that typified neoclassical ideals. In place of
monolithic puritanism, Machiavelli pictured a rigorous morality
of public life joined to a slack morality of private life.

At the beginning of the *Art of War*, the process by which
Machiavelli toned down the Spartan outlook of neoclassical thought
may be observed. First we hear the words of Cosimo, whose
nostalgia for the hard ways of Sparta leads him to an uncompromising denunciation of the corruption rife in his age. Then Fabrizio, spokesman for Machiavelli's viewpoint throughout the
dialogue, holds forth. He voices certain reservations about the
"severe methods" of the Spartans and proclaims that modern ways
are "more humane."[88] The modern republic, he adds, can do
without a full-fledged Spartanism and flourish nonetheless. Eventually Fabrizio carries the day with his very un-Spartan argument
that only on holidays should citizens be subject to military discipline.

In his letter of January 31, 1515, to Francesco Vettori, Machiavelli justified his oscillations between political and amorous
concerns by proclaiming that Nature is "variable." With that

statement he had, in effect, returned to the "happy versatility" of which Pericles spoke when defending Athenian ideals in the Funeral Oration. And Machiavelli returned to the doctrine of happy versatility the hard way when he infused happiness and versatility into the very Spartan and Roman outlooks that were bywords for somber rigidity.[89]

— V —

CONVERSATIONS WITH THE ANCIENTS

FROM BEGINNING to end, the Italian Renaissance was characterized by the notion that dialogue is the path to knowledge, that wisdom is acquired through conversing with the wise, and that the most engaging and rewarding conversation a modern can have is with the ancients. Petrarch's letters to Cicero and Livy initiated this trend,[1] and Machiavelli's famous letter of December 10, 1513 to Francesco Vettori is one of its most remarkable culminating points.

> On the coming of evening, I return to my house and enter my study; and at the door I take off the day's clothing, covered with mud and dust, and put on garments regal and courtly; and reclothed appropriately, I enter the ancient courts of ancient men, where, received by them with affection, I feed on that food which only is mine and which I was born for, where I am not ashamed to speak with them and to ask them the reason for their actions; and they in their kindness answer me; and for four hours of time I do not feel boredom, I forget every trouble, I do not dread poverty, I am not frightened by death; entirely I give myself over to them.[2]

Our present concern is to elucidate the intellectual significance of Machiavelli's give-and-take with the classics of Western thought, to determine which concepts and themes he borrowed from the ancients, which he neglected, why, and with what consequences. Thus far we have studied the *contents* of Machiavelli's writings—his notions of the admirable and the despicable in public life, and of the joyous in private life; now we turn to the classical *forms* of thought that he drew upon as he created his outlook.

It is time to climb the ladder of abstraction and ask not simply what Machiavelli said but how he said it and what he was unable to say. Almost everything he wrote was uttered through the language of the classical tradition, the ancient pagan authors, among whom the Roman republican writers were his most beloved mentors; hence it is in terms of his Latin heritage that his identity, limitations, and genius are best understood. In the present chapter we shall address the oft-debated question of Machiavelli's prowess as a political analyst, a "scientist" of politics as he has sometimes been called, and it will be argued that his accomplishments within this sphere of inquiry were as unremarkable as those of his Roman teachers. This negative lesson will then be superseded in the following chapter by the claim that Machiavelli learned from the Latin classics how to turn Roman history into a powerful mythology and ideology, and used his mythical Rome to beckon moderns to overthrow Christianity and restore pagan virtue.

Dialogues in Latin

WRITING to Vettori, Machiavelli described his exchanges with the ancients as a "conversation." He did not, however, indicate precisely who were the classical authors he chose to talk to, nor did he mention the names of those whom he elected to ignore; but with the help of his major works, the parties participating in the evening conversations sponsored by Machiavelli may be unmistakably identified. Livy, Tacitus, Sallust, and Polybius were present at every one of these meetings; Cicero was sometimes present; Plato, Aristotle, and Thucydides—the masters of Greek political thought—were almost never invited to attend. Machiavelli's classical learning was Roman rather than Greek, so his conversations with the ancients were conducted solely in Latin. Among Greek thinkers only Polybius was systematically included in Machiavelli's nocturnal discussions, an exception being made in his case for the reason that he was an honorary Roman and the initiator of Roman political thought. Among Roman thinkers the formidable reputation of Cicero, precisely to the extent that it was based on an immersion in Greek philosophy, did not automatically earn its bearer an invitation to the nightly debates held in the Machiavelli household.* Cicero's offense was that he was eager to incorporate Plato and Aristotle into Roman thought, whereas Machiavelli sided constantly with the Roman historians and was himself something of a Roman historian in his *Discourses on Livy* and *Florentine History*.

The silence of Plato and Aristotle in the pages of Machiavelli is no less significant than the volubility of the Roman historians. From the moment Machiavelli chose to clothe himself in Roman attire and to speak in the Latin language, he committed himself to an intellectual tradition stressing action over contemplation. Within Greek thought, a satisfactory answer was never given to the question of why the philosopher should return to the cave once he succeeded in escaping from it. Plato's answer, that the philosopher had to rule lest he be ruled by inferior men,[3] was more clever than convincing. For if, as Plato argued, knowledge of universals was the highest form of wisdom and wisdom the highest form of excellence, then it is difficult indeed to understand why the philosopher should quit his contemplation of the unchanging, eternal, perfect world and plunge back into the morass of a changing, temporal, and imperfect world. In Roman thought, on the contrary, the impulse to soar above temporal events was never present, and the world of shadows was much more likely

* On the other hand, Cicero the moralist, rhetorician, and author of *De Officiis*, was a primary target of Machiavelli the ideologue. See chapter VI (below).

to be located by Roman thinkers in Plato's extraterrestrial sphere of ideas and forms than in the workaday sphere of human intercourse where Plato found it. Already in its most civic moments the theoretical side of Greek speculation threatened to undermine its practical side. Conversely, by virtue of its relative indifference to philosophy, Roman thought was rarely tempted to sacrifice the *vita activa* to the *vita contemplativa*. Pupils of Aristotle could justify withdrawal from public affairs by forgetting their master's assertions that the good life is political while remembering those passages in which Aristotle proclaimed contemplation the most perfect activity.[4] Pupils of Cicero, however, could not quote Cicero against Cicero, for his message was always the same, that a life devoted to public concerns was the only one befitting a superior man.[5] And what was true of Cicero's writings was, if anything, even truer of the writings of the Roman historians, all of whom regarded it as axiomatic that politics and military affairs are the meaning of life.

"I am well aware," writes Sallust, "that by no means equal repute attends the narrator and the doer of deeds."[6] To the Romans a man wrote about politics when he could not do politics. Disgraced and removed from the senate, Sallust devoted himself to the lesser fame that is due the historian. Earlier, Polybius had assumed the occupation of writer because as a hostage of the Romans he could not continue the direct participation in public affairs that had been the joy of his first forty years. Later, Tacitus wrote because imperial Rome, a monarchy in all but name, had no meaningful use for him as a senator. Much the same is true of Machiavelli. His writings are the fruit of his bitter political unemployment, which began with the return of the Medici in 1512 and never ended. Gladly Machiavelli would have sacrificed his writings for a political job, almost any political job, however humble. His letters abound with anguished complaints that he, now a private man, is of no use to his family, friends, or city.[7] Most of his major works are, among other things, pleas to the

Medici for a political position, and he cannot prevent himself from inserting into *The Prince* the claim that the most loyal servants a princely family can have are to be found in the ranks of those who, having originally opposed the new political regime, are eager to prove themselves to their new masters by extraordinarily diligent service.[8]

According to the Romans, treatises on politics should be written for current men of action by former men of action, and in this view there was no room for Plato's notion of philosophers who would be kings or kings who would be philosophers. "Plato," asserts Polybius,

> tells us that human affairs go well when either philosophers become kings or kings study philosophy, and I would say that it will be well with history either when men of action undertake to write history . . . or when would-be authors regard a training in actual affairs as necessary for writing history.[9]

Much the same sentiment was responsible for Machiavelli's statement that Plato and Aristotle each conjured up a speculative political vision "to show the world that if they have not founded a free government, as did Solon or Lycurgus, they have not failed through their ignorance but through their impotence for putting it into practice."[10] At the very moment when Castiglione was turning Plato and Aristotle into courtiers—Plato the courtier of the kings of Sicily, Aristotle the courtier of Alexander the Great[11]— Machiavelli was turning them into political theorists of the Roman variety, authors forced to write on politics because they lacked opportunity to do politics. Neither Machiavelli nor Castiglione was accurate in his reading of Plato and Aristotle, but both Italians succeeded in creating a Plato and Aristotle in the image of their political outlooks.

If Roman thought, despite its indebtedness to the Greeks, deleted the philosopher-king from its agenda, it was hardly more receptive to Plato's and Aristotle's discussions of the utopian but unrealizable community. In this regard it was again Polybius who set the tone of all subsequent political thought emanating from Rome.

> Just as we do not admit to athletic contests artists or athletes who are not duly entered and have not been in training, so we have no right to admit [Plato's ideal republic] to the competition for the prize of merit, unless it first gave an exhibition of its actual working. Up to the present it would be just the same thing to discuss it with a view to comparison with the constitutions of Sparta, Rome, and Carthage, as to take some statue and compare it with living and breathing men. For even if the workmanship of the statue were altogether praiseworthy, the comparison of a lifeless thing with a living thing would strike spectators as entirely imperfect and incongruous.[12]

Livy was an exception to the Roman rule that history should be written by men of political experience, yet even he had not the slightest use for either the philosopher-king or for philosophical discussions of the theoretically best regime:

> If there should be a city-state of sages, such as philosophers imagine rather than actually know, I am inclined to think that neither could leading men possibly be of more solid worth and more self-controlled as regards the lust for power, nor could the populace show a higher character [than in early Rome].[13]

Hence, concludes Livy, it is from the history of the early Roman republic, not from any abstract notion of an ideal republic, that the politician should learn his lessons. In the same vein is the pride Machiavelli takes in not adopting the idealizing tone of his humanistic predecessors. Taking note that "many have fancied for themselves republics and principalities that have never been seen or known to exist in reality," he congratulates himself on "depart[ing] very far from the methods of others."[14] Moreover, both Polybius and Machiavelli choose as their model state the Aristotelian polity, the mixed and balanced government, which to Aristotle was the best practical state but far from truly ideal. While following Aristotle in refusing to proclaim polity a formula for political perfection, Polybius and Machiavelli diverge sharply from him when they conclude that discussions of the truly best but never-to-be community are pointless. Roman thought responds to utopian speculation with an uncomprehending and dismissive shrug, and so does Machiavelli's neo-Roman thought.

When Roman thought downgraded the philosopher, it fundamentally revised the Platonic scale of values. It demoted the proposed ruling class of the *Republic* to a secondary rank while at the same time it promoted Plato's middling class, the timocrats savoring honor, glory, and heroism, to the first rank. Self-consciously or not, the emphasis of Roman historians on military deeds as the highest form of goodness was a restoration of pagan values to their original and pre-Platonic meaning. Plato and Aristotle denounced the Spartan way of life[15] for stopping short of the highest excellence, philosophical wisdom; but in so arguing they were quarreling with all of Greek culture from Homer on, and their efforts at redefining *areté* were clearly acts of purposive revisionism. The retrieval of heroic and warlike values by Sallust, Livy, Tacitus, and others, militaristic values which before the advent of Greek philosophy had always been understood as the highest form of excellence, may be viewed as an act that followed automatically and perhaps unthinkingly from their Roman reverence for tradition. Since the Latin word *virtus* meant almost exactly what *areté* had meant in popular Greek usage, simply to use the Latin language as it had always been used had the effect, whether intended or unintended, of undoing the Platonic and Aristotelian effort at reworking and philosophizing pagan values.

Once again "excellence" was synonymous with all that is heroic, noble, warlike, and great.

For his part, Machiavelli was merely accepting the role of a good Roman son when he stressed the militaristic implications of *virtù*.[16] He further displayed his fidelity to Roman definitions of virtue when he rank-ordered intellectuals in the *Discourses* well below generals, political leaders, and founders of republics and religions.[17] In the *Florentine History*, to top off his Romanizing performance, he wrapped himself for a moment in the toga of Cato as he suggested that "the virtue of military courage cannot be corrupted with a more honorable laziness than that of letters, nor with a greater and more dangerous deception can this laziness enter into well-regulated cities."[18]

To recognize Machiavelli's credentials as a Roman thinker is fruitful in still another way, namely, that it makes his preoccupation with war and empire perfectly predictable. The theme of both Polybius and Livy is the glory and grandeur of universal Roman conquest, and if Tacitus writes of the period of imperial and monarchical Rome rather than of republican and empire-building Rome, he does not fail to bemoan his lot. The author of *The Annals of Imperial Rome* laments that his subject matter is despicable.

> I am not unaware that very many of the events I have described, and shall describe, may perhaps seem little things, trifles too slight for record; but no parallel can be drawn between these chronicles of mine and the work of the men who composed the ancient history of the Roman people. Gigantic wars, cities stormed, routed and captive kings . . .—such were the themes on which *they* dwelt, or digressed, at will. Mine is an inglorious labor in a narrow field: for this was an age of peace unbroken or half-heartedly challenged, . . . of a prince careless to extend the empire.[19]

Such is the voice of Roman paganism, just as St. Augustine's complaint that from the founding of Rome to Caesar Augustus the gates of Janus were closed* for only one year, is the voice of the Christian repudiation of paganism.[20]

As champions of imperialism, Machiavelli and the Roman historians are at odds not only with Christianity but with Plato and Aristotle as well, both of whom abhorred imperialism and cited the decline of Athens and Sparta as evidence of the extravagant price that foolhardy ambition exacts. Here once again Polybius is a crucial figure, for he was Greek, familiar with the works of Plato and Aristotle, and yet believed Roman experience proved that world conquest was far from a ridiculous dream. Native Roman intellectuals eagerly seized upon the Polybian break with the anti-imperialistic attitudes of Greek philosophy, making his enthusiasm for empire their own; and they did the same with the one aspect of Aristotelian philosophy that Polybius saw fit to import from Greece to Rome, the notion that Roman institutions were an accidental but nonetheless magnificent embodiment of Aristotle's ideal of mixed government. All of Roman republican thought accepted the Polybian theory, at once Aristotelian and anti-Aristotelian, that Rome was a polity and as such was properly equipped for achieving a long succession of triumphs, ending only when no one was left to conquer.

The Romans also had some limited use for Thucydides. His depiction of the warlike but unsuccessful Athenian republic became the paradigm in Roman political theory of how a city with a popular government should not proceed in world affairs, just as Rome became the self-congratulatory paradigm of how a city with a popular government should proceed.

To all these comings and goings of Roman thought Machiavelli added his wholehearted approval, along with his sorrow that Roman democratic glory was a remembrance of things past, and

---

* Closed gates signified peace, open gates war.

his scorn that Athenian democratic incompetence had been reborn in the Florentine present.

The Deficiencies of Latin Discourse

THAT MACHIAVELLI was a Roman rather than a Greek thinker accounts for his intellectual weaknesses as a political analyst. Scholars have long recognized that Roman thought, although apprenticed to Plato and Aristotle, produced works of lesser quality than those of the Greek masters. Much of the intellectual brilliance and analytical genius of Plato and Aristotle were lost somewhere along the road from Athens to Rome, and the losses of the Romans were Machiavelli's as well. His decision to converse constantly with the authors of the Latin classics but rarely with the authors of the Greek classics set limitations beyond which his thought could only with difficulty reach.

At Rome the thought of the Greeks was first diluted, then frozen. One mark of this debasement may be observed in the Polybian alteration of Aristotle's modest scheme for classifying governments into a pretentious law of political change. Regimes may be grouped under headings, Aristotle suggested, on the basis of the number of rulers and the manner in which the rulers govern, whether for the public interest or for their private interest. Monarchy, aristocracy, and democracy are the governments of the one, the few, and the many, each regime aiming at the well-being of the whole polis, whereas tyranny, oligarchy, and mobocracy are the one, the few, and the many serving the one, the few, and the many—they are corrupt governments, dictatorships of varying degrees of popularity.[21] By the time Polybius finished assimilating this harmless scheme of classification, it had become an explanation of the inevitable and endlessly repetitive course of all history, beginning with monarchy which quickly degenerates into tyranny, then moving on to an aristocratic regime which soon yields to oligarchy, yielding next to democracy from which mob rule ensues, ¿nd finally to a restoration of one-man rule, thus completing one full rotation of the cycle.[22] If this ironclad scheme does not redound to the glory of Polybius, neither does it to Machiavelli, who uncritically reproduced it in the *Discourses*.[23]

The Roman reconceptualization of Aristotle's notion of polity is another example of how rigid Greek thought became when Romanized. It was to Aristotle's credit that he could squeeze the best out of two existing corrupt forms of government, oligarchy and democracy, and show how they might be combined into something much better, polity. It was not to Polybius's credit that he insisted on finding ingredients of each good form of government, monarchy, aristocracy, and democracy, in the Roman constitution, and failing to do so invented the obviously missing monarchical element through a trumped-up argument for placing the consuls in that niche.[24] So dominated by his arbitrary formulas was Polybius that he falsified reality rather than reconsider his preconceptions, and Machiavelli was content to repeat rather than correct the error of his half-Greek, half-Roman predecessor.

Likewise the noble lie by which Plato hoped to legitimize his utopian ideal, the fable that Plato knew could be sold to the masses only with the greatest difficulty, and not at all unless the philosopher-king was handed a generation of children minus their parents,[25] hardened in Polybius into the assumption that Roman religion had in fact been created by Numa for the purpose of manipulating the masses.[26] On this occasion, the consequence of a faithful replication in the *Discourses* of a view originally enunciated in the *Histories* of Polybius was that Machiavelli made himself as much the dupe of a myth as its analyst. Religion may have been the opium of the Roman people, but belief that the Roman leaders invented religion was the opium of Machiavelli. Much was lost in the translation of Greek writings into Latin, and for Machiavelli as well as for his Roman forebears.

On the problem of explaining the cause and cure of political degeneration, the Roman imitation of Greek thought again proved a pale copy. By and large Aristotle's treatment of the struggle of social classes for political power, his skillful analysis of contrasting interpretations of distributive justice—oligarchs equating wealth with merit, democrats proclaiming that simply to be a citizen was adequate qualification for all public offices[27]—fell out of the Polybian and subsequent Roman accounts of political change. Discussions of classes and ideologies largely gave way in the thought of Polybius to a scheme tracing the corruption of governments to no deeper cause than the passing of power from talented ruling class fathers to their untalented sons by hereditary succession. Why such a shallow explanation convinced Polybius is unclear, unless it was because he was consistently predisposed to believe that the composition of the ruling class explained all political phenomena, or because he believed the leaders somehow stood outside society and therefore were exempt from all social determination, as he in effect argued when he interpreted religion as an invention of the political elite. The same loss of Aristotle's social understanding is apparent in the predilection of Polybius for treating power in abstraction from its social milieu.[28] A more or less mechanical formula for the parceling out and balancing of power satisfied Polybius, who lacked sufficient sociological insight to realize that both the aristocratic and the democratic elements of the Roman constitution were controlled by the same oligarchical group.[29] And where Polybius went wrong Machiavelli was sure to follow.

Since Polybius took little notice of the role of collective beliefs in causing conflict, we should not be surprised to learn that he largely neglected their role in maintaining cohesion. The Roman deletion of Aristotle's discussion of class ideology was matched by the deletion of his concern for political education. In place of civic participation and a law internalized and beloved,[30] Polybius initiated that very Roman emphasis on interests, punishments, rules, claims, and contracts, which was later to assert itself more fully in Cicero's republican thought and in the Roman law of the empire.[31] As for Machiavelli, his limitation of political education to military service and pagan religion places him in the camp of Polybius rather than Aristotle. Moreover, although Machiavelli shared with Aristotle an immunity to the pitfalls of the legalistic mentality, they were exempt from the Roman belief in law as a universal panacea for different reasons, Aristotle because he realized law could be systematically biased along class lines,[32] Machiavelli because he realized that law is a form of power and not its opposite.[33] Even in those moments when Machiavelli saw beyond the Romans, he did not avail himself of the riches of Greek thought. Aristotle's sociological genius was wasted on Machiavelli no less than on the Romans.

Equally wasted was Plato's prowess in psychology. Machiavelli repeats the Polybian belief that the assumption of power by the younger generation sparks political decline, but no more than Polybius did he recover the Platonic psychology explaining the rift between generations. Plato grounded his explanation in a psychology postulating that in addition to the socialized self presented in everyday life there is "in all of us, even in good men, . . . a lawless wild beast nature, which peers out in sleep."

> Then the wild beast within us . . . starts up and . . . goes forth to satisfy his desires. And there is no conceivable folly or crime—not excepting incest . . . or parricide . . . which at such a time . . . a man may not be ready to commit.[34]

When Plato lit up the darkest corners of the psyche, he came face to face with Oedipus, author of incest and parricide. From myth and drama, the *Republic* transfigured the Oedipus of Sophocles into psychological analysis; for Plato knew Oedipus is not fictional or distant but is everyman, and he nightly re-enacts his drama as many times as there are human beings.[35]

The divided self and the rebellion of sons against fathers were central concepts in Plato's psychology, and their politicization

scope and longer lasting than anything found in Greek history, that the Romans prided themselves. Were Rome gifted with historians as able as those of Greece, the world would soon know that events originating in or impinging upon the city of Romulus and Scipio overshadowed all other happenings ever recorded; or so Sallust believed.

> The acts of the Athenians were indeed great and glorious enough, but nevertheless somewhat less important than fame represents them. But because Athens produced writers of exceptional talent, the exploits of the men of Athens are heralded throughout the world as unsurpassed. . . . The Roman people never had that advantage, since their ablest men were always most engaged with affairs; their minds were never employed apart from their bodies. . . .[41]

Livy's designation of the Greeks as "a race more valiant in words than in deeds"[42] and his comment that the deaths of the Greeks at Thermopylae were more memorable than the battle they waged against the Persians,[43] are a continuation of Sallust's attempt to claim for Rome the lion's share of antique glory. The grandeur, greatness, and glory of Roman arms, conquests, and empire was the master theme of Latin literature, particularly of the *Aeneid*, Virgil's epic poem which Machiavelli enjoyed quoting, and of Livy's *History*, that epic in prose upon which Machiavelli erected his theory of politics. Yet for all the Roman preoccupation with imperialism, so starkly contrasting with the few asides of Plato and Aristotle on the topic of expansion, and for all the efforts of the Romans to represent their history in the high and sublime style of epic, as the greatest epic of all times, the issue may still be raised whether it was not the Greeks whose treatment of the politics of imperialism was the more penetrating.

At the aesthetic level, the epic tale of Roman triumph was less moving than the tragic tale of Greek defeat related by Thucydides. One shortcoming of Roman self-congratulation was that it injected a quantitative criterion into the center of qualitative judgment: the Roman standard of sublimity and grandeur was based upon the number, the amount, the quantity of Rome's victories. Another shortcoming of the Romans was that they could only see sublimity in defeat and nobility in failure when the loss of one party to a conflict was the gain of another, usually the Romans. As opposed to this, Thucydides dramatized a conflict that was especially awesome precisely because both the Spartans and the Athenians lost, a conflict of lesser compass than those of the Romans but nevertheless more significant because its grandeur was tragic. Sparta and Athens represented mutually exclusive and equally worthy political principles which should not have been, and yet were, set against one another by a tragic turn of fate, and from this disastrous collision of a magnificent aristocracy with a magnificent democracy the death of the polis itself threatened to ensue.[44]

By contrast, neither the peaks nor the valleys of Roman thought were sharply drawn. Too democratic and too willing to hire mercenary soldiers, corrupt Carthage was not, Polybius writes, a truly worthy opponent to the Roman republic, still ruled by the astute senators and fighting its wars with native troops organized as a citizens' militia.[45] Therefore we should not expect his *History* to evoke the emotions aroused by Thucydides. So much the better, Polybius might respond, since he was contemptuous of the many Hellenistic histories that sacrificed truth for literary effect.[46] Artistry, however, was the paramount concern in the historical writing of Livy, so the Polybian defense for not eliciting the deepest emotions—that literal truth might be lost—could not be pleaded by Livy. Weakness of art thus constitutes a devastating charge against Livy, and it is a charge that must be levied. Livy at his best painted Rome's enemies in heroic colors, the better to congratulate his city on her conquests, but the tragic sense of life was as foreign to him as it was second nature to the

Greeks,[47] and at his worst Livy made the foes of Rome into villains, thereby reducing his *History* to melodrama.[48]

Florentine by birth but Roman at heart, Machiavelli was not tempted, as Livy had been, to read too much heroism into the deeds of his native city, and he scrupulously gave voice in his *Florentine History* to the charges of Italians that the ambition of Florence, if successfully asserted, would mean the end of their freedom.[49] He knew, too, that the moment of Italy's chastisement by Northern powers might well be at hand.[50] Yet tragic sensibility is fully as absent in Machiavelli's work as in those of his Roman teachers and mentors, and since glory for him as for them was measured quantitatively, by the number of cities a republic holds in subjection, he rarely experienced the blood and gore of heroic values as deeply problematic, especially not when his side was doing the goring.[51]

At the level of causal argumentation it was again the Greek philosophers who had something important to say about empire, and the Romans-cum-Machiavelli who were satisfied with an evasive generalization. Faced with the disconcerting realization that the final triumph of Rome over her archenemy Carthage inaugurated an era of civic corruption, the Roman historians overlooked the potential Platonic and Aristotelian explanation of this event that was theirs anytime they wanted it. They did not want to know that their imperialism had always been self-destructive. Rather than accept the painful argument of the Greek philosophers that the expansion of a republican city-state entails the end of its civic way of life—frugality, simplicity, and dedication to the public good inevitably losing out to luxury, ostentation, and self-interest—the historians of Rome substituted the less exacting, and less devastating, theory of the *metus hostilis* (fear of the enemy).[52] Seen through Roman eyes, the irony of human existence is that bad grows out of good, so that the triumph of virtue signals the onset of corruption. Once the Roman people had no enemies to fear, their virtue became expendable and almost inevitably faded into memory. Thus to tell the story of Roman degeneration from virtue to corruption was to turn historiography into an exercise in political irony and paradox. Machiavelli reproduced this Roman argument in his *Discourses on Livy*,[53] and not surprisingly, for he was as anxious as the Romans themselves to remain ignorant of the self-destructive implications of empire. Irony suited Machiavelli because it suited his temperament; and it suited him all the more when it permitted him to evade responsibility for the less desirable consequences of the politics he advocated.

Plato and Aristotle were so intent on warning against empire, and Thucydides so intent on recounting the deleterious effects of the conflict between the Spartan and Athenian empires, that they had no incentive to develop theories explaining the machinery and workings of imperial administration. To the very end their thought remained parochial, and proudly so. The political theorists of Rome, on the contrary, had every reason to be dissatisfied with parochialism and to strive to comprehend the new large-scale political structure that had gradually supplanted the old republican and city-state governmental forms under which they had acquired their far-flung possessions. Nevertheless the Roman historians remained as tied to the city-state perspective as their Greek predecessors had been. Although Tacitus lived under the emperors, he showed not the slightest interest in anything happening outside Rome, with the exception of wars, of course.[54] What the emperors did, the machinations at court, the progressive servility of the once haughty senate, encompass the entirety of his field of vision. Rather than struggle to enlarge the field of vision of republican thought to account for imperial administration, Tacitus made it an explicit principle of historical writing that as the collective leadership of the republic shriveled to the one-man rule of the empire, the focus of political thought should likewise grow more narrow.[55] Not without reason did St. Jerome organize the writings of Tacitus under the title *Lives of the Caesars*.

And after Tacitus, Roman historical thought ceased to exist, its place in intellectual life filled by philosophies of natural law and by legal thought. Henceforth there was no republic to laud and no great deeds for historical writing to save from forgetfulness. The historiography of Tacitus is the swan song of republican thought; his works are decidedly not the beginning of an effort to shift focus to a new political structure.

Living much later than the Romans and benefiting from historical hindsight, Machiavelli had opportunity to remedy the nearsightedness of republican thought, its inability to peer over the walls of the city and observe the surrounding political units, so large as to dwarf the autonomous cities of ancient and modern Italy. Machiavelli both enlarged and failed to enlarge the horizon of classical thought from Plato to Tacitus. He did take some account of the territorial and almost national monarchies north of the Alps, especially of France on whose institutional arrangements he frequently commented,[56] although never at great length. It is possible, moreover, to discern in his distinction between the monarchical governments of Turkey and France, the former governed by a prince and servants, the latter by a prince and barons,[57] the seeds of Montesquieu's later models of despotic and feudal kingship. But surely it would be wrong to equate Machiavelli's scattered intimations of later theories explaining the Old Regime with matured insight into the transalpine governments that had succeeded in overflowing the narrow confines of the city-state. Fundamentally the focus of Machiavelli was rigidly fixed on the city-state republic, and he accounted for the factor of size by speaking of the city-state expanded into a regional state in the manner of Florence, or into a universal empire in the manner of ancient Rome.

How seriously Machiavelli's city-state blinders could mislead him is glaringly evident in his comments on Switzerland. Amazingly, he contended that the disjointed Swiss government was the nearest approximation in the modern world to the expansionary Roman republic. He would have his friends believe the Swiss boasted they would do one day what the Romans did, take all.[58] For extra measure he attributes to them a use of the methods which in the *Discourses* and *Art of War* he credited Rome with inventing during her unrelenting quest for imperial glory, particularly the securing of associates that would later be reduced to subjects, and the exploitation of mutual suspicions among allies,[59] so that the Swiss imperialists would have a "ladder for their own greatness and the ruin of others."[60] Chided by Francesco Vettori,[61] Machiavelli would modify his position only to the extent of saying "I do not, indeed, believe they will produce an empire like the Romans, but I do believe they can become masters of Italy."[62] There is in Machiavelli's remarks on Switzerland a determination to misunderstand the modern world totally if that is the only way to preserve the hope that Roman legions might once again cover the earth.

Before ending our efforts to overhear the dialogues routinely held in Machiavelli's study, we would do well to note how misleading discussions of Machiavelli the political scientist are when his identity as a classical thinker is ignored. "Machiavelli studied political actions in the same way as a chemist studies chemical reactions,"[63] asserts Ernst Cassirer, writing from a neo-Kantian standpoint. Similarly, contemporary scholars of positivist persuasion have delighted in suggesting that Machiavelli charted the movements of political bodies in much the same spirit as Galileo studied the movements of physical bodies.[64] What the positivists and Kantians share is the assumption that a sharp distinction may be drawn between facts and values, phenomena and noumena, science and ethics. This same set of distinctions is central to the arguments of those scholars who contend that the moral passion of Machiavelli, his hatred of corruption and love of virtue, proves that science was not his foremost concern.[65]

Both parties to the foregoing debate are mistaken, and mistaken for the same reason: they wrongly impose upon Machiavelli a bifurcation of fact and value which is foreign to classical thought and therefore foreign to Machiavelli, a neoclassical thinker. Explaining politics and judging it morally were always part of the same process in Greek and Roman political theory. For example, when the Greek thinkers Plato and Aristotle highlighted the methods of rule employed by the tyrant, when they drew attention to the permanent purge by which he destroyed not merely some social bonds but society in general, they condemned tyranny at the same time as they explained it.[66] For their part, Roman authors saw no contradiction between explaining political events and stirring the passions of their readers. Given the classical credentials of Machiavelli, it cannot be said, then, that his passionate moral concern is at the expense of his interest in understanding the interconnections of political phenomena. What can be said is that since his efforts to explain political phenomena were pursued through Roman rather than Greek concepts, his achievements as a political scientist were less than remarkable. In order to discover the secret of his appeal, we shall have to search elsewhere.

Monumental History

IT IS TIME to return to the beginning, to Machiavelli's letter to Vettori where his intentions are explicitly stated. In Machiavelli's own words, he conversed with the ancients because he wished "to ask them the reason for their actions." Worthy of note in Machiavelli's statement of purpose is his implied use of the classical authors to bypass them and come into direct contact with men of action. To Machiavelli, there was no point in striving to understand the past for the sake of historical comprehension itself. Rather, the study of the past was for the sake of learning how to act, and action pertains to the here and now, the present. Whatever theories one derives from past action have value insofar, and only insofar, as they guide present action to a successful conclusion. An ex-politician studies history, which is to say past politics, so that he may act politically with all the more effectiveness upon his resumption of power, and may in the meantime be politically useful by teaching those holding public office how to wield power. The union of theory and practice was Machiavelli's intent, and the method of achieving it was a combination of a lengthy "experience" of modern things with a continual "reading" of ancient ones.[67]

The fault of the Florentines, in Machiavelli's opinion, was that they were content to admire the political riches of ancient Rome without giving a thought to reproducing them.

> I see that in the differences that come up between citizens in civil affairs, or in the illnesses that men suffer from, they ever have recourse to the judgments or to the remedies that have been pronounced or prescribed by the ancients; for the civil laws are nothing else than opinions given by ancient jurists, which, brought into order, teach our present jurists to judge. And medicine too is nothing other than the experiments made by ancient physicians, on which present physicians base their judgments. Nonetheless, in setting up states, in maintaining governments, in ruling kingdoms, in organizing armies and managing war, . . . in expanding an empire, not a single prince or republic now resorts to the examples of the ancients.[68]

In one field of inquiry after another the moderns had blazed a new path as they demonstrated that ancient wisdom could be recovered and adapted to the needs of the fifteenth and sixteenth century present, but in political studies, which constituted the branch of classical learning on which the ancients prided themselves the most, the Florentines were content with a passive admiration of ancient deeds. In consequence, the Renaissance was in danger of proving to be less a rebirth than an abortion.

Insofar as Machiavelli was determined to unite theory and

practice, he had affinities with both Greek and Roman political thought, especially with Polybius, whose writings were an attempted mediation between the abstract victories of Greek theory and the concrete glories of Roman practicality. Neither Polybius nor Machiavelli had any reason to object to Aristotle's division of wisdom into speculative and practical knowledge, nor to the Greek master's placement of politics under the heading, and at the top of the list, labeled practical. To Polybius and Machiavelli as to Aristotle before them, politics pertained to the order of those things which, since they could be other than they were, allowed for the assertion of human will, whereas speculative wisdom, since it aimed at understanding what cannot be other than it is, presupposed no action other than the act of contemplation. Yet Aristotle had not, from a Polybian and Machiavellian point of view, sufficiently forced theory to descend from the ethereal heights of philosophy into the mundane world of praxis; above all, Aristotle had failed to write a handbook for statesmen that went beyond general exhortations to a delineation of specific strategies and tactics. It was not enough to outline the principles of the good life or to uncover the inner logic of various types of regimes, as Aristotle had done. Unless how-to-do-it manuals were added to Aristotle, no one would ever learn how to direct practice to its destination by the light of theory.

Prudence and discretion gained during years of public service, Machiavelli and Polybius believed, have traditionally been the intellectual capital of the political actor. Sometimes the everyday experience of the politician rises conceptually to the level of rules of thumb, that is, to low-grade generalizations, but the political practitioner will never of his own accord climb the ladder of abstraction to a more comprehensive theory of action; nor could he if he would, because his knowledge is so bound to particulars that an explicit articulation of his unstated assumptions, even if successfully undertaken, would not yield maxims of action underpinned by high-grade theory. Therefore Polybius and Machiavelli provisionally abandoned the actor's perspective, hoping later to return to the particular situations a politician faces, armed the second time around with the advantage of a theoretical knowledge previously unavailable to the man of action. Crucial to their procedure for linking theory and practice was the subsumption of history under the category of nature, specifically through the notion of cyclical history, a doctrine found time and again in pagan thought[69] and used by Polybius to claim that changes of political regimes are as regularized and predictable as the periodicity of the seasons.[70] Thus the political actor, if trained by Polybius, would have little difficulty in understanding the political possibilities of his period; knowing what could and could not be realistically striven for, he would neither chase after windmills nor be driven to resignation. Likewise Machiavelli, taking his cue from Polybius, sought in nature the foundation of a theory of action.

> He who considers present affairs and ancient ones readily understands that all cities and all peoples have the same desires and the same traits and that they always have had them. He who diligently examines past events easily foresees future ones in every country and can apply to them the remedies used by the ancients or, not finding any that have been used, can devise new ones because of the similarity of the events.[71]

Effective politicking had been regarded as an art prior to Polybius in classical Rome and prior to Machiavelli in neoclassical Florence. After them, if all went well, it would be a science. For if history runs in a cycle, repeating itself endlessly in the manner of nature, then political events are only apparently unique. Whatever is has been before, so the deeper we dig, the more likely it is that the claims of the supposedly unique situation will capitulate to the claims of the typical occurrence—the theory-blocking particular will succumb to the theory-building generalization. Realizing there is nothing new under the sun, we will seek out the old in what appears new, ask which actions were previously effective in this type of situation, which ineffective, and then apply the proper remedy.

Without question, Machiavelli's discussions of a science of political action, reiterated constantly throughout his works, are the conceptual foundation upon which he based his hopes that the successful politics of the Roman republic could be retrieved by the failing republics of modernity. For him it was comforting to know that "every science has its general rules," because then "a rule and a method" of conducting affairs, a practical wisdom, could be derived from scientific theory.[72] Unfortunately for Machiavelli, his own historical findings, particularly those reported in the *Florentine History*, had the effect of calling into question the central assumption underlying his science of political action. The assumption that history and nature are one, that historical events repeat themselves endlessly, that the same situations occur again and again, that whatever happens is therefore typical and falls under a general rule—all these variations on the same notion easily won the credence of Polybius, for whom all history was recent and classical, but could be upheld by Machiavelli, who had investigated both classical and modern times, only by suppressing his own most insightful comments on the differences between Rome and Florence.

Although Machiavelli was a proponent of the cyclical theory of history, he had within his grasp all the ammunition necessary to explode the view that history was closed and repetitive. While writing the *Florentine History* he verged on discovering that with the humiliation of the nobility and the coming of age of the guilds, the era of economic man had dawned and the era of political man had receded into the past. Here was his opportunity to recognize that as city-states come and go, "the city-state" does not stay the same—it is not a Platonic form, a single "substance" persisting in its identity throughout various reorderings of its "accidents." City-states old and new represent radically different ways of life, different cultures, different values. Surely the mores of ancient Rome have little in common with those of modern Florence if the Romans put politics first, economics second, the Florentines economics first, politics second. Rather than forge ahead to make this discovery for which his own researches into the Florentine past had thoroughly prepared him, he backslid into the position of interpreting the Florentine present as a corruption of ancient virtue. That the Florentines valued privacy and economic activity had to be evidence of the decline of an old world rather than the rise of a new world, otherwise the man of action and the student of the past had parted company; time spent conversing with the ancients would henceforth be time diverted from political activity, and political activity would be an exercise not in following rules but in improvisation. Machiavelli shrank from so painful an insight.

Machiavelli's problem, that the more he mastered history, the less the past was relevant to the present, was that of the Renaissance in general, dating back to Petrarch. Following every victory of the humanists in restoring a classical text to its context, there was that much additional evidence of the absence of a common denominator between ancient and modern ways of life. Forever insisting there were lessons to be learned from the classics, the humanists were constantly in danger of learning the one lesson they were unwilling to learn, that the past was irrevocably past. By abusing Justinian's code, the unhumanistic Bartolists had rendered it applicable to the circumstances of Italian cities; by recovering the original meaning of Roman law, the humanists denied it life. Such was the type of dilemma humanism repeatedly created for itself.[73]

Machiavelli's problem was this humanistic dilemma in an exceptionally severe form. For while the humanists could be satisfied with moral inspiration gained from a retelling of Roman deeds as a way of bridging the gap between past and present, Machiavelli could settle for nothing less than a retrieval of Roman political techniques and a resurrection of antiquity. Hence he did the only reasonable thing, which was to refrain from following his reason where it beckoned him. He refused to learn that if Renaissance city-states were as radically dissimilar to the city-states of the ancient world as he contended, this was a reason to forget Roman politics and to begin addressing Florentine politics in Florentine terms.

Guicciardini, who liked Machiavelli but also found him annoying, was not about to let his fellow statesman-writer get off so easily. In his *Ricordi* Guicciardini repudiated Machiavelli's methodology in memorable terms.

> How wrong it is to cite the Romans at every turn. For any comparison to be valid, it would be necessary to have a city with conditions like theirs, and then to govern it according to their example. In the case of a city with different qualities, the comparison is as much out of order as it would be to expect a jackass to race like a horse.[74]

The historicist understanding of historical epochs as each differing from every other because marked by a distinctive *Zeitgeist*, spirit, or culture may have been present in embryo, as has frequently been argued,[75] in the attempts of humanists to comprehend ancient Rome in its own terms; but such reputed premonitions of modern historical scholarship were utterly foreign to Guicciardini who, despite the jackass and horse quotation, continued to believe that "the world has always been the same, and everything that is and will be, once was; and the same things recur, but with different names and colors."[76] To the end he clung to a pagan, naturalistic, and cyclical view of history,[77] and then proceeded to argue that nothing followed from it by way of a science of action. From Machiavelli's standpoint, nothing could have been more devastating. Either a discontinuation of the conversation with the ancients or a nonactivistic rationale for continuing it was the choice implied by Guicciardini, but neither alternative was acceptable to Machiavelli.

Summarizing in his *Ricordi* what he had learned from a lifetime of politics, Guicciardini taught lessons that were mainly negative. "How different theory is from practice!"[78] he exclaims. "Reading" is one thing and "experience" another in Guicciardini's view, which is directly opposite Machiavelli's proud marriage of the two in the dedications to *The Prince* and *Discourses*. For purposes of political action, "experience" is, in fact, the only thing. No one can learn from the history of the Romans or from any other history how to conduct political affairs. No handbook purporting to reduce political wisdom to usable formulae can be other than dogmatic—and Guicciardini, with admirable consistency, therefore warns readers against taking his own *Ricordi* too seriously.[79]

Whereas Machiavelli is forever dramatically announcing the discovery of "a general rule that never fails,"[80] Guicciardini's *Ricordi* repeatedly asserts that cases are not identical, so rules of action cannot be derived from political experience. The only book of use to the political actor, Guicciardini notes, is "the book of discretion,"[81] written in letters legible in the world but illegible in the study. Actions once undertaken have consequences so remote, complex, and unpredictable, Guicciardini adds, that not even the wisest politician can control all the consequences of his initiatives. "Unanticipated events affect us incomparably more than those we foresee,"[82] and presumably always will, no matter how often we read Livy or Machiavelli on Livy.

What Guicciardini could not say, but which we can on the basis of linguistic studies of the *Discourses* and other writings, is that Machiavelli's literary style created the very rules it pretended merely to express. His incessant use of the disjunctive statement, noted by modern scholars,[83] created the illusion of discoverable rules of action as it arbitrarily excluded every possibility lying somewhere between the rule-producing poles of an either/or construction. "Often—perhaps the majority of times—events will take a third or fourth course that has not been foreseen,"[84] wrote Guicciardini, warning politicians against assuming a decision must lead either to this or that result. He might have gone on to observe that the disjunctive statement favored by Machiavelli automatically stopped short at the first two courses of action and artificially omitted the third and fourth. As for Machiavelli himself, there was no chance he would realize that his style, rather than eternally recurring political reality, was the source of his rules. Busily fending off the fainthearted Florentine slogan of the "middle way," he fought back with the counterslogan of the disjunctive statement, legitimizing it by transferring his taste for extreme solutions to the Romans. Polemical necessities prevented Machiavelli from being self-critical and encouraged him to elevate timely diatribes into timeless rules of action.

It may be added that even if Machiavelli's rules of political conduct were true, they would hold only for the opening moves of a protracted conflict. Renaissance diplomacy has been likened to a "game at chess,"[85] with moves and responses, strategies and counterstrategies, and one can find something of this attitude in the many letters in which Machiavelli calculates the interests of various European states.[86] But when Machiavelli writes his political treatises he forgets politics is give-and-take, and assumes that the opening move, if clever and crafty, will win the game. He goes further: in effect he eliminates competition from the game by assuming the opponent is a poor player, easily duped. If Rome subjugated Italy, Machiavelli rushes to the conclusion that it was by tricking the Latin peoples. Rome won by default.

Rome won by default in the *Discourses* just as Callimaco did in *Mandragola*, and in both cases for the same reason: Nicia is a fool and so were the Latins. Similarly, Machiavelli not only drove Fortuna off his comic stage; he also drove her out of Roman history. Machiavelli's premise in *Il Principe*, that *fortuna* decides half of all outcomes,[87] is implicitly deleted from the *Discorsi*, where Roman *virtus* in the sense of military might and political virtuosity dictates all significant outcomes.[88] It is not Machiavelli but Guicciardini who spells out the power of *fortuna*, which is so great that the fool sometimes wins and the wise man sometimes loses.[89] Machiavelli gives neither the fool his deserts nor Fortuna hers because then the ablest politician would likely not receive his. Machiavelli cheats fortune and cheats the game of politics. He takes the spirit of the *beffa*, the trick played on the fool, and transfers it from comedy to politics, while forgetting Boccaccio's frequent warnings that one trick provokes another and the trickster is often tricked.[90]

Nevertheless, there is something singularly compelling in Machiavelli and his Romans, something undeniable if elusive, which can be identified by thoroughly examining the critique of Machiavelli that Guicciardini began in the *Ricordi* and completed in the *Considerations on Machiavelli's Discourses*. At one level, Guicciardini's examination of Machiavelli's commentary on Livy is simply an elaboration of what the *Ricordi* briefly but forcefully argued against his fellow Florentine. At another level, the *Considerations on Machiavelli's Discourses* introduces an entirely new criticism of Machiavelli that Guicciardini doubtless thought was particularly devastating, as indeed it is of Machiavelli's claim that he was the founder of a scientific unity of theory and practice. Yet this new and potentially destructive critique, meant to silence Machiavelli's Romans once and for all, unintentionally provides us with an invaluable clue as to how Machiavelli kept his Romans alive and his thought vital.

The *Ricordi* states the conclusion of Guicciardini's evaluation of the *Discourses on Livy*, which was that Machiavelli expected a jackass to run like a horse; it also implies, in its dismissal of the search for political rules, the basis on which Guicciardini arrived at his conclusion, but it does not actually examine the content of Machiavelli's writings. In the *Considerations on Machiavelli's Discourses* Guicciardini fills in what is missing in the *Ricordi* as he moves chapter by chapter through Machiavelli's treatise, taking the maxims of the *Ricordi* and with telling effect applying them to Roman history. His was a methodology of courteous and understated destruction. Where Machiavelli found historical parallels, Guicciardini answered softly that "cases are . . . different, and the author does not distinguish properly between the examples."[91] Where Machiavelli found in the classical texts political principles of such shining clarity that by their example hotly debated contemporary issues could readily be resolved, Guicciardini could not help but see "many examples on both sides" and he noted that "each side has its good reasons."[92] Sometimes Guicciardini adds so many qualifications to a bold generalization Machiavelli drew from Roman history as to wear the reader out— a rhetorically astute tactic in boredom, proving the point that the complexities and permutations of politics are an eloquent refutation of Machiavelli.[93] Equally effective was the very playable game of showing how one of Machiavelli's Roman examples "can be turned around completely":[94] what "works" and why it "works" is frequently so ambiguous that the opposite tactic might have been even more successful, and the successful tactic might readily have failed. Along the same lines, Guicciardini has no trouble showing that Machiavelli's maxims sometimes cancel out one another; for example, even though Machiavelli repeatedly states it as a general principle that action should be decisive and that hesitation implies indecision, he also counsels a policy of temporizing here and there throughout his works.[95]

In sum, Guicciardini's argument was that there are "decisions which cannot be taken by a firm rule, but conclusions must be drawn from the mood of the city, from the state of affairs which changes according to the state of the times, and other mutable circumstances."[96] Simply to reverse the process by which Machiavelli supposedly arrived at his generalizations was Guicciardini's method of criticism: a reimmersion of Machiavelli's general rules in the historical circumstances whence their author supposedly derived them served to drown those rules in the swirling waters of political uncertainty.

Thus does Guicciardini complete the argument begun in the *Ricordi*, an argument driving a wedge between "experience" and "reading" and denying, in the name of the former, the relevance of the latter as a guide to perplexed political actors. But this is only half of what Guicciardini held against the author of the *Discourses on Livy*. Having attacked Machiavelli from the vantage point of "experience," Guicciardini went on, hoping for a rout, to outdo him as a "reader" of the classics—indeed, on the basis of a cold, skeptical and detached reading of Livy, Guicciardini was able to charge the enthusiastic Machiavelli with drastically misreading Roman history. Not only had Machiavelli failed to demonstrate how the classical past could be adapted to the needs of the present; he had even failed, and failed egregiously, to rise above a "Machiavellian" falsification of what the Romans did and why they did it.

Precisely because he was himself so much a lover of Latin literature, Guicciardini noticed the ways in which Machiavelli had refashioned the image of Rome presented in the classics. A good and faithful reader, Guicciardini quickly hit upon the vital difference between Machiavellian and pre-Machiavellian Rome, which was that the Romans of his compatriot were excessively given to the use of fraud and violence. Latins entering into alliances with the Romans had not been duped, Guicciardini noted; they were merely buying time—a perfectly prudent policy when they chose it, no matter how badly it may have turned out for them in the long run.[97] Arguing backward from result to intention in the most arbitrary manner feasible, Machiavelli had made the Latins incredibly foolish and the Romans incredibly cunning, so that he might make a policy of systematic fraud credible.

Machiavelli's interpretation of Roman religion as a fraud acted out by the ruling class against the people was also thrown out by Guicciardini, even though he hated the political influence of the Catholic church as much as Machiavelli, believed in the necessity of an astute ruling class no less than Machiavelli, and as the advocate of an aristocratic republic was even more skeptical of the people than Machiavelli. For all that, it was unbelievable that the early Roman rulers were religious skeptics.[98] Machiavelli, it seems, was the one who was too credulous, too susceptible to discovering in ancient Rome the actual existence of what he felt ought to be.

In Machiavelli's eulogy of Roman fraud Guicciardini saw, besides blatant historical inaccuracy, a pseudo-"realism" that was likely to redound to the political disadvantage of anyone dogmatic enough to take the *Discourses on Livy* seriously.

> But as for fraud, it may be questionable whether it is always a good means of attaining power, for while by deception one may bring off some fine things, too often a reputation for deceit spoils one's chances of attaining one's ends.[99]

Too undemocratic to argue that one cannot fool all the people all the time, Guicciardini states his argument in the aristocratic form that all of the rulers cannot be fooled all the time. The habitual trickster inevitably alerts his opponents, and establishes a negative reputation for himself. Hence systematic trickery is self-defeating.

Guicciardini also takes Machiavelli to task on the question of violence, chastising the author of the *Discourses* "who was always extremely partial to extraordinary and violent methods."[100] Such criticism would have meant nothing if written by a pacifistic Christian; written by Guicciardini it was very meaningful. Not one to be squeamish about the facts of political life, Guicciardini maintained that all political order, not excepting republican order, had its origins in violence and could not be maintained by following the dictates of conscience.[101] Violent, too, according to Guicciardini, was the republican treatment of subject peoples.

Best of all is not to be born a subject. But if it must be, then it is better to be the subject of a prince than of a republic. For a republic represses all its subjects and gives only its own citizens a share of power. A prince acts more equably towards all; the one is as much his subject as the other.[102]

So wrote Guicciardini, sounding as Machiavellian as Machiavelli did in the *Discourses*, where one reads that the only fate worse than subjection to a republic is subjection to an Oriental despot.[103] Yet, in his commentary on the *Discourses*, Guicciardini advised the reader not to heed Machiavelli's violent proposals, since they habitually exceeded what was necessary. It was one thing to face up to the inescapability of violence; it was another to give violence a good conscience.

Guicciardini came to the *Discourses on Livy* ideally prepared to speak to Machiavelli's meaning and to offer meaningful criticism. The empathy that is a precondition of good criticism was second nature when Guicciardini spoke of Machiavelli, since he resembled the author of the *Discourses* in so many ways: Guicciardini's education was classical, his life was devoted to politics, his political commitments were republican yet he was willing to serve the Medici, his hatred of the papacy was implacable, and he believed as strongly as Machiavelli that violence and politics are inexorably linked. When Machiavelli and Guicciardini met, each man saw himself in the other and the other in himself. Criticism coming from Guicciardini could not be easily dismissed, for it was the kind of criticism Machiavelli might have written of himself, and doubtless that is why the *Considerations on Machiavelli's Discourses* remains one of the finest, and most devastating, documents ever written against Machiavelli. After reading it, no one can continue to believe Machiavelli is to be congratulated on pioneering a science of policy.

After reading Guicciardini we can also understand, as never

before, why Machiavelli's brand of power politics is so striking. It was Guicciardini, not Machiavelli, who accepted power politics because the *verità effettuale della cosa* left him no other choice.[104] Machiavelli's power politics is of a very different sort; it has far less to do with a frank acknowledgement of what is given than with a deep sense of ideological mission to change what exists. Antiquity was Machiavelli's myth of a power and greatness that could give moderns the capacity to transform reality, rather than accept it or cope with it "day by day,"[105] as Guicciardini was satisfied to do. Machiavelli, who interpreted pagan religion as a political myth of the Romans, made a myth of the Roman republic for use by the moderns; and he was both the first to believe in this myth and its greatest propagandist.

Machiavelli's writings on Rome constitute a perfect example of the kind of mythological account of the past that Nietzsche called "monumental history."

> What is the use to the modern of this "monumental" contemplation of the past, this preoccupation with the rare and classic? It is the knowledge that the great thing existed and was therefore possible, and so may be possible again. He is heartened on his way; for his doubt in weaker moments, whether his desire is not for the impossible, is struck aside.[106]

Antiquity was Machiavelli's myth as the general strike, much later, was Sorel's,[107] and for both thinkers the value of a myth lay in spurring men to action. The difference between them is that Sorel knew his myth for what it was, an untruth having no connections with science, whereas Machiavelli was himself a believer in the myth of antiquity and remained convinced that a science of "general rules," distilled from examples of ancient virtue, was his greatest discovery.

Contrary to Machiavelli's expectations, a theory of how to act effectively in public affairs, a practical science of politics, did not prove to be the medium through which activistic moderns eventually communicated with the shades of the ancients. Rather, it was antiquity transformed into myth and transfigured into ideology that provided an action-inducing link between the old world and the new. Monumental history moved out of the study and into the world when memories of Rome excited eighteenth-century Frenchmen to revolutionary acts. Machiavelli's conversations with the ancients had become conversations with the moderns—conversations eventuating in political actions, as he had always hoped; but it was his genius as a civic ideologist, not as a scientist, that eventually inspired those who sought to change the world.

Once we recognize that Machiavelli unified theory and practice by ideology rather than science, his deviation from Polybius, ostensibly the father of scientific statecraft and thus Machiavelli's inspiration, becomes both evident and highly revealing. In order to make historical study "the soundest education and training for a life of active politics,"[108] Polybius did everything he could to shake off the moralistic and rhetorical dross that Hellenistic historiography had substituted for the vigorous labors of Thucydides to demythologize the past. That same moralizing and rhetorical bent of mind characterized Roman historiography which in this instance was too eager for suitable heroes and villains to remember its tutelage under Polybius. As a Polybian living after the Romans, Machiavelli presumably had as one of his primary tasks the purging of those moralistic and rhetorical encumbrances from Latin historiography that Polybius had purged from Hellenistic historiography; then and only then could the naked facts of power be mastered. Yet Machiavelli attempted nothing of the sort. He shows not the slightest interest in demythologizing the past, not the slightest intention of challenging the conventions of a rhetorical—and necessarily inaccurate—retelling of ancient deeds. Not for a moment did Machiavelli stray from the conventions of Latin historiography, which perpetuated Roman myths and used them to arouse the young. He simply put Roman myth and the

suasive powers of rhetoric to his own use by substituting a Machiavellian Rome, a "Machiavellian" reading of ancient deeds, for
Livy's.

Guicciardini politely refrained from writing his critique of the
Discourses until after Machiavelli's death. This left the field clear
for Machiavelli to use his great rhetorical skills in conversations
with men of "experience," the members of the Florentine ruling
class, and with men of "reading," the humanists who educated
the rulers. It was Machiavelli's hope that the man of action and
the man of ideas might yet become one and the same, that the
ruling class might be re-educated in a *studia humanitatis* taught
along Machiavellian lines, that is, on the basis of a Machiavellian
(mis)reading of the past, and in accord with the demand that a
man and his education should be inseparable, practice should be
inseparable from theory, and the moderns should be inseparable
from the ancients.

—VI—

CONVERSATIONS WITH THE MODERNS

Ancients and Moderns

MACHIAVELLI intended that his conversations with the ancients should also be conversations with his compatriots, part-time students of the Latin classics. Florence might yet be saved if his fellow Florentines unburdened themselves of Christian virtue and girded themselves with the armor of pagan *virtus*. Let *virtù* take on more fully the connotations of strength and efficacy that it frequently had in Tuscan usage, let it forget the connotations of Christian virtue that were equally common in the Italian language, and Latin *virtus* would once again dominate and rule. Through imitation of the Romans, the glories of ancient politics might be resurrected in modern times. Only "the weakness of the present religion" and a failure to read classical authors with an eye for political lessons stood in the way.[1] Machiavelli was a politician and a humanist, a man of affairs and a devotee of the *studia humanitatis*, who hoped to effect a union between the political actor and the new type of intellectual as he conversed with each, exhorting the politician to read the classics, the classicist to think politically, and both to overcome their Christian consciences.

Of course, to a considerable degree the members of the Florentine ruling class were already readers of the classical and neoclassical authors, and the Florentine humanists did in fact have political concerns. Yet neither group measured up to Machiavelli's specifications, and one may infer why they failed to satisfy him. For the established families, sponsorship of humanist scholarship was a route to social esteem in much the same way that tasteful attire, graceful manners, and splendid architecture were—as so many proofs of a refined, patrician, superior mode of existence.[2] Consequently classical learning was constantly in danger of demotion by the patricians to the status of ornamentation. The humanists, too, disappointed Machiavelli. Those of the earlier generations were so enamored of the past, so convinced that only Rome merited a writer's attention, that it never occurred to them to consider whether their cherished antique furniture could one day be housed in buildings constructed by a political architect who knew how to re-create not just the decor but the foundations of ancient Rome. Worshiping at the altar of the past, the earliest humanists ignored Florence,[3] made a church of the classical world,[4] and upon entering it bowed down in passive reverence, when all the while they could have been making new political structures on the model of the Roman republic. Later humanists, including Machiavelli's contemporaries, thought their Latin eulogies of Florentine politics were a service to the moderns, a proof that the classics were of more than antiquarian interest, yet all their exercises in rhetoric had done was to offer glorifications of the very deeds that demanded criticism and radical change. Humanism was indeed the basis upon which Florence might be saved, but a new type of humanist was the precondition of evoking what the *studia humanitatis* had thus far withheld from the moderns.

Machiavelli must have felt particularly annoyed by the oscillation of humanists between statements of political convictions sometimes strikingly similar, sometimes strikingly dissimilar to his own, often within the same essay. Near the beginning of *On the Family*, Alberti saluted the Romans, referring to them as "our most excellent Italian forebears [who] conquered and everywhere subjected all peoples."[5] But before he finished composing his treatise on the household, he congratulated the Florentines on preferring leisure and peace to struggle and war.[6] Likewise Bruni's *Praise of the City of Florence* is a work expressing two apparently opposing points of view: Florence the guardian of all free peoples[7] versus Florence the modern heir to Roman "lordship of the world."[8] To the extent that the inconsistency of humanistic argument was the result of a failure of nerve, of an unwillingness to face up once and for all to the Machiavellian implications of a classical education, Machiavelli was out to goad, chide, and cajole the humanists whenever the opportunity arose. To the extent that their inconsistency was the result of their professional commitments to oratory and rhetoric,[9] to form over content, to how something is said over what is said, to words over actions, to arguing equally well either side of a question, Machiavelli could hardly take them seriously. It was bad enough that patricians often treated humanist scholarship as decoration; it was worse that the humanists themselves should encourage, albeit unintentionally, an interpretation of their social function as ornamental.

Worst of all, the humanists left to themselves could hardly be expected to transform the consciousness of the Florentine ruling class. Neither the self-definition of the humanists nor their social standing promised to yield substantial political influence. So enticing to the humanists were the claims of both the medieval *vita contemplativa* and the Roman *vita activa*, so much did they value rhetoric for the opportunity it afforded them to cross over into the world of politics without being forced to cut their ties to the cloister,[10] that their need to participate in politics was far from unlimited, whereas their ability to act independently in public affairs was very limited as a consequence of patronage.

In Machiavelli's judgment the man of classical learning was charged with a mission, a burdensome mission the humanists had refused to accept, namely, to instil heroic values into the members of the governing elite and to curtail the prevalence of commercial calculations in political decision-making, especially where foreign policy was concerned. Both in and out of office Machiavelli embraced this mission and acted as the self-appointed link between humanists and rulers. During his years of active service to the republic, he demonstrated how to saturate a policy statement with classical examples teaching "Machiavellian" lessons in *Del modo di trattare i popoli della Valdichiana ribellati*, a paper urging the Florentines to adopt the decisive measures republican Rome used against cities balking at the prospect of forfeiting their freedom. Afterwards, having fallen into political limbo, he spent his time there writing the *Discourses*, which is his position paper on Valdichiana all over again, more systematically argued, and dedicated "not [to] those who are princes, but [to] those who because of their countless good qualities deserve to be"[11]—the aristocrats resentful of Medicean rule, who might in the future govern a restored republic. His efforts to render the modern world classical in its actions as well as in its scholarship were unrelenting.

Unlike Machiavelli, who struggled so valiantly to unite theory and practice, the humanists were forever disuniting thought and action. For instance, despite their eulogies of cities successful in glorious feats of aggrandizement, the humanists were frequently silent about means. And although they spoke of politics, none of the humanists, not even those in the chancellery, were makers of policy.[12] Worse, at the end of a day spent writing a history of battles, wars, and glorious deeds, a humanist made the sign of the cross before retiring. Given his propensity to return to Christian virtue, a humanist might even find himself in the strange position of praying the day would come when he would have no more acts of *virtus*, no more glorious military deeds, to celebrate.[13] Above all, the humanist—a professional man of words—was satisfied with words; indeed, he made of rhetoric an end in itself and of speech an activity intrinsically worthwhile, as he in his self-interest was perhaps bound to do; and which he, in his indecision between an active and a contemplative life, needed to do in order to have it both ways.[14]

Machiavelli, however, had no more sympathy for ambivalence between the *vita activa* and the *vita contemplativa* than did the classical Roman authors, and he turned the tables on the humanists by locating rhetoric squarely within the realm of means. If the humanists were silent about means, Machiavelli would retaliate by taking the rhetorical and suasive powers of humanism and using them as means to his ends. Under his direction, the entire repertoire of humanist scholarship, the accent on rhetoric and persuasion, the imitation of classical genres and art forms, the extraction of *exempla** from the writings of ancient authors, were enlisted in the service of Machiavellism. By no other method could the classical world be raised from the grave.

Machiavelli's major works, masterpieces of rhetoric, eloquence, and persuasion, are similar to and competitive with those of the humanists. The prize in this competition was the younger generation of Florentines, a generation of young aristocrats destined to political prominence, classically educated, and convinced force is the essence of politics.[15] To Machiavelli, it was good that the young should be so ready for the sort of matter-of-fact power politics that, in the older generation, was represented by Francesco Guicciardini and Francesco Vettori. Much better, however, was his own novel, inspirational, and ideological power politics that fused the lessons of "reading" with those of "experience" and held out the promise of a radically new order. It was these future leaders who provided Machiavelli with just the kind of audience he desired and which he wrote for when compelled to watch politics from the perspective of the spectator.

How To Think Unhistorically

Only if the earth always began its drama again after the fifth act . . . could the man of action venture to look for the whole archetypic truth in monumental history. . . . Till then monumental history . . . will always bring together things that are incompatible and generalize them into com-

* *Exempla* are examples, typical instances, and models drawn from history and mythology. Their purpose is to teach by example.

patibility. . . . Its object is to depict effects at the expense of the causes—"monumentally," that is, as examples for imitation.[16]

There is no evidence that Nietzsche's words were written with Machiavelli specifically in mind, but they do apply perfectly to him. Examples for imitation were Machiavelli's explicit objective; and the myths Machiavelli accepted, of Sparta created by Lycurgus, and Roman religion invented by Numa, were surely cases of effects depicted at the expense of causes; finally, the master assumption of all Machiavelli's thought, that commercial Florence and militaristic Rome were two horses, one lethargic and the other spirited, rather than a jackass and a horse, amounts to a bringing together of incompatibles and a generalizing of them into compatibility. Behind all this stood Machiavelli's notion of cyclical history, which was his way of asserting his belief that the human drama is a never-ending performance of the same play, perpetually reenacted every time the curtain falls on the fifth act. All Machiavelli's hopes and dreams rested on an historical method that by modern standards is profoundly unhistorical. To keep his dreams alive he had to mine every resource available to unhistorical thought, since the alternative was to see the ancients recede into a past that could not be recaptured.

"Monumental history lives by false analogy,"[17] wrote Nietzsche, and Machiavelli proved his point by piling one fallacious comparison between Florence and Rome upon another. The secretary's entire method of analysis and argumentation presupposed the interchangeability of ancient Roman and modern Florentine experience. What was good for Rome was good for Florence because they were both city-states, both republics, both inclusive of the many, both hopeful of aggrandizement; and their differences could readily be accounted for by the classical terminology of virtue and corruption—Rome representing virtue and Florence corruption. Circumstances peculiar to Italian history also played a role in encouraging Machiavelli to slide from one illicit analogy to another. Roman municipal civilization died out less completely in Italy than elsewhere, and feudalism took more shallow root south of the Alps than to the north, so the impact of the centuries in radically altering ways of life was not so glaringly apparent in Machiavelli's country. Moreover, there had in fact been a time when the citizens of Florence, like those of ancient Rome, were organized as a militia and fought their own wars, sometimes with considerable valor, as when they fended off the emperor and, again, when they cleared the countryside of troublesome feudatories. Nor can it be denied that a struggle between patricians and plebeians was common to all urban civilization, ancient and modern, to the cities born during the late Middle Ages as well as to the cities of antiquity. Truly "the city," a self-governing, autonomous political unit, did exist in the Western world both before and after feudalism. Comparisons between city-states ancient and modern can therefore be legitimately made, but the contrast of the ancient city of warriors with the modern city of traders is equally important,[18] and to dispose of it by accusing moderns of a fall from virtue, as Machiavelli did, was to use history by abusing it.

While writing the *Florentine History* Machiavelli came very close to a realization that Rome and Florence represented two different worlds, one classical, the other not, instead of a virtuous and a corrupt version of one and the same classical world. His contrast between ancient Roman democracy on the one hand, in which the values of the aristocracy trickled down to the populace, and Florentine democracy on the other, with its aristocracy forced to enter the guilds and accept a commercial ethos, seemingly signaled a need to question the applicability of Roman standards to modern circumstances. Quickly he retreated from the insight that would have increased his historical sensibility at the cost of shattering his *Weltanschauung*. The road of retreat chosen by Machiavelli had been paved by previous humanists, who inured him to the belief that the prominence of the trader in Florentine politics could be recognized without provoking a crisis for classically educated intellectuals. "For or against the citizen-trader?" was a familiar polemic among the sympathizers of humanism;[19] yet neither side to this debate ever stepped back far enough from the heat of controversy to ask whether the political preeminence of the trader signified the historical obsolescence of classical thought. Machiavelli opted for making his exceptionally penetrating contrast of ancient with modern social structure merely the most sophisticated version of these myopic polemics, thereby escaping the need to question his fundamental assumptions.

Even when Machiavelli painted the local colors of Florence in the most un-Roman of shades, no evidence exists demonstrating he realized the significance of what he had done. There is a speech in *Clizia*, quoted time and again to prove Machiavelli had a strong feeling for the local realities of Florentine society, in which Sofronia describes Nicomaco's daily concern to balance his books.[20] Critics of our day may be right in asserting that Machiavelli has in this passage portrayed a distinctively modern type, the bourgeois;[21] even so, it does not follow that Machiavelli himself believed he was representing a human type who had not walked the streets of ancient Rome. So far as he could tell, the husbands and fathers who appeared on the stage of Plautus or Terence were also "bourgeois"—most of their everyday lives were devoted to lawsuits and business, not to war and politics. Possibly, too, Machiavelli was familiar with those passages in Polybius and Horace that highlighted the materialistic, penny-pinching, profit-seeking—in brief, the bourgeois—aspects of the Roman character.[22] The important point, to him, was that all Romans knew how to behave on the battlefield, and some of them knew how to direct public affairs; what they did with their private lives was therefore unimportant. A bourgeois in the private sphere, a Roman was unbourgeois in the public sphere, which was all Machiavelli demanded of his compatriots. If today historians sometimes protest that the terms "bourgeois" and "middle class" are used indiscriminately, covering far too many centuries, times, and places,[23] that very lack of discrimination was to Machiavelli's advantage because he needed to blur the distinctions between eras. Comedy, said Cicero, was "the mirror of custom"; Machiavelli agreed and added the assumption that ancient and modern customs were interchangeable. When there were continuities between ancient and modern mores he discovered them; when there were not, he presupposed or invented them.

In his comedies as elsewhere Machiavelli assumed that a journey across time from modern Florence to ancient Rome was no more difficult an undertaking than a journey across space from contemporary Florence to contemporary Venice. Scratch a street sign etched in Italian letters and Latin letters appear underneath. As proof of his attitude, we need only cite Machiavelli's own words, as stated in the prologue of *Clizia*.

> If into the world the same men should come back, just as the same events come back, never would a hundred years go by in which we should not find here a second time the very same things done as now.

Clizia is a remake of Plautus's *Casina*, the story of

> a gentleman who, having one son and no other children, by chance took into his house a little girl whom, until she reached the age of seventeen, he brought up very carefully. It then happened that all at once both he and his son fell in love with her. . . . What would you say if, only a few years ago, this same thing happened in Florence?[24]

By substituting the Italian tongue for the Latin, by superimposing the local colors of Florence upon a canvas dating from antiquity, Machiavelli effortlessly bridged the gap between antiquity and modernity. It was, so it seemed, as easy to pass from old Rome to new Florence as it was for Philocomasium, in the *Braggart*

Soldier of Plautus, to pass from the house of Pyrgopolynices to the house of Periplectomenus by means of the hole in the wall common to the two houses.

The nonspecificity of comic settings lent additional support to Machiavelli's efforts to plaster over the gaps between the ages. When Terence and Plautus borrowed plots from Meander and other Greek dramatists, they borrowed the Athenian setting as well. In truth, however, the setting of Roman comedies is so general that it brings to mind the idea of "the city-state" rather than the idea of Athens, Rome, or any specific city-state.[25] Similarly, although Machiavelli's comic characters are Florentine, the plot of *Clizia* is borrowed from Plautus, and the setting of both *Clizia* and *Mandragola*—the intersection of two streets with a house on either side—might just as well be located in ancient Rome as in Renaissance Florence. Abstraction[26] and universalization saved Machiavelli from a painful recognition of the historicity of societies.

The idea of nature provided Machiavelli with another unhistorical bridge spanning the centuries, and across it he frequently traveled. A cyclical view of history and an assurance that human nature is as it always has been and always will be were the staples of Machiavelli's pagan naturalism. Had he actually tried to fit all of history from early antiquity to his own age into a cyclical scheme of history, he would have encountered infinite difficulties. It was much more comforting simply to assert the closed and repetitive nature of history and then to concentrate on whatever social phenomena were characterized by an apparent fixity, permanence, and continuity suggestive of unchanging nature. The family, love, and politics were all historical phenomena that could very readily be misconstrued as ahistorical.

Aristotle deemed the patriarchal family of his preference the "natural" family, a perfect illustration, he believed, of his principle that the worth of custom and tradition were guaranteed by nature. The Romans, if they disagreed at all with the Greeks on the family, did so by affirming more vigorously and less critically the sanctity of the traditional family. Machiavelli followed his usual procedure of initially agreeing with the classic texts and then adding something of his own—the conviction that the fixity of the family licensed the activities of the adulterous lover. To the types and roles of the father, mother, and child Machiavelli added that of the seducer. The family was forever; and it was, so Machiavelli thought, one and the same in Florence as in Rome. Henpecked husbands, lovesick sons, and jokes about mothers-in-law have a timeless and cross-cultural flavor. Whatever questioning of the family one finds in Machiavelli is comic questioning and nothing more; that is, it is a form of questioning that presupposes the inevitability of the family. In his tale *Belfagor*, a devil marries in order to understand why so many new arrivals in Hell blame their woes on their wives. Ultimately the devil, who has assumed human form and character, is driven to financial ruin by his desirable but demanding wife. The hilarious story assumes the permanence of the family and marriage even as it pokes fun at them. Likewise the type of the lover was forever: his story was the old one of boy meets girl, man seduces woman; and the perpetually Machiavellian nature of the lover's activities is assumed even today in the saying that all's fair in love and war. Machiavelli's writings nowhere show the slightest inkling of recognition that the eros of chivalry and romance was vastly different from the earlier pagan eros; nor does he see the possibility of different types of families.

A politics of favors, deals, and the manipulation of power for personal advancement is yet another activity that even today is spoken of as if it were timeless and constituted the sum total of politics rather than one style of politicking. Like love and the family, politics seemed to Machiavelli to travel well across space and time, and to retain its identity while doing so. His presupposition of the oneness and ubiquity of politics enabled him to wrap together eras and cultures that otherwise might have asserted their uniqueness. The Middle Ages mingles indiscriminately with the Renaissance in the first book of the *Florentine History*, in which Machiavelli relates stories of intrigues, assassinations, and conspiracies. For one brief moment, admittedly, it does dawn on Machiavelli that during medieval times "Italy and the other Roman provinces . . . not merely changed their government and their prince, but their laws, their customs, their way of living, their religion, their speech, their dress, their names."[27] This passage, however, neither concludes nor introduces a chain of reasoning. It is an isolated statement in the midst of a discussion of endless centuries of politics-as-usual.

If there is a topic that receives special attention in Machiavelli's treatment of the feudal period, it is the rise of the papacy in political power, its falls into nepotism, and its guilt, even before the Renaissance, of inviting foreigners into Italy and of preventing Florence or any other city from seizing an Italian empire.[28] In short, Machiavelli utilizes the technique of foreshadowing, a literary device that when applied to history ties the past to the present, the Middle Ages to the Renaissance, at the expense of obscuring the differences between them. Anachronism also helped: antiquity was little different from the Renaissance after Machiavelli finished reading the Renaissance politics of vengeance, violence, and conspiracy[29] back into the history of Greece and Rome. Sometimes the ancients summoned to Machiavelli's study were requested to speak Italian.

In studies of what may be termed national character, Machiavelli reduced temporal history to atemporal nature while putting his education in the classics to work. The Germanic peoples of his day figure in his work as do the Germans of Tacitus, as republicans whose still intact virtue is a reminder of the corruption of the Latin peoples, the Italians most of all.[30] Similarly, his Frenchmen are seen through the prism of Caesar writing on the habits and character of the Gauls.[31] Machiavelli's incessant references to modern France as Gaul and to ancient Gaul as France are far more than a literary nicety. Gaul in fact was France and France in fact was Gaul because "men born in any region show in all times almost the same natures." Thus the Florentines could learn how to deal with the French, Machiavelli advised, by learning how the ancient Tuscans dealt with the Gauls. Since the Gauls had been treacherous, the Florentines of Machiavelli's day should have been prepared for the refusal of modern Frenchmen to honor their agreements with foreigners. Machiavelli was convinced that "if Florence . . . had read or learned the ancient habits of the barbarians, she would not have been deceived by [the French] . . . , for they have always been of one sort and have under all conditions and with everybody shown the same habits."[32] Through the notion of national character Machiavelli managed, so he believed, to render the classical authors vital to modern tacticians and strategists. Through the notion of national character he managed, so we believe, seemingly to absorb culture into nature, thereby blocking the development of historical consciousness.

Encouragement to think of history as repetitive and of a given historical circumstance as an instance of a typical occurrence sometimes came from unlikely sources. Although Guicciardini the practical statesman vigorously objected to Machiavelli's bookish appeal to the Romans, Guicciardini the lover of the classics appealed to ancient example when he needed words to console Machiavelli, who had once been politically influential but in 1521 was charged with the minor and ironic task of persuading the friars of Carpi to send a noted preacher to Florence.

> When I read your titles of orator of the Republic and the friars, and consider with how many kings, dukes and princes you have formerly negotiated, I remember Lysander who after so many victories and trophies was charged with the care of distributing meat to the same soldiers whom he had so gloriously commanded, and I say: see how only the faces

of men and outer colors change, the same things recur, and we see nothing happen which has not been seen before.[33]

Guicciardini's letter of aid and comfort was more comforting than he knew, since it reinforced the unhistorical methodology upon which Machiavelli depended for his intellectual life.

Appeals to atemporal nature, whether by Machiavelli or his classical ancestors, were all the more attractive for the facility with which their authors circumvented the danger of a static and rigid outlook. An emphasis on movement and change was quite compatible with classical naturalism, so long as something persisted throughout all changes, the substratum called nature. In the Aristotelian account of changing regimes and constitutions, change is abrupt and nearly total, the only unmoving point being the polis itself, which Aristotle regarded as the eternal gift of nature to mankind. Though "the city-state" is forever, different types of city-states come and go so rapidly that the reader of the *Politics* may find all the change he wants in the midst of permanence.

Roman literature expressed its longing for a nature alive with movement in the likes of the Ovidian theme of metamorphosis, and its need for permanence in an overriding concern with foundations laid by ancestors on which the living built into the future by extending the past.[34] Machiavelli the poet was far from spurning the notion of metamorphosis;[35] Machiavelli the Roman was attentive to foundation; but Machiavelli the Florentine had no foundation upon which to build and no tradition to preserve and embellish. Consequently he stressed the violence of foundation and renewal. That Romulus slew Remus was the event that typified Roman foundation, Machiavelli believed,[36] and he stressed the violence of Rome's periodic returns to her origins rather than the supposedly unbroken chain of continuity over the centuries. Disruption and upheaval, will and power, are central in Machiavelli's thought; tradition, even in the case of the feudal monarchies of the North, is little more than forgetfulness of violent origins,[37] he asserted. No wonder, then, that everything about Machiavelli appears to be in motion, so much so that the static element in his writings lies hidden beneath the surface.

So far removed was Machiavelli from vulnerability to the charge of adhering to a static philosophy of nature that it was he who charged others, and in the name of nature, of failing politically because of the inflexibility of their natures.

> I believe that as Nature has given each man an individual face, so she has given him an individual disposition and an individual imagination. From this it results that each man conducts himself according to his disposition and his imagination. On the other hand, because times vary and affairs are of varied types . . . , he is fortunate who harmonizes his procedures with his time, but on the contrary he is not fortunate who in his actions is out of harmony with his time and with the type of its affairs.

A changeable nature was therefore the formula of unending political success.

> Certainly anybody wise enough to understand the times and the types of affairs and to adapt himself to them would have always good fortune . . . and it would come to be true that the wise man would rule the stars and the Fates.[38]

One is reminded of the words of Ovid:

> Hearts have as many fashions as the world has shapes; the wise man will suit himself to countless fashions, and like Proteus will now resolve himself into light waves, and now will be a lion, now a tree, now a shaggy boar.[39]

It is fitting that a discussion of Machiavelli's fusion of antiquity with modernity should end with a quotation from Ovid, a Roman poet, for it was the Latin Middle Ages that bridged the two eras.[40] Latin literature did not die with the fall of Rome and did not have to be reborn during the Renaissance. Most of Rome crumbled when lords and peasants replaced citizens and slaves, but Latin literature continued to prosper and provided Western culture with the continuity that Machiavelli attributed to nature.

A World-View

LESS WHAT Machiavelli thought than how he thought it enabled him to glue disparate historical eras into a seeming oneness. Machiavelli thought the world through the categories, concepts, and genres of Latin literature, which sorted, classified, and ordered his experience so symmetrically that his thought, while not constituting a vast philosophical system in the manner of Aristotle or Hegel, nevertheless puts forth something closely resembling a world-view.

In a romantic theory of art for art's sake, literature is too much a world unto itself and too isolated from social existence to offer a world-view. Not so with classical art: the literature of Machiavelli and the Romans harks back to the Greek notion of mimesis,[41] according to which art imitates life and represents reality, and the reality it represents and the life it imitates are social existence. The New Comedy of Meander, Plautus, and Terence represents the sphere of private activity, particularly in the household, while Greek tragedy and Roman historical writings represent the sphere of public activity, the realm of war and politics. Taken together these genres depict—or were thought to depict—every aspect of social existence worthy of commentary.

Not only was the scheme of genres thought to exhaust the varieties of meaningful human behavior. At the same time as the genres represented reality they evaluated it and gave lessons in moral conduct: they rank-ordered values and instilled them into the audience. To attend a comic performance was to learn the role of father, mother, or servant; to read the epic of Roman struggle was to familiarize oneself with *virtus*. Without being propagandistic or indifferent to artistry, Roman art was an exercise in civic education. From comedy one learned how to be a good member of a family, from history—understood as a literary genre—how to be a good citizen, and from the contrast of the low style of comedy with the high style of history one learned that public duty overrides private duty whenever the two conflict.[42] The highest emotions and the most elevated style are reserved for public affairs.[43]

Frequently cut off from society and disdainful of it, given to breaking reality into discrete fragments, prone to believe in truths but not in truth—such is the romantic artist. Much different is the classical artist. Iconoclasm does not tempt him. The genres he abides by structure reality and interlock into a kind of additive world-view. Comedy and tragedy, humor and politics, domesticity and public affairs are the sum total of existence; the masks representing them mask nothing and reveal everything. That much is true of classical art in general and applies to Machiavelli with particular force because he was Plautus (*Mandragola* and *Clizia*) and Livy (the *Discourses on Livy*) at the same time. In the past the historian Livy was one man, the comic playwright Plautus another, and the twain infrequently met until the coming of Machiavelli, who not only wrote in both genres but recognized the "Machiavellian" potential of each—the theme of virtuosity in deception—and penned all his works in the same racy, abrupt, and lean intermediary style. Thus Machiavelli had an uncanny capacity for transforming parts of reality into the status of parcels of a single reality, which at any moment could be retrieved and packaged into unity.

It does not suffice to say that, in the classical view, art is an imitation of life. Equally important and equally productive of a world-view was the belief of Machiavelli, also classical in inspiration, that life should imitate art. Ancient literature abounds in discussions of the art of agriculture, maintaining a household, painting the face, making love, and making war. The "general rules" Machiavelli sought had been sought many times before him by Roman authors; if Ovid's comments on how to gain and hold a woman sound much like Machiavelli's writings on how to seize the state and maintain it, the reason is that in either case the rules of art, of art lived and put into effect, are at stake. Other authors of the Renaissance were also concerned to make life an imitation of art, foremost among them Castiglione, whose *Book of the Courtier* has been aptly termed an attempt to make the self a work of art.[44] Machiavelli would make the state a work of art,[45] and the politician an artist molding his clay into a magnificent form.[46]

Because life imitated art, literature could never become, for Machiavelli, "mere" literature. Literature was lived, and constituted not just the intellectual life of a cultured elite but the practice, or the potential practice, of a ruling elite; under the sponsorship of enlightened rulers, it might even one day become the practice of the total community. Machiavelli aimed to make imitation a path to political artistry for all of Florence. His entire methodology was premised on the assumption that imitation of the actions of the noble Romans, if rigorously pursued, could prove the salvation of the moderns. Reading the Latin classics and living the most worthy form of life were part of one and the same process, a process that was not complete until what was read was acted out on the stage of everyday civic existence.

Popular as well as aristocratic, the writings of Machiavelli flow so fluidly across class lines that they much more readily conjure up a comprehensive overview of reality than do the works of the humanists, written in disdainful disregard of the culture of the populace. Whereas the humanists deliberately excluded the many from their audience by writing in Latin, Machiavelli included the most talented of the people in his potential readership by writing in Italian. And surely it is significant that included in the audience of *Clizia* were not only distinguished leaders of the government, but middle-class citizens and representatives of the populace as well.[47] Let it be remembered that the conversation with the ancients which is the climax of a typical day in Machiavelli's life is preceded by a morning spent trading hard luck stories with field hands and an afternoon spent at an inn where "there is the host, usually a butcher, a miller, furnace tenders, [and] with these I sink into vulgarity for the whole day, playing . . . [games which] bring on a thousand disputes and countless insults with offensive words."[48]

The use of the *Decameron* is a perfect example of Machiavelli's willingness and the humanists' unwillingness to discern what was popular in the literature of high culture. Romantic and chivalrous love may be found in the humblest hut as well as in the most refined circles of society, Boccaccio had suggested.[49] Humanists turning to the *Decameron* for stories to dramatize on the stage of a revived classical comedy therefore had ample opportunity to clear the way for an equality of amorous opportunity unknown during feudal times. Fundamentally they refused to do so, refusing not so much in their plots as in their choice of audiences, which were usually courtly or academic rather than popular.[50] Machiavelli did write for a popular audience and made use of the *Decameron* in doing so: not, however, through invoking Boccaccio's theme of an amorous love that elevated private affairs above public ones. Democratic or not, such a love was uncivic and unacceptable. Democratic and perfectly acceptable was Boccaccio's humor which preceded Machiavelli's in crossing and leveling class lines. It was the wit of comedy, not its frequent amorous content, that in Machiavelli's hands was an egalitarian force. A peasant outwits a devil in *Belfagor*, a tale at odds with the penchant of urban humor in Machiavelli's day for making the country yokel the butt of jokes.[51] A man who in common with the humanists is enthralled by any words spoken in Latin is made a cuckold in *Mandragola*.[52] Wit, trickery, and connivance belong to the people no less than to those educated in the classics.

How very popular Machiavelli's humor is may be appreciated

by a comparison with the courtly humor of Castiglione. In common with jokes told on street corners, Machiavelli's comedies laugh at someone, at Nicia in *Mandragola*, at Nicomaco in *Clizia*. Malice and insult were keenly ingrained in the popular life of the quattrocento and early cinquecento,[53] and Machiavelli responded to the vitality of *malizia* (malice) with the mock threat at the beginning of *Mandragola* that if his audience can be malicious, he can too.[54] Castiglione, on the contrary, warns the courtier to forgo the bite of malice.[55] At court personal relations are an exercise in diplomacy and tact, and that alone is enough to make malice imprudent, even in jokes. Humanism in its monarchical guise, as represented by Castiglione, advises the courtier to shun the crowd and all its ways, its laughter included.[56] Republican humanism sometimes speaks favorably of the populace, but in Latin and from a safe distance. Machiavelli, however, shares in the laughter of the people.

Why Machiavelli should empathize with popular humor is not mysterious. Hungry for entertainment, the popular audience had stripped the moralist of his moral, the better to concentrate on the good fun of storytelling for its own amoral sake.[57] And the content of these popular stories was the trickery, deception and dissimulation of the *beffa*. Thus the humor of the people was thoroughly Machiavellian and might be considered a preparation for the entry of the most talented commoners into the ranks of the ruling class. Machiavelli was indeed a believer in the equality of political opportunity, and it may be that it was the nature of popular humor, so appreciative of sleight of hand, that led to his conviction, stated in the *Discourses*, that outstanding rulers may be born in humble huts.[58]

The incorporation of popular humor into aristocratic culture distinguishes Machiavelli from the humanists, who, even when of humble birth, believed that nobility was acquired by an education cleansing the self of all that was common. Humanist thought, in consequence, lacks that impulse toward comprehensiveness which was present in Machiavelli's work. He was not the only figure of his age to reach out to popular culture; Aretino the master of scandal and ribald humor did too, but then Aretino was a rebel against the conventions of humanism. Machiavelli merged the classical with the popular, the result being that classical thought enlarged its field of vision. It attempted, under his aegis, to take all of social reality as its province, where before it was more than content with a single slice, the upper crust.

In forms of thought, Machiavelli's was a mind that conceptualized the world and expressed itself through the classical literary genres, which to him were not just one way of stamping coherence upon perceptions but the correct way. Machiavelli poured all his experience into the thought-forms of Latin literature, especially comedy and historiography, which in turn ordered and structured his experiences so systematically as to perform the tasks assigned to ontology and epistemology in a philosophical worldview. That being the case, we must once again question the claim, frequently made, that what Machiavelli's thought amounts to is the assertion of "the autonomy of politics." In this view, Machiavelli spoke of politics for politics' sake much as others were later to speak of art for art's sake. Reality, then, is broken up into various fragments, each with its own logic, and it is impossible to constitute a whole by adding them together, however hard we try, because where the parts are totally different there is no totality. To this it must be objected that Machiavelli would find such a view incomprehensible. Though much was out of place in his native Florence, where religion and business often ruled the politician rather than the other way around, yet everything had a place, a place both its own and also a distinct part of an all-encompassing whole, the immortal city-state, which was forever because nature guaranteed its undying existence; and the parts, spheres, and realms of this city, carefully parceled out by the genres of Latin literature, could instantly be reconstituted as a whole by adding those genres together.

Politics, as understood by Machiavelli, is ubiquitous rather than autonomous. Hence, far from shattering reality into bits and fragments, his preoccupation with politics actually contributes to his sense of offering a view of all reality, a *Weltanschauung*—in his case one entering through the back door, perhaps, but a *Weltanschauung* nonetheless. Politics belongs to all realms, the private as well as the public, as we have previously noted when examining Machiavelli's comedies, private letters, and biography. The politics of public life is heroic or contemptible, the politics of private life mock-heroic and laughable; but there is no sphere in which Machiavellian deception, dissimulation, and trickery, well-done or ill-done, do not exist.

To the objection sometimes made to Machiavelli's writings, that there is more to life than the spheres of the state and the family, and more activities to engage in than politicking and womanizing, the answer must be that such an objection speaks past Machiavelli and not to him. So far as he knew or cared, his interests were the only ones that mattered; anything else was bound to be trivial.[59]

To the claim that Machiavelli's thought was addressed to only one historical period and one type of politics, the violent politics of the usurping Renaissance prince, the answer must be that Machiavelli wrote for all times, about what was, is, and always will be; and to which the only alternative to doing it well is doing it poorly.[60]

When Machiavelli spoke to the moderns, he addressed himself to all men of *virtù*, no matter what historical era they lived in, and he spoke to the totality of their lives, offering them a worldview.

Machiavellism and the Classics

MACHIAVELLI'S method of conversing with his contemporaries, of persuading, cajoling, and winning them over to his point of view, was to insinuate his message into their conversations with the ancients. Thus the dialogues of the Renaissance humanists with the classical authors would become a dialogue with Machiavelli, and the more the humanists read the classics, the more humanism would become Machiavellism. The constant effort of Machiavelli was to underscore, intensify, and dramatize what was Machiavellian in Latin literature, ancient and modern, Roman and humanist.

Happily for Machiavelli, the Roman and humanist theme of grandeur, glory, and greatness had done much preparatory work for his message. Machiavelli the typical humanist was therefore already well along the way to a doctrine of power politics, and when he infiltrated his most strikingly atypical thoughts into the tradition of Italian humanism, he did so with a deftness inviting the erroneous but not implausible conclusion that some two centuries of humanist scholarship had been struggling to make Machiavelli possible. Machiavelli's teaching was not that humanism must face up to its opposite, Machiavellism; it was that humanism is Machiavellism. However novel this thought, it was as old as the ancients and as fresh as the Renaissance once Machiavelli had finished tampering with the classical and neoclassical texts.

When offering a literary representation of the private sphere, Machiavelli followed the humanists, who combined Roman comic form with Boccaccian content. But he also went beyond the humanists as he turned the moralistic and didactic comic theory of the Renaissance upside down. If comedy preaches the duties of fatherhood, it also teaches the methods of seduction, and may thus be said to be a training in the Machiavellism of the household. From such a conclusion the humanists had retreated to an idealizing theory of comedy, Ciceronian in origin, which was contradicted time and again by their literary practice in the comic genre. As usual, Machiavelli did not retreat, and it was perhaps from the strict moralist Cicero's reluctant concession in *De Officiis* that, alas, though born for grave affairs, a citizen does need his occasional amusements, that Machiavelli derived his notion of a variable nature best served by daytime seriousness and nighttime folly.

Nature [asserted Cicero] shaped us not to give the impression that we were made for jokes and games but rather for seriousness and all kinds of grave and important matters [cf. *cose grandi*]. Of course, it is permissible to enjoy relaxation and amusements [cf. *cose vane*], but we should enjoy them like sleep and other refreshing pastimes, after we have devoted enough energy to important and serious affairs.

Cicero concludes with a cautious endorsement of reading Plautus and going hunting as recreations. Machiavelli concludes by putting Plautus into practice and hunting women.[61]

In historiography, too, Machiavelli followed the humanists, the better to lead them. Other histories of Florence, notably Leonardo Bruni's and Poggio Bracciolini's, had been written before his by authors who took their theory of historical writing from the ancient Roman authors and the content of their histories from Villani and the medieval chroniclers.[62] For every such historical work, the Roman values of *virtus*, glory, grandeur, and military prowess were the primary concern; economic concerns, regardless how important in the medieval chronicles, were removed from the history of Florence by the Roman filter through which the Florentine past was forced to pass. Bruni, for instance, made little of the guilds in his Florentine history.[63] Here Machiavelli found that both the humanists and the chroniclers had cleared away the obstacles to his message. He had only to insert the chroniclers' history of the political triumph of the guilds into a humanist history to transform Bruni's panegyric of Florentine virtue into a resounding condemnation of Florentine corruption.

What was wrong with un-Roman Florence could be traced back to her Roman origins. Bruni and the republicans had taken pride in countering the traditional monarchical genealogy of Florence, the child of Caesar, with a republican genealogy tracing the beginnings of Florence to an earlier date, preceding the downfall of the Republic.[64] A disenchanted republican, Machiavelli located Florentine origins in the era of transition from the corrupt

Roman Republic to the monarchical Roman Empire, and argued that Florence suffered both from a despicably corrupt parentage and from an unfree beginning,[65] quite unlike the beginning of the Roman Republic, a city born of itself and hence free to do great deeds.[66] To the humanists, who placed so much emphasis on establishing a noble genealogy for their city and believed the origins of a people followed it throughout the centuries, Machiavelli's comments on the genesis of Florence were devastating.

While the Romans could well afford to be satisfied with perpetuating their past, the Florentines had to overcome theirs. This message, a recurring theme in Machiavelli's writings, explains why his adaptations of the classics to modern circumstances were as radical in thrust as those of the humanists, who pretended Florence was similar to Rome, were conservative. Whereas Roman virtue could be traditional and limit its violence to acts committed against other cities, Machiavellian virtue had to be radical and willing to resort to violence within the city. His brand of *virtù* could hardly be credible and persuasive to humanists unless an argument for it could be squeezed out of classical thought.

That was precisely what Machiavelli set about doing. He called upon the classics for assistance as he depicted a man of *virtù*, expert in the use of internal violence—a "new" prince, a usurper who ideally would exercise his illegitimate power to reinvigorate a fading republic. Cesare Borgia is the name this man bears in *Il Principe*, but in truth he is an abstraction Machiavelli created by taking elements from both Greek and Roman thought and compounding them into a creation all his own. The ideal Machiavellian prince is the foundation-builder lauded by Roman historians, combined with the tyrant execrated by Plato and Aristotle. Those teachers of eloquence, the modern humanists, admired Isocrates, who used his rhetorical powers to exhort Philip to defend Greece from the Persians. Machiavelli went further than the humanists; he used his eloquence to specify the violent and tyrannical measures a virtuous prince needed to master, and urged him to use them not only against foreigners but also against his own people if they were corrupt.

What Machiavelli had to say in praise of the internal violence that humanists disdained was said, then, through the classical forms of thought the humanists cherished. Realizing the humanists might nevertheless remain reluctant to listen to him, he made his message less jolting by calling their attention to the violence of Romulus killing Remus at the beginning of Roman history. Since to humanists the Roman way was always right, the bloodiness of Roman foundation constituted proof that violence was essential to the welfare of republicanism. Moderns should be Machiavellians because the Romans had been. Surely that was an argument the humanists could not ignore.

No strategy of persuasion is more common in Machiavelli's writings than that of imposing a Machiavellian reading upon Roman history and Roman ideals. Occasionally, as for instance in the notion that politicians invented and manipulated pagan religion, a mere repetition of the words spoken by Polybius or some Roman author sufficed to achieve a Machiavellian Rome. At the other end of the spectrum he sometimes dared build his case for a Machiavellian Rome by explicitly disagreeing with classical authors, as when he argued against Plutarch that Rome's conquest of the world had little to do with *fortuna*.[67] But his favorite method of turning Romans into Machiavellians was to invert the idealizing and moralizing mentality that was congenital to Latin literature. Livy, Tacitus, Virgil, and the other masters of Latin literature, understanding their function as that of moralists and censors, carried out their assigned tasks in portraits of characters presented as incarnations of good or evil. Perfectly consistent with the accepted understanding of the historian's duty was the announcement of Tacitus that he would omit from his *Annals* whatever was neither particularly virtuous nor scandalous.[68] His Tiberius is the embodiment of corruption and his

Germanicus the embodiment of virtue because there was no place for moral ambiguity in the didactic universe of Latin literature. Machiavelli's so-called "realism"[69] is simply this Roman moralism turned upside down. No more than his classical forebears did Machiavelli paint portraits of individuals in all their complexity, individuality, and self-contradiction.[70] His individuals are as much types, abstractions, and exemplars as were those of the Romans, the single difference being that Machiavelli's heroes are good at being bad. Heroism and villainy merged into oneness in Machiavelli's idealizations.

The greatest hero-villain to appear in Machiavelli's works is not Cesare Borgia or Romulus; it is not a person but a collectivity, republican Rome, which rose from humble beginnings to grandiose finale by using—so Machiavelli argued—the methods of force and fraud. Doubtless this portrayal of Rome as a ferocious lion and a deceitful fox was Machiavelli's most spectacular gambit in his bid to win the game of constructing the image of Rome that would hold sway among his contemporaries.

Just how radically Machiavelli altered the Renaissance image of Rome cannot be appreciated unless we recall that the thought of the classical authors to whom the humanists were indebted for their image of Rome was deeply imbued with Stoicism. Challenging all of classical and neoclassical Latin literature, Machiavelli boldly substituted Machiavellism for Stoicism as the inner meaning of Roman history. Despite their imperialism, Virgil and Livy felt the need to justify their politics by appeals to the destiny of Rome, taking their notion of destiny from Stoic philosophy.[71] Probably it was Stoicism, again, that led Livy to uphold the law of nations and the sanctity of treaties—which he could do and still champion the Roman imperial cause if he accused the enemy of faithlessness and barbarity.[72] Livy was a Stoic humanitarian and yet he could without inconsistency rejoice in the Roman takeover of Greece, because he understood that episode as a war of liberation fought by republican Rome for the sake of freeing her fellow republics.[73] Machiavelli's determination to reverse Livy is nowhere more evident than in his reinterpretation of Rome's actions in Greece, which he cited as an example of the willingness of the Romans to expand their empire by destroying free, republican cities:

> They were forced to destroy many cities of that province in order to hold her, because in truth there is no certain way for holding such [free] states except destruction; and he who becomes master of a city used to being free and does not destroy her can expect to be destroyed by her.[74]

Stoic, too, in Livy's *History* was the frequent antithesis of the expedient (*utile*) with the honorable (*honestum*),[75] and the claim that the virtuous Romans never sacrificed the latter to the former. In Cicero's *De Officiis*, a work familiar to all humanists, the Stoic preference for the honorable over the expedient is used to stop Machiavellian thoughts before they start. "It is extremely shameful not only to value what seems profitable more highly than what is right conduct, but also to compare these with each other and to debate inwardly about them."[76] Nobility and Machiavellism, Cicero believes, are mutually exclusive because "the mere act of mentally equating immorality and advantage is devastating to the character."[77] Machiavelli, then, is Stoicism inverted; grandeur and nobility, he proclaims, are impossible without fraud practiced on a grand scale, and he calls the history of republican Rome, as interpreted in the *Discourses on Livy*, to bear witness to the truth of his testimony.[78]

Cicero's argument was that since goodness is useful for the soul, no conflict is possible between the *honestum* and the *utile*.[79] Machiavelli's crushing counterargument is that to be good is often useful not to oneself but to one's enemies, while to be bad is often the prerequisite of doing good.[80] Utility answers to goodness in Stoic thought, goodness answers to utility in Machiavelli's.[81] Whenever Livy swells with pride as he relates a story of Roman

kindness to the enemy, Machiavelli alters the meaning by stressing that the magnanimous act induced the enemy to surrender[82]—
goodness was good because it was successful as a strategy of
domination. Again, when Livy sees the Romans acting as arbi-
trators in a troubled city and concludes that "not merely [Roman]
arms but Roman laws were dominant," Machiavelli quotes him,
only to draw a moral as Machiavellian as Livy's was Stoical: "Men
so much the more quickly throw themselves into your lap as you
appear the less inclined to take possession of them; and they fear
you so much the less, with respect to their liberty, the more
humane and friendly with them you are."[83] Law, justice, and
mankind were grouped together in the Stoical philosophy that
Cicero and Livy used to justify Rome's empire. To Machiavelli,
on the contrary, Roman law outside of Rome was a method of
achieving domination under cover of righteousness. In *The Prince*
Machiavelli argued that force belongs to the animals and law to
men;[84] in the *Discourses*, it seems, a turn to law in foreign affairs
signified less the assertion of the human half of the Romans than
a recognition on the part of their bestial half that the fox in them
could succeed where the lion was bound to fail.

"In praise of deception" is a leitmotif in Machiavelli's writings
because "in denunciation of deception" is in Roman and humanist
writings. Fraud and deception figure in Livy's history as the
methods of the enemies of Rome, particularly Hannibal, and any
evidence of Roman deceitfulness is accounted for by terming it
un-Roman.[85] Sallust frequently speaks of Roman fraud and deception,[86] but does so because he is forced to by his task of
recording the increasing corruption of once virtuous Rome. The
old ways, he assures us, were different: Rome "had grown great
through toil and the practice of justice,"[87] virtue had reigned in
the city, and as late as the time of Cato the Romans produced a
man who "preferred to be, rather than to seem, virtuous."[88]
During the Italian Renaissance Latini argued, in imitation of the
classical texts, that the ruler "must actually be as he wishes to

seem";[89] and Alberti never doubted that "a noble spirit prefers to be virtuous rather than just give that impression."[90] "To gain fame," Alberti adds, "we must have virtue; to obtain virtue we must wish to be, not appear to be, what we want others to think we are."[91] Against this backdrop of classical and neoclassical quotations, Machiavelli wrote the celebrated eighteenth chapter of *The Prince* which promotes *parere* (to appear) to inclusion in the list of virtues and ranks it higher than *essere* (to be). Success and greatness are rarely attained in the absence of fraud, which is why seeming is more important than being. A great man is, among other things, "a great simulator and dissimulator."[92]

Machiavelli's rout of Stoicism and humanism, begun in *The Prince*, was completed in the *Discourses*, an essay in the interpolation of his opinions into the classical texts. As paraphrased by Machiavelli in the *Discourses*, Xenophon advocates the pursuit of greatness through systematic fraud,[93] even though the actual text of the *Cyropaideia* limits trickery to military strategy[94] and maintains that the best way to seem to be something is to be it.[95] Guicciardini's complaint that Machiavelli had misread Xenophon[96] was correct but irrelevant. All Machiavelli cared about was that before him Xenophon was perfectly compatible with the humanist creed, and after him Xenophon was a Machiavellian.

Still more striking was Machiavelli's transformation of Roman history into a showcase of masterful fraud and conspiracy, planned in the earliest days of the republic and so effectively carried out as to culminate in the greatest empire ever known. Such a reading of Livy, if it had anything to do with his text, was derived from the speeches he occasionally wrote to dramatize the hostility of the enemy. A speaker for the Samnites denounces Roman foreign policy for its despicable record of Machiavellian misdeeds.

> Will you never . . . lack excuses for not holding to your covenants? You gave hostages to Porsinna—and withdrew them by a trick. You ransomed your city from the Gauls

with gold—and cut them down as they were receiving the gold. You pledged us peace, on condition that we gave you back your captured legions—and you nullify the peace. And always you contrive to give the fraud some color of legality.[97]

Machiavelli, in effect, takes this moral outrage of the Samnites, victims of the Romans, and turns it into a eulogy of the Romans, masters of Machiavellian methods.

Livy, of course, believed the Samnite spokesman could hardly have been more mistaken in his characterization of the Romans since they—by Livy's account—carried Stoic humanitarianism with them wherever they went and almost never unleashed their full destructive fury unless it was against an enemy guilty of Machiavellian crimes. "See to it that no one survives from whom either force or fraud may be feared,"[98] a Roman urges his fellows just before the massacre at Henna. Elsewhere in Livy's *History* it is Philip, the tyrant determined to rob Greek republics of their freedom, whose actions are explained as resulting from "either force or fraud."[99] Livy's Rome fought to make the world safe for republics and to rid it of Machiavellians.

Machiavelli's Rome was a republic that devoured all other republics by making full use of the methods of force and fraud. Before Machiavelli arrived on the scene of Italian humanism, Livy had been a humanist and Rome an embodiment of humanism; after the *Discourses on Livy* was written, Livy was a Machiavellian and Rome an embodiment of Machiavellism.

Tradition and Innovation

MACHIAVELLI'S work was innovative and destructive of tradition precisely insofar as it belonged to an intellectual tradition, that of classical and humanist thought. Myths, symbols, vocabulary—these and more were furnished him by an established tradition of thought, and upon this tradition he incessantly drew even as he rebelled against it, knowing full well that his classically educated audience was ideally prepared to appreciate his provocative and disturbing performance. His very formula of entering upon a "new path" is symbolic of his overall rhetorical stance: it is a formula used repeatedly in Latin literature,[100] a mere formula when uttered by previous writers, but truly meant by Machiavelli who throughout all his writings took what others had said and said it again in ways that created radically new meanings.

The classical tradition against and through which Machiavelli rebelled was both pagan and Christian. It was a tradition begun by the Greeks, revised by the Romans, and then selectively absorbed into Christian doctrine. In the largest sense Machiavelli's originality can only be appreciated when his thought is studied in terms of the contending varieties of paganism—Greek and Roman—and of the conflict between pagan and Christian viewpoints, all contained within the classical tradition.

While Machiavelli's fusion of the hero with the immoralist would not have been striking had he been working within the Greek tradition, it was remarkably subversive given that he asserted his views through Roman materials. The contrast of the Ulysses of Virgil with the Odysseus of Sophocles is telling and explains the novelty of Machiavelli's thought. In the play *Philoctetes* Sophocles places on stage two heroes, Neoptolemus and Odysseus. Their object is to save the cause of the Greeks against the Trojans by taking possession of the bow of Heracles, held by Philoctetes, who is unlikely to yield it voluntarily. Cast out of society, isolated, abandoned, condemned for the last ten years to live like a beast, Philoctetes has no desire to aid and abet his countrymen. Odysseus therefore decides to take the bow from Philoctetes by the most promising means, trickery, cunning and guile, only to be thwarted at the last moment by his erstwhile fellow conspirator Neoptolemus, who as the son of Achilles and a representative of heroic ideals is willing to defeat Philoctetes by the noble means of force but not by the ignoble means of fraud.[101] By the end of the play, however, Odysseus has been vindicated, and the ability to outwit and deceive others has been firmly ensconced in the heroic code. Heroism without guile, whether that of the adolescent Neoptolemus or the mature Achilles is criticized as incomplete heroism, especially when guile well-done can be of service to the whole city. So says Sophocles, spokesman for the ideals of the Greek city-state.

By contrast, Virgil, spokesman for Roman tradition, castigates Ulysses as cruel, merciless, and even blasphemous, much as Livy treated Hannibal. Rome was built, Virgil proclaims, by the survivors of once great Troy, that noble city finally sacked after ten years of glorious defense when tricked by Ulysses, perpetrator of the despicable deceit of the horse. Coroebus, a Trojan fighting frantically to save his burning city, asks "Who cares whether what we do to an enemy is treachery or valor?"[102] But his words are those of desperation and suggest that the noble Trojans would stoop to the level of Ulysses only if forced to, and were not, as he was, cunning and contemptible by their very nature. Aeneas is as upright as Ulysses is underhanded, which was Virgil's way of communicating that Greece is ignoble, Rome noble, and that the heroic ethic has no room for craft, guile, and deception. Rome deserves to rule Greece as surely as nobility deserves to rule ignobility.

Neither in Virgil's epic poetry nor in Livy's epic history was the immoralist allowed to figure other than as a villain. Within Latin literature a less censurious attitude toward the immoralist was inconceivable except when the writer descended from the sublime to the ridiculous—from epic to comedy. Laughing at the immoralist was permissible provided his wrongdoing was much ado about nothing and the act of laughing an exercise in social conformity. Usually, too, the schemer of comedy was a slave, so that the Roman comic stage offered the upper classes an opportunity to equate deceitful behavior with their social inferiors and to congratulate themselves on their superiority and nobility.

That deceitfulness could be an aspect of virtue was simply unthinkable to the Romans. Their prephilosophical tradition of rigid moralism could abide no such notion; their philosophy of Stoicism erected a wall between the good and the useful, and sided in favor of the former; and although their Aeneas adds *sapientia* to his *fortitudo*, wisdom to his bravery, and contrasts sharply with his arch-rival Turnus who is pure *fortitudo*, this Roman development of the image of the ideal hero differs from the Greek preference for Odysseus over Achilles exactly insofar as wisdom differs from cleverness and cunning. An ability to rule others falls under the jurisdiction of *sapientia*, but the use of fraud in ruling receives no warrant from the Romans.

Machiavelli went far beyond declaring the political necessity of sometimes engaging in acts of ignoble fraud for the sake of survival. He proclaimed fraud essential to nobility, greatness, and heroism, making his argument not by recovering Greek ideals but by taking the standard Roman literary materials and reshaping them in the image and likeness of Machiavellism. The Roman fraud of conquering the outer reaches of the known world by means of allies against whom Rome later turned, trapping their armies between Rome and the peoples they conquered in Rome's name,[103] outdid the Greek trick of the Trojan horse and was less overtly mythological.

Machiavelli regarded it as a point in favor of modern times that Count Francesco of Milan, bent on expanding his empire, did not hesitate to commit fraud; from this incident the Florentine drew the conclusion that "great men call it shame to lose, not to gain by trickery."[104] Republican fraud, especially if it was as high-minded as Florentine fraud was petty, was of course much more to Machiavelli's liking than any fraud committed by a tyrant; particularly blameworthy, in his view, was the refusal of a modern Roman republican, one Stefano Porcari, a man pas-

sionately devoted to the ideals of the Latin classics, to employ
the fraud that was necessary to achieve his noble goal of overthrowing the pontiff.

> He wished, according to the nature of men who long for
> glory, to do, or to attempt at least, something worth re-
> membering. And he judged he could attempt nothing other
> than the delivery of his native city from the hands of the
> prelates, and her restoration to her ancient government. He
> hoped through such a deed, if he succeeded, to be called
> the new founder and second father of that city.

Despite the grandeur of Stefano's designs, his conspiracy against
the papacy failed, largely because his conception of nobility had
no room for dissembling. "Having taken up this idea, he could
not conduct himself in so cautious a fashion that through his
words, his conduct and his way of living he did not reveal
himself."[105] One can only wonder what Stefano might have accomplished had he been born a few decades later and learned
from the *Discourses on Livy* that his beloved Romans were the
perpetrators of the greatest and most noble fraud ever known.

With the advantage of hindsight, the generalization may be
ventured that what Machiavelli did to Latin literature was the
reverse of what Euripides had done to Greek literature. Disgusted
with the barbarity of the Athenians at Melos—the city Athens
saved for her empire by destroying its helpless inhabitants; disgusted with the war fever consuming Athens on the eve of the
Sicilian expedition, Euripides poured a torrent of unforgettable
abuse on *areté* and power politics in *The Trojan Women*. The glory
of war and conquest is reduced to little more than a slaughterhouse
of senseless, revolting carnage in Euripides's superb deflation of
the heroic ethic; and the unspeakable horrors of power politics
are piercingly represented by Odysseus's command that the innocent boy Astyanax, son of Hector, be hurled to his death lest
future Trojans seek their vengeance against Greeks. Henceforth

areté could retain its traditional meaning and associations of excellence and virtue only if Euripides was ignored.

Machiavelli, on the other hand, inserted into Roman literature that very missing Machiavellian motif which Euripides had attempted to delete from Greek culture. *Virtus* in Roman literature implied prowess in most any activity,[106] particularly arms and ruling, but did not, before Machiavelli, imply virtuosity in the use of political violence. *Virtù* did imply skill in violence for many modern Italians who, in their un-Christian moments, could designate almost any activity effectively pursued a proof of the *virtù* of its doer,[107] including the violent activities of a usurping prince. In effect Machiavelli took this meaning of *virtù*, attributed it to the word *virtus* in Latin literature, and then used the rewritten Roman classics to judge his contemporaries wanting in excellence. When it came to having the determination to be Machiavellians wholeheartedly, systematically, and uncompromisingly in the pursuit of the grandeur of empire, the Florentines were abject failures. Nevertheless, their inability to kill the rebels of Arezzo was a weakness that might yet be atoned for, if they but recalled the violence Rome used against those who rebelled against her.

The exceptional rhetorical force of Machiavelli's writings is based on its grounding in Roman values. This finding, already apparent, is reinforced by a comparison with the pattern of Greek values, which contemporary scholars have placed under the concept of a "results-culture."[108] To the Greeks good intentions were never good enough, not just in politics but everywhere, because in the virtuous man's unending competition for honor and glory there could be no acceptable alternative to success. Courage, honesty, or any other value was valuable—the Greeks believed—only so long as it led to success. "Good" meant to the Greeks "good at" or "good for," never "good" in and of itself[109]—good had to be useful, and since guile, craft, and deceit were sometimes essential to success, they were part of *areté*. In Greek culture, it follows, there was no need for a Machiavelli; at Athens or Sparta his rhetorical powers would have been nil, and his notoriously shocking words would have been so ordinary as to make him a bore.

Stoicism, by separating virtues from their results, made Machiavelli possible and necessary, and the Christian belief in a pure good, a good indifferent to results, greatly increased his necessity. Unlike Christians, Roman Stoics had at least attempted, however feebly, to reintegrate the good and the useful with the claim that virtue succeeds, an assumption Renaissance humanists added to the Christian "mirror-of-princes" genre, which before their time had spoken of virtue but not of utility.[110] Machiavelli shattered both Christian and humanist outlooks in one deft blow with the argument of *The Prince* that success is mandatory, and virtue, Stoic and Christian, its nemesis. All his life Machiavelli spoke in the vocabulary of Stoicism and Christianity turned inside out and upside down. He could not do otherwise since he knew little or no Greek, and even had he known how to recover the Greek moral vocabulary fusing virtue with result, that would merely have led to his speaking past his contemporaries, not to them.

Defining himself against Christianity, Machiavelli never escaped totally from Christian expressions. He had no reason to attempt a purge of all Christian symbols from his language since to do that would have been to run the risk of losing his audience. A master of rhetorical techniques, he chose the more promising strategy of stealing Christian symbols, exactly as he stole those of Stoicism, for the purpose of incorporating them into his brand of paganism.

Frequently Machiavelli appropriated the Christian vocabulary of exhortation and disapprobation and used it for his own un-Christian ends. His favorite technique was to invoke Savonarola's charge that Italy's woes were a punishment for her sins, adding a characteristic Machiavellian twist. "Italy in our times . . . has been sacked, ruined and overrun by foreigners for no other sin than that she has given little attention to soldiers on foot and put all her soldiers on horseback." These words appear both in the *Art of War* and the *Discourses*,[111] and in the latter work they are complemented by the chapter entitled "The sins of the people are caused by their princes."[112] For every occasion on which the word "corruption" was suggested by classical republican vocabulary, the Christian word "sin" could also be spoken, and frequently was, by Machiavelli who sometimes took off his Roman toga to put on the frock of a monk and feign the voice of a prophet. And as a prophet he spoke not only of sins but of "redemption," especially in the final chapter of *The Prince*, where he again assumed the tone and uttered the words of Savonarola: the ideal Machiavellian prince would be the "redeemer" of his people. Ever the ironist, Machiavelli delighted in the thought of watching Savonarolans assemble under a banner held high by a power politician.

Machiavelli's absorption of Christian symbols into his un-Christian philosophy was much more than simply a rhetorical device. It was nothing less than an attempt to displace and supplant the Christian world-view with an alternative world-view, one reminiscent of ancient paganism. Parceling out one's life, as the humanists did, between immersion in the pagan past and loyal adherence to the Christian present was not Machiavelli's way.[113] Rather, he attacked Christianity, sometimes quite openly, as in his devastating contrast of the greatness of pagan *virtù* with the smallness of womanish Christianity; sometimes more covertly, as in his claim that a truthful "interpretation" of Christian doctrine would yield a modern religion sharing the ancient pagan contempt for humility. After violently denouncing Christian values and championing the cause of pagan standards in *Discourses* II, 2, Machiavelli rounds out that chapter with a castigation of those "who have interpreted our religion according to *ozio* and not according to *virtù*." Machiavelli's disingenuous argument was that Italian *ozio*—a word meaning the same as the Latin word *otium* (leisure, inactivity, contemplation)—would give way in a

correctly understood Christianity to Italian *virtù*, a word interchangeable with the Latin word *virtus*. How could the distinction
between paganism and Christianity be maintained if in modern
Christianity *virtù* were to drive out *ozio*, just as in ancient paganism *virtus* had driven out *otium*?[114]

Christianity interpreted according to *virtù* rather than *ozio* was
represented in the Bible by Moses and David, and in modern
times by various worldly and warlike popes. A prophet armed,
Moses knew how to free the Hebrews from the Egyptians,[115] and
knew, too, how to commit violence against his own kind. "He
who reads the Bible intelligently sees that if Moses was to put
his laws and regulations into effect, he was forced to kill countless
men who, moved by nothing else than envy, were opposed to
his plans."[116] As for David, "so great was his *virtù* that [he]
conquered and crushed all his neighbors," bequeathing to his
successor Solomon an exceptionally powerful throne.[117] Indeed,
David was the very model of a Machiavellian prince, for he not
only used external force successfully but also violently disrupted
the unacceptable patterns of domestic politics and made "everything in that state anew."[118]

Julius II, a warrior pope, "a man of courage . . . who wants
the Church to expand and not to grow less in his time,"[119]
fascinated Machiavelli the writer of the *Legations*. Later, Machiavelli would outgrow his infatuation with Pope Julius, seeing
in him a rash man whose very rashness happened to fit in with
the times, but who lacked the flexibility to adapt to new circumstances.[120] Thus the very successes of Julius were more the
result of *fortuna* than *virtù*. Yet Machiavelli never doubted that
Julius possessed *virtù* or that he lived a life suggestive of what a
pope who interpreted Christianity according to *virtù* could accomplish.

Julius used *virtù* to serve the papacy; Alexander VI and his son
Cesare Borgia used the papacy to serve *virtù*. In truth, Machiavelli
was less interested in Christianity interpreted according to *virtù*

than in Christianity the slave of *virtù*. The corruption, in Christian terms, of the papacy, its frequent subservience to worldly and dynastic ambitions, might be the opportunity Italy needed to regain her *virtù*.[121] Had Cesare Borgia, the dark hero of *The Prince*, lived to unite his empire in the Romagna with the papal chair held by his corrupt father, advantages might have accrued to all Italy. Were Leo X, son of Lorenzo the Magnificent, to pool his resources with the younger Lorenzo de'Medici, the arbiter of Florentine affairs to whom *The Prince* was dedicated, a great empire might be the upshot. In Leo X Machiavelli saw "a Pope . . . who is young, rich and justly eager for glory and for not making a smaller display of himself than his predecessors have made, and [who] sees that he has brothers and nephews without territory."[122] It is well to remember that in those passages in which Machiavelli blames the papacy for keeping Italy disunited, he also chides it for failing to bring about unification; clearly the political sins of the popes are sins of omission as well as commission.[123] What "new" prince was better armed with the confidence of the masses, more able to draw upon and manipulate popular belief, and more likely to be a successfully aggrandizing prince than a Machiavellian ruler, preferably Florentine by birth, wearing papal robes? Particularly if such a pope made the papacy an annex of Florence, rather than Florence an annex of the papacy, he was bound to meet with Machiavelli's approval.

Virtù could be injected into modern Italy by either Julius II and his militant Christianity or by Alexander VI and his corrupt Christianity, one pope being the servant of the Church, the other its master, both being ecclesiastical princes answering to the worldly standards of greatness and success. Only the Christianity of the reforming orders, forever striving to restore Christianity to its original, antiworldly, pacifistic, and enervating values, was flawed beyond hope of redemption. Every recovery of uncorrupted Christianity, even if successful, was a destruction of *virtù*, a triumph of weakness that was despicable in itself and guilty, besides, of teaching passive acceptance of evil.

"This renewal, then, has maintained and still maintains our religion."[124] Maintaining Christianity is a mistake; taking it over and using it for Machiavellian purposes, on the other hand, is not a mistake. Machiavelli's statement that the moment of the punishment or fall of the Church was at hand,[125] had all the urgency of Savonarola's preaching and sounded rhetorically the same, even though Savonarola's fist clenched in anger against the papacy was as Christian in its potential violence as Machiavelli's was anti-Christian while feigning Christian sympathies.

By force and by fraud, by violence and dissembling words, Machiavelli hoped to absorb Christianity into a new paganism. He robbed the Christians of their rhetoric because he intended, eventually, to rob them of the papacy. As a first step along the road to a new world, or the restoration of an ancient one, he sought to reduce the Christian world-view to a set of symbols useful in propagating his own all-encompassing faith. No greater rhetorical offensive against the Christian stronghold was ever undertaken by Machiavelli than when he substituted "fame" and "immortality" for "eternity." Many another figure of his day had sung the praises of fame, of course—indeed, so many did that Burckhardt cited the clamoring for enduring reputation as a distinguishing characteristic of the Italian Renaissance.[126] Machiavelli did not create but he did alter the craving for fame, making it more anti-Christian, more pagan, more Machiavellian. His *Florentine History* contains a number of examples of Italians face to face with death, whose only concern is to do "something worth remembering";[127] and each such incident comes as a kind of heroic relief in his dramatization of the Italian comedy. Such passages are striking but do not in themselves differentiate Machiavelli from other humanists, Alberti for instance, who commanded that a man of *virtù* strive to be extraordinary and to raise himself above "the common nameless herd."[128] Machiavelli's innovation was that he underscored how a name can be gained by committing evil acts as well as good ones; he showed, moreover, how evil sometimes rises to a plane of greatness beyond good and evil; and he not only refused to back down, in cowardly humanist fashion, from a sometime ideal of fame to an all-the-time fear of eternity— he actually took the symbols of eternity and put them to work promulgating the ideal of immortality.

Consider what he says of Giovampagolo Baglioni, tyrant of Perugia and enemy of Julius II. Offered the chance to destroy the pope, Giovampagolo failed to do the deed that would have earned him "everlasting fame." Despite his personal history of crime and violence, Giovampagolo proved too fainthearted to accept his opportunity to be "splendidly wicked."

> So Giovampagolo, who did not mind being incestuous and an open parricide, . . . did not dare . . . do a deed for which everybody would have admired his courage and for which he would have left an everlasting remembrance of himself. . . . And he would have done a thing the greatness of which would have transcended every infamy. . . .[129]

It is the nature of greatness to transcend morality, and no greatness is more beyond good and evil or more deserving of immortality than that which destroys the man whose existence symbolizes the belief in eternity, the pope.

Truth be told, Dante had unwittingly laid a trap for Christianity in the course of glorifying its world-view, a trap Machiavelli was quick to seize upon. The damned souls of the *Inferno* are more concerned with what is being said about them on earth than with the unworthiness before God that has plunged them into the abyss.[130] Machiavelli needed nothing more to prove that damnation and salvation have to do with this world and not the next, with posterity and not with eternity. The most fortunate of men is he whose violence is like that of Romulus, creator of a city, and unlike that of Caesar, its destroyer. Stretching out in front of those men in a position to choose whether they shall be the reincarnation of Romulus or Caesar are "two roads . . . : one makes their lives secure and after death renders them famous; the other makes them live in continual anxieties and after death leaves an ill repute that never ends."[131] The heaven and hell that matter are located on this side of eternity, as the greatest of founders and rulers have always known, and as even the feeble Florentines once knew in the past when they challenged the religious sanctions Pope Gregory XI had imposed upon them. "They were called saints, even though they had little regard for the Censures, stripped the churches of their property, and forced the clergy to celebrate the offices. So much higher did those citizens then value their city than their souls!"[132]

Max Weber, in his memorable essay "Politics as a Vocation," cites the preceding quotation from the *Florentine History* as a "beautiful"[133] recognition of the enormous torment any politician must suffer who is responsible enough to accept his calling of mediating between idealism and power politics: hands forever stained, a soul permanently soiled, and a cross of exceptional heaviness to bear are the wages of the sins that are necessarily committed by a responsible political leader. To this reading it must be objected that Weber's Machiavelli was more Machiavelli as Weber wanted him than as he was. The image of losing one's soul is used several times by Machiavelli, but he never means it; he simply means to restate his very un-Christian thought in Christian imagery. Whoever recalls Machiavelli's statement, "I love my native city more than my own soul,"[134] would do well to remember that his Hell is hardly an undesirable place in which to take up residence. Certainly Callimaco finds Hell so little terrifying that neither he nor any other seducer in his right mind has cause to reconsider his wrongdoing:

> The worst you can get from it is that you'll die and go to Hell. But how many others have died! And in Hell how many worthy men there are! Are you ashamed to go there?[135]

Callimaco's vision of an agreeable Hell was later Machiavelli's on his deathbed, where he is said to have told the last of those tall tales that had always delighted him and the telling of which was not the least of the joys he took in everyday existence. He said he had had a dream in which, first, a group of poor, miserable, and humble people appeared, formerly the salt of the earth and now the blessed souls of Paradise. Then, on the spot where the humble had stood a moment before, a second group of men appeared, wearing regal robes and discussing affairs of state, and among them were numbered Plato, Plutarch, Tacitus, and many other famous ancients, who despite their greatness on earth had been condemned to Hell by Dante. Asked with which group he wished to spend eternity, he chose the second.[136] Better to continue conversing with the ancients, even in the environs of Hell, than to suffer through an eternity of Paradise in the company of ignoble saints. Without exception, Machiavelli's references to Hell are comic,[137] and if his treatment sometimes slides toward seriousness, that is by way of making the *Divine Comedy* so comical and so submissive to pagan reinterpretation as to deflate its pretensions.

Machiavelli loved the poetry of the *Divine Comedy*, knew much of it by heart, and quoted it frequently. Every time he took Dante's meaning and changed it to his own, it was as a deliberate act of subversion and one that his contemporaries, who shared his familiarity with Dante's masterpiece, were certain to appreciate. The use and abuse to which we have seen Machiavelli subject the image of Hell was not lost on his fellow Florentines; nor could they fail to understand his hilarious and yet serious misappropriation of Dante's canto on Limbo. Souls consigned to Limbo, suggests Dante, are those which on earth had known how difficult and demanding are both the good and the evil life, and knowing this, were unable to commit themselves to either choice or to do anything other than be indecisive. For such as these, too weak to be evil, not even the devils have any use. "Deep Hell rejects so base a herd"—they must remain, therefore, in the waiting room of the Inferno for all eternity, as is only proper in the case of men so indecisive during their lives as to earn "neither praise nor infamy."[138]

So we read in the *Divine Comedy*, and it is as a mischievous footnote to Dante that Machiavelli's rhyme of "Soderini" with "bambini" must be read.

> The night when Piero Soderini died, his spirit went to the mouth of Hell. Pluto roared: "Why to Hell? Silly spirit, go up into Limbo, with all the rest of the babies."[139]

Piero Soderini, formerly head of the Florentine republic and Machiavelli's boss, was the epitome of indecision. Too weak to purge his enemies, too given to a wait-and-see foreign policy, Soderini was as undeserving of either praise or infamy as a child. Upon entering Hell, his insignificant soul was therefore decisively rejected by Pluto and rerouted to Limbo. Machiavelli's joke is far more than a joke; it tells the truth about Soderini (and about Florence in general, the indecisive republic)[140] and exemplifies one of Machiavelli's favorite intellectual strategies, that of politicizing Christian imagery and pressing it into the service of ideals anything but Christian.

However often the reader travels forward and backward across Machiavelli's writings, there is one location in *Tutte le opere* that is privileged. To it we return time after time, necessarily and inescapably, and that is the eighteenth chapter of *Il Principe*, which takes the virtues as its subject matter and proceeds to argue for virtuosity in seeming and dissembling. This same chapter also contains Machiavelli's single most brilliant exercise in the fine art of innovation through inverting and subverting the images of his intellectual targets, Stoicism and Christianity. There is in Machiavelli no passage more quoted than his insistence, in this chapter, that the prince must avail himself of the force of the lion and the fraud of the fox. Not a single humanist had excuse to miss the significance of Machiavelli's words, which were taken from Cicero's *De Officiis*—a work known to all students of the classics—and turned upside down.

> Wrong doing [writes Cicero] originates in one of two ways: either by force or by fraud; fraud is like a little fox, force like the lion. Both are most uncharacteristic of man, but fraud should arouse greater contempt. Taking all forms of injustice into account, none is more deadly than that practiced by people who act as if they are good men when they are being most treacherous.[141]

Machiavelli's image of the lion and the fox is, then, Cicero's Stoicism stood on its head.

Machiavelli was not the first to play tricks on Cicero's *On Duties*. Shortly before the fall of Roman civilization, St. Ambrose rewrote *On Duties* under the revised title *On the Duties of Priests*. Cicero's pagan and Stoical treatise, after its conversion to Christianity by St. Ambrose, became the companion of monks in their cloisters and of preachers in the world all through the Middle Ages. Its holy life ended only when the quattrocento humanists restored the text to its original meaning, but in the meantime its identity had been irreversibly linked with Christian religion. From Machiavelli's point of view, the decisive baptism of Cicero was the one sponsored by Dante:

> Of all malicious wrong that earns Heaven's hate
> > The end is injury; all such ends are won
> > Either by force or fraud. Both perpetrate
> Evil to others; but since man alone
> > Is capable of fraud, God hates that worst;
> > The fraudulent lie lowest, then, and groan
> Deepest.[142]

Thus did Dante christen Cicero's denunciation of force and fraud, which were the means of the lion and the fox, respectively, in Cicero, and of the lion and the wolf in Dante. The deeper Dante descended into the pit of Hell, the more the sins of force were left behind, and the more it was the sins of fraud that pointed the way to the ultimate depths of damnation, until at last, having slipped past Geryon, the monster with a just man's face and a hideously bestial body,[143] Dante encountered those among the damned who were teachers of fraud,[144] Ulysses for one; surely Dante, given the chance to peer into the future, would have added Machiavelli for another. When Machiavelli advocated the use of force and fraud, and expressed his admiration for the man who could play both the lion and the fox; when he reserved his deepest admiration for those who were able to dominate by resorting to the subtle methods of the fox rather than the crude methods of the lion, he was overturning both Cicero and Dante, Stoicism and Christianity, in one efficient and brilliant move. And he did so using the imagery (the lion and the fox) and the language (either force or fraud) of *On Duties* and *The Divine Comedy*, two works with which every educated person in Renaissance Italy was conversant.

At the same time that Machiavelli was writing his major works, Thomas More was writing *Utopia*. Though neither wrote in knowledge of the other, their works nevertheless epitomize the difference between Christian and pagan humanism. In warfare the Utopians fight using every trick and deception that Machiavelli attributed to the Romans. Yet they are not Machiavellians, but the denial of everything Machiavelli stood for. Utopians prefer to hire mercenaries if a battle must be fought, and they take as much satisfaction in bloodless conflict as Machiavelli feels contempt for mock battles. Externally, the objective of the Utopians is harmony and peace among peoples; when they go to war it is against their will and for the sake of liberating foreign peoples from their tyrannical masters. Internally, their aim is the rooting out of pride, including the yearning for glory and distinction, which is pride so unabashed as to mistake itself for idealism. Earnestly humanitarian, the Utopians use trickery against their enemies because each trick is a means of saving lives. To fight, they argue, is to lower oneself to the level of the beasts, whereas to outwit the enemy is to make use of what is distinctively human, the intellect.[145] Had More and Machiavelli written to negate one another, they could not have done so more totally. Only a favorable judgment of cunning unites them, and even this is misleading; virtuosity in cunning is admired by Machiavelli less because it saves lives than because it is the most sophisticated expression of *virtù*.

Machiavelli was as enamored of heroic ideals as Christian thinkers were inimical to them. Whether one reads St. Augustine, who cannot lament the sinfulness of human nature too often, or Thomas More, whose Christian humanism comes close to positing natural goodness, pride is blamed for the downfall of mankind— pride, the reason why Eve ate the apple, is the root of all evil. Therefore both Augustine and More heap scorn on wars fought for glory, no matter whether the glory in question is the civic glory of the Roman republic or the feudal glory of European princes and nobilities. For his part, Machiavelli cares passionately that glory should be republican rather than monarchical because only then will it be true glory, the kind that puts Christianity to shame. Machiavelli prays as the ancients did, standing upright, if he prays at all.

The Latin classics acknowledged glory as an end and then proceeded to repudiate its means. Cicero's constant urging of his countrymen to the enactment of deeds meriting fame and glory was unfortunately accompanied by a denunciation and denial of the beast within man. Yet it was this beastly nature that had to be aroused and purposively directed if humans were to accomplish great things. Half man, half beast, the centaur is Machiavelli's symbol of the great man, the man of *virtù*, who knows "how to put to use the traits of animal and of man."[146] For an image of an entire people that was virtuous and manly Machiavelli turned to the ancient Romans, greatest of all conquerors because their religion, unlike Christianity, brought out the beast within man.

> The pagans, greatly esteeming honor and believing it their greatest good, were fiercer [than the men of today] in their actions. This we infer from . . . the magnificence of their [religious] sacrifices, compared with the mildness of ours. . . . [Theirs were] full of blood and ferocity in the slaughter of a multitude of animals; this terrible sight made the men resemble it.[147]

By no means was Machiavelli's image of a Rome that conquered because it was a lion in its force and a fox in its fraud sanctioned by Latin literature read literally. Nevertheless, Livy's endless descriptions of battles abound in predatory verbs of slaughter and butchery[148] that give the lie to his Stoic morality and beckon a Machiavellian revision. Furthermore, it is not impossible that Machiavelli took some of his inspiration for a revised estimate of Rome from the figures of speech of the *Aeneid*, Virgil's eulogy of Roman foundation and expansion, a poem Machiavelli loved. Images of animals stalking their prey, of jaws tearing and shredding their victims, are common in Virgil,[149] as common as in Homer's *Iliad* despite the many intervening centuries during which the Romans toned down the competitive and violent heroic ethos, especially by yoking it to the cooperative and law-abiding standards of justice. Feasibly Machiavelli's predatory Roman republic is Virgil's Rome shorn of its moralistic veneer and reinterpreted through the poetic images of the *Aeneid*. If so, power politics may be the covert message of that very Latin literature which overtly, and even in its most jingoistic moments, understands Roman expansion as the divinely ordained extension of law and civilization across the known world.

In general, however, Machiavelli's ploy was not to discover a hidden meaning in Latin literature, but to take its outspokenly idealistic and Stoical message and invert it, changing it to power politics, to Machiavellism; he then idealized that Machiavellism through incorporating its methods of force and fraud into the heroic code. The force and fraud Cicero hated were, in Machiavelli's judgment, the heart and soul of Roman greatness.

When Machiavelli dealt with the Roman historians, with Livy for instance, he discovered a militaristic conception of *virtus* combined with a Stoic morality, and he inverted the latter while faithfully reproducing the former. In the case of the Roman moralists, Cicero or Seneca, for example, who were full-time Stoics, Machiavelli devoted his energies to an unrelenting program of subversion through inversion.[150]

After the Roman classics had been inverted, Machiavelli had one other task to accomplish before his radically innovative thought had spent its force. He had to annex Christianity to his worldview by acts of intellectual imperialism. This, as we have seen, he did in fact do, using every rhetorical trick available to him, notably the transformation of Christian images and the restatement of his thought in Christian terms. In *De doctrina Christiana* St. Augustine had turned classical rhetoric into the vehicle of the preacher; in *Il Principe* and the *Discorsi* Roman rhetoric savored a belated revenge against Christianity. Beyond rhetoric, Machiavelli more than hinted that the time had come for a political takeover of the church. Where Stefano Porcari and Cesare Borgia had failed, others could succeed.

Machiavelli's thought could hardly be more frightening. It takes humanism and turns it into the all-devouring power politics of a people forever on the march, its energies directed by a ruling class willing to use any means promising success. Such limitations to violence as are enjoined by Machiavelli are fundamentally those flowing from the heroic code, which forbids meaningless slaughter but finds slaughter frequently meaningful as a proof of greatness. No man is great because he says he is but because others say he is, and they will not say so unless they witness great and manly deeds, which more than anything else are acts of domination.

In effect, the unusually barbarous acts of the Athenians at Melos become the ordinary actions of the Romans against the Latins in Machiavelli's interpretation of ancient history.[151] The ordinary citizens of an exceptional republic are extraordinary. Such men once were and might be again if only the moderns would read Machiavelli and refrain from saving him. Salvation was never his concern; immortality was.

—VII—

INTERPRETING
MACHIAVELLI

TO REINTERPRET Machiavelli is to quarrel with other scholars over the meaning and significance of Machiavelli's thought; over what he originally meant, what he means to us, and the proper relation between the two; over which interpretive methods can yield fruitful results, which are doomed to sterility. Explicitly, some of these disagreements have already been aired (chapter I, above); implicitly, other disputes have followed us throughout this book, and it is best that we end by making the implicit explicit. Against whom have we been arguing, and to what avail?

Most of all, our quarrel is with the heirs of the Enlightenment, liberals and socialists in particular, who inhabit the academy and have conjured up the standard Machiavelli of courses on the history of political thought: a Machiavelli teaching us how to face up to the inescapable reality of power in politics, all politics, even the most humanistic; a Machiavelli much needed, so it is thought, because he speaks to a pressing moral dilemma, the problem of "dirty hands," the moral necessity of sometimes contravening morality for the sake of establishing or maintaining a just and humanitarian order. This view of Machiavelli is bound to be a persuasive one since it makes him a forerunner of ourselves; it is also bound to be one we shall never tire of, no matter how often it is repeated, because so long as the adjective "Machiavellian" continues to mean underhanded and sinister in the popular mind, there will be academic minds eager to save him from his reputation. Yet our findings in the present study give us strong reasons to reject this standard interpretation of Machiavelli—to reject it in all of its several noteworthy formulations, even though each one has been argued by astute scholars.

The first variation on the theme of a standard, humanistic Machiavelli takes the form of underscoring the moral ends that supposedly excuse the immoral means discussed at length in *The Prince*.[1] In this view Machiavelli qualifies for absolution once we realize that the evil tactics sanctioned in *The Prince* have as their end the reestablishment of a republican order, as demanded in the *Discourses*. Completely overlooked in this interpretation, however, and fatally so, is the predatory nature of Machiavelli's republic. From the moment interpreters hear Machiavelli speak of liberty and constitutional order, the assumption is made that we are in the presence of a kindred spirit, when nothing could be further from the truth. Restoration of republican rule, for Machiavelli, is not the end justifying the means; nor does the forcible unification of Italy, which was little more than an afterthought, play such a moral role in his writings. The end is greatness, and Italian unity is merely a possible byproduct of the glorious, violent, and aggrandizing deeds that are better performed by republican citizens than monarchical subjects.

Not that any violence will do, of course. Small-minded, petty, and poorly-done violence such as was characteristic of the Florentines and the Italians in general is, indeed, resoundingly condemned in the pages of Machiavelli. The violence of a tyrant who seizes power for purely personal reasons and crushes all men of *virtù* so that he may rule alone and rule notoriously rather than gloriously is likewise forbidden. But the great, glorious violence of a conquering republic is strongly praised, and the chief constraint placed upon such a usurping republic is that the methods of mercy and clemency—the ways of the fox in Machiavelli's reworking of Stoicism—are recommended whenever they are more efficient and effective than the ways of the lion. There simply is no sense of a dilemma of violent means versus humanistic ends in Machiavelli's thought, and not so surprisingly as it might seem; for in an heroic ethic the end itself is violent.

Moreover, inasmuch as glory by its very nature is simultaneously style and substance, means and end, there is another reason why a moral dilemma does not arise in Machiavelli's world; where the quest and the achievement are one and the same, both are present or both absent in a given instance, and one cannot possibly be sacrificed to the other. Robert Michels,[2] Milovan Djilas,[3] and Maurice Merleau-Ponty[4] worry whether the means of socialists have displaced their ends; Machiavelli did not worry. At most, what one finds in him, after setting modern preconceptions aside, is the recognition that it usually takes one kind of man to seize a corrupt government by violence, another kind to establish a good political order.[5] But this is a bemoaning of the rigidity of human personality—it is not a moral statement, and even less is it an encounter with a moral dilemma.

Glory needs no excuses; it requires nothing outside itself to justify its ways. Therefore all Machiavelli asked of glory was the one thing that could be asked, that it be true glory, the highest glory, the kind that makes the most of the maximum number of persons, is most disciplined, and leads to the most magnificent results. In short, he asked that the sham glory of monarchs and feudal nobilities be outshone by the true glory of a republican people led by an astute ruling class. The discussion of an end justifying the means is our discussion, not Machiavelli's.

To dispel the illusion that Machiavelli taught lessons about a dilemma of means and ends is simultaneously to disabuse ourselves of the belief that his thought can be properly understood in terms of a pitched battle between "realism" and "idealism."[6] What, after all, is the realism/idealism interpretation—the second variant of the standard Machiavelli—if not the first variant, the means/ends dilemma, all over again? Common to all arguments that revolve round a dichotomy of "realism" versus "idealism" is the notion that the ideals, the ends, are one thing, and the "Machiavellian" means used to achieve them are another, and contradictory, thing. The moral so often drawn in our times, and which Machiavelli is given the credit of having discovered, is that we must, despite our revulsion, resort to power politics in some situations—for example, for purposes of survival in the jungle of international politics. We must, it is said, spurn the foolishness of assuming that the methods of force and fraud pertain to the monarchies of the old regime and the dictatorships of the new regime but not to democratic, just, and humane polities. Against our wills, we must sanction an unholy alliance of realism with idealism. This is an argument that, by now, we know by heart; but no matter how familiar it may be to us, it is alien to Machiavelli's thought.

Machiavelli doesn't need to struggle to bring his realism and idealism together since they were never apart; no conflict can exist between the two since, in truth, they are one, and that one is the child of the *studia humanitatis*. In place of Stoicism, *humanitas*, and an accretion of Christian humanitarianism, Machiavelli offered a reading of the classics that idealized power politics. When we watch him accentuating the military and imperial side of *virtus* while simultaneously tearing away the Stoical and humanitarian masks hiding the power politics of Rome, his model republic, we have come into contact with an author for whom the realism/idealism dichotomy has no meaning.[7]

Historically, it is Christians such as St. Augustine and Reinhold Niebuhr who have found the realism/idealism distinction meaningful,[8] which is another reason to doubt that such a dichotomy has anything to do with Machiavelli, and reason, too, to suppose that the ideologies growing out of the Enlightenment owe more to the Christian religion the *philosophes* despised than to Machiavelli, whom some scholars have treated as a forerunner of the anticlerical intellectuals of the eighteenth century.[9] Realism versus idealism is a theme running through Christian, liberal, and socialist thought; in Machiavelli's case, it has been read into his thought.

The heroic and violent values Machiavelli espouses refuse to be confined within the formulae of the end versus the means or idealism versus realism. Those same heroic values shatter yet another formula applied to Machiavelli and which constitutes a third variant of the standard interpretation: the notion, brilliantly argued by Sheldon Wolin,[10] that Machiavelli pleaded for an "economy of violence."

What has been viewed as an economizing frame of mind in Machiavelli's comments on violence is in reality an aspect of the heroic code and its call for glorious action. One of the characteristics of heroic and glorious action is that it is elegant; one of the characteristics of elegance is that it is economical in its means. Subsumed under the rubric of glorious action, economy in politics is an aesthetic principle; its quantitative calculations are dictated by qualitative considerations of beauty, grandeur, and the fame that is their reward. It must be remembered that to Machiavelli's mind the economy of violence was in fact, and to his consternation, practiced by the commercially-minded ruling class of Florence against which he constantly polemicized, as in his adage, or rather counteradage, that not money but men and arms are the sinews of war.[11]

Surely, moreover, the presence of an economizing mentality in Machiavelli's thought should not be understood as substantially curtailing the quantity of violence implied by his political stand; for where unlimited conquest, growth, and aggrandizement is the objective, the economical use of violence at each given moment is canceled out by the endlessness of violent moments. For anyone who inhabits a universe of heroic values, violence comes to an end only when there is no one left to conquer, at which moment an Alexander the Great is reduced to tears.

The concept of an economy of violence voices our dread that sometimes to act morally is to count the number of corpses entailed by alternative political strategies. What it involves is the treatment of human beings, in the most literal and brutal sense, as means rather than ends, even though we wish to be Kantians rather than Machiavellians.[12] Horrible though it is, this concept does speak to genuine political realities, particularly those associated with revolution. Thus we are irresistibly drawn into discussions of the economical use of violence. Nevertheless, it is not Machiavelli who is doing the talking; it is ourselves.

The fourth version of the standard Machiavelli comes in the form of the familiar argument from "necessity." Its *locus classicus* is the fifteenth chapter of *The Prince*, quoted time and again in defense of Machiavelli:

> There is such a difference between how men live and how they ought to live that he who abandons what is done for what ought to be done learns his destruction rather than his preservation, because any man who under all conditions insists on making it his business to be good will surely be destroyed among so many who are not good. Hence a prince . . . must learn how not to be good, and understand when to use this knowledge and when not to use it, in accord with necessity.

So Machiavelli says in the fifteenth chapter, and so, argues the noted Renaissance scholar J. H. Whitfield, he says on almost every page of *The Prince*; by Whitfield's count, the word "necessity" occurs no less than seventy-six times, as noun, participle, or adjective, in the short span of *The Prince*.[13]

Having by linguistic and quantitative analysis rendered *The Prince* respectable, Whitfield quickly concludes that he has accomplished his goal of placing Machiavelli above reproach; for if the notorious *Prince* is as unobjectionable as he makes it out to be, how much more innocuous must the *Discourses* and other republican works be, suffused as they are with the spirit of liberty. Unfortunately, Whitfield's central assumption could not be more erroneous. It is precisely in the republican *Discourses* that Machiavelli kicks over the traces and, after a brief initial discussion of "necessity," in which that concept is twisted beyond recognition, he turns his ideal republic loose upon a world ill-prepared to cope with Roman force and fraud. The republican Machiavelli, reluctant to make any concessions to the argument from "necessity" so nicely phrased in *The Prince*, makes just one: notably in the claim, stated in the first pages of the *Discourses*, that a city-state must conquer all other cities or be conquered.[14] Reduced in this manner to a rationalization of unlimited aggression, the republican invocation of "necessity" has too hollow a sound to be meaningful. In truth, Machiavelli's hopes for republican greatness override all considerations of "necessity" (chapter II, above). On this point the *Florentine History* and the *Discourses on Livy* are in full agreement, the only difference being that the latter work applauds greatness achieved, whereas the former scorns greatness aborted (chapter III, above). In sum, the republican works are Machiavelli at his most Machiavellian, *The Prince* Machiavelli at his least Machiavellian; that being the case, Professor Whitfield's defense of *The Prince*, far from a masterstroke, is an evasion of the real issues.

For a Machiavelli who needs "necessity" to excuse violence and fraud, one must read the monarchical Machiavelli; the republican Machiavelli is well-represented in the closing words of Book II, chapter 4 of the *Discourses*, where Machiavelli condones doing all that is "necessary" to achieve "greatness," including the practice of fraud on an unprecedented scale. "Greatness," not "necessity," is the key word in Machiavelli's vocabulary. No matter how frequently the word "necessity" occurs in the republican writings, it is nearly always a servant of the word "greatness." Usually, in the *Discourses, Art of War*, and *Florentine History, necessità* means a situation in which human nature, despite its chronic weakness, is forced into acts of greatness and heroism, much in the manner that a cornered animal fights with exceptional intensity and courage, sensing that anything less will mean certain death.[15] A good general, therefore, never leads enemy troops to believe they must conquer or be conquered, but often leads his own troops to believe there is no alternative to success.[16]

"Necessity," then, is useful because it yields strategies for achieving greatness, and this is true not only in the case of the general in the field but of the ruling class at home. In their competition with the ruling classes of other cities, the Roman senators resorted to a strategy related to but just the opposite of that employed by the Roman generals. While the generals zealously kept open the options of the enemy rank and file, thus giving cowardice an opportunity to assert itself, the senators closed the options of their noble ruling counterparts in enemy cities, forcing enemy statesmen to act (or react) in necessary, predictable, and consequently vulnerable ways, ways leading to their shame and to Roman glory.[17]

"Necessity" is the key word in contemporary discussions of the conditions under which the tolerant liberal state cannot afford to be tolerant;[18] it is central in discussions of why a democratic state must practice secret diplomacy,[19] and of why the logic of humanism sometimes dictates acts of terrorism.[20] Machiavelli's uses of the word "necessity," however frequent, belong to another world, one farther removed from ours by ideology than by time.[21]

All four varieties of the standard Machiavelli—necessity, the economy of violence, realism versus idealism, the means versus the end—perform the same function in contemporary scholarship, that of helping liberals and socialists address a "Machiavellian problem" that is certainly theirs but was not Machiavelli's. All varieties of the standard Machiavelli likewise share an inadequate appreciation of the significance of heroic values in Machiavelli's thought. Admiration of antique glory, grandeur, and fame pervades almost every page of the *Discourses*; concern for the absence of those same heroic virtues in the modern world weighs so heavily in the *Florentine History* that Machiavelli ends up championing the cause of the nobility even though he has just traced the origins of Florentine factionalism to the doors of its noble families (chapter III, above). Yet, since no present dilemma of twentieth-century humanism has much to do with heroic values, "glory" and "greatness" have been largely deleted from Machiavelli's writings, the better to give us the Machiavelli we desire, one who is a precursor of ourselves.

When "honor" and "glory" are now and then recognized as central words in Machiavelli's terminology, the conclusion all too often drawn is that since his thought is therefore demonstrably moral, not amoral as some neo-Kantians and positivists have insisted, he cannot be someone who should inspire fear.[22] His thought, so this line of argumentation runs, is far more than a dispassionate examination of the efficacy of this or that means of wielding power; rather, it is passionately censurious of wrong and committed to right.[23] As such, Machiavelli must be reckoned a moralist misunderstood, and our unmistakable scholarly duty is to explain to the public why he should be brought in from the cold.

Usually missing from the foregoing apology for Machiavelli is a recognition that "honor" and "glory," far from placing him within our moral universe, figure in his thought as expressions natural to a heroic and pagan moral code. Always missing is an account of how disconcerting, how dangerous, how explosive, Machiavelli's morality is from a liberal or socialist point of view. It is Machiavelli's moral utterances that are disturbing, not his amoral calculations of the method of overthrowing any regime, republican or princely. It is Machiavelli's very "humanism," his morality derived from and imposed upon the classics, that is so incompatible with our humanism. Lashing out against the weakness of Florence, against a millennium and more of a bad Christian "education," and more than two centuries of oscillations between an ignoble commercial republic and a monarchical Medicean government perched atop the coffin of civic hope, Machiavelli was a pagan with a vengeance. The incipient power politics of ancient pagan culture, which Plato and Aristotle had tried to bring under philosophical control, Euripides under dramatic control, the Romans under the control of Stoicism, and the Christians under the control of an antithetical set of values, was set free by Machiavelli.

Set free for use by the moderns. In his historical writings Machiavelli had no trouble detecting a theme of power politics running throughout Florentine and Italian history; his complaint is simply that the omnipresent power politics of his compatriots was petty, half-hearted, vacillating, irresolute, and weak. To their credit, the Italians Machiavelli depicts in the *Florentine History* do not suffer from an anguishing problem of "dirty hands"; to their discredit, they suffer from a weakness and small-mindedness preventing them from pursuing a high-spirited and unflinching policy of power politics. Despite the scorn and contempt he frequently heaps upon the Florentines, Machiavelli never abandons hope, remaining convinced throughout his life that imitation of the Greeks and Romans can still provide deliverance.

Yearning for the moderns to resemble the ancients, Machiavelli actually overshoots the mark and, at times, makes his moderns more Machiavellian than the ancients. In the famous Melian dialogue written by Thucydides, the vulnerable citizens of Melos assert the claims of justice against the Athenian claim that "you and everybody else, having the same power as we have, would do the same as we do."[24] In the *Florentine History* the spokesman for Lucca, a republic threatened by the much stronger republic of Florence, tells his fellow citizens that "if we could, we would do the same or worse to them."[25] When the Athenians universalized the will-to-power, they did so as the spokesmen of those who are strong; when Machiavelli's Italians universalized the will-to-power, it was as the ultimate step in universalization, since the weak give voice to the law of domination and submission.

Machiavelli was not just like us. Until this lesson is taken to heart, Machiavelli studies will take us along a path that is well-lighted and familiar but which constantly leads back to where we started.

UP TO THIS point, our argument has been that a certain mistaken pattern of generalization—a certain incorrect "synthetic" interpretation, as it might be termed—has characterized many studies of Machiavelli. To this must now be added the charge that a second body of scholarly literature has erred by overindulging the "genetic method" to Machiavelli's texts; and that, in consequence, much research either lacks significant generalizations or assumes the validity of the standard, revisionist Machiavelli even as it issues disclaimers of interpretive preconceptions and prides itself on generalizing with the greatest circumspection.

The genetic approach is one of two styles of interpretation that may be discerned in the secondary literature on Machiavelli. It is at work when, as in much recent scholarship, the investigator pulls out a text from the complete works and then dwells on the order in which its chapters flowed from Machiavelli's pen, or on the question of whether the text was written before or after another of Machiavelli's works, or on the particular historical circumstances surrounding the work at the moment of inception—all in the name of charting the evolution of Machiavelli's thought. Which came first, *The Prince* or the *Discourses*, and in response to what conditions, are typical concerns of those scholars who employ the mode of interpretation variously labeled the genetic, the chronological, or the biographical.

The alternative approach may be termed the structural or the synthetic. It sees Machiavelli's works as interrelated parts of a whole and does not refrain from using one work to assist in elucidating the meaning of another. Typical of this approach is the claim that the monarchical means of *The Prince* have as their ultimate objective the republicanism of the *Discourses*, so that to study *The Prince* in isolation from the *Discourses* is to risk misconstruing Machiavelli's meaning.

The respective dangers of the two methods would seem to be obvious enough. Left to itself, the genetic approach may pile fact upon fact, while never concerning itself with increasing our understanding; and the synthetic approach, unchecked by the genetic, may inadvertently lead to the imposition of generalizations upon the corpus of Machiavelli's writing that never existed in his mind. Whence the conclusion would seem to follow that the synthetic approach divorced from the genetic is empty, and the genetic approach divorced from the synthetic is blind.

Nevertheless, there are some proponents of the genetic approach who are reluctant to concede anything to the synthetic approach. Quentin Skinner, in his well-known essay "Meaning and Understanding in the History of Ideas," takes it for granted that *The Prince* and *Discourses* should be studied in separation from one another.[26] His reason for doing so is that he is combating the methodological viewpoint, represented most ably by Ernst Cassirer, which postulates a vital center from which all the individual works of a given thinker radiate as do the spokes from the center of a wheel. In opposition to Cassirer's interpretive technique, Skinner rightly objects that the various writings of a given thinker were composed on different occasions with different purposes in mind. As a corrective to Cassirer, Skinner's point is well-taken. It is to Skinner's apparent reversal of an a priori assumption of unity into an a priori assumption of disunity that we must object.

Presumably Skinner's argument, if further articulated, would be made in some such fashion as this: most thinkers, including the formidable authors of the "classic" texts, the great books, were not system-builders. Consequently, an interpreter of these texts who posits a systematic Machiavelli, Rousseau, or Marx has in truth invented the unity he claims to have discovered, and all such synthetic interpretations must therefore be deemed ahistorical, except insofar as the manner in which the living play tricks on the dead is itself a piece of history. Surely an argument along these lines would be welcome were it to relinquish its universal sweep—its claim that it need not examine specific cases.

The case of Machiavelli proves how wrong it is to determine in advance that a thinker who was not a system-builder was therefore unsystematic. For Machiavelli's works, though each one has its particular intentions and history, are intimately interrelated. While *The Prince* is hardly a republican work, it is nonetheless true that Machiavelli counsels the prince in the *Discourses* that his greatest glory lies in establishing or reestablishing a republican order; and for good measure Machiavelli adds his *Discourse on Remodeling the Government of Florence*, in which he urges the Medici to restore the Florentine republic. Thus *The Prince* and the *Discourses* are complementary, and the same may be said of the *Discourses* and *Florentine History*: for if the *Discourses* shows the methods and means of democratic greatness, as embodied by ancient Rome, the *Florentine History* shows the methods and means of democratic mediocrity, as embodied by modern Florence. Even the lighthearted *Mandragola* has a theoretical significance linking it to the general corpus of Machiavelli's works; for, when read along with his advice in the familiar letters on how a spirited citizen may spend his private hours, Machiavelli's laughter signifies a relaxation of the repressive demands of civic virtue (chapter IV, above).

Skinner's belief that the synthetic approach necessarily leads to overgeneralization is misplaced when the man whose thought is under investigation is Niccolò Machiavelli. Indeed, it might even be said that since Machiavelli's works are so much all of a piece, the study of his writings one by one, in isolation from one another, is bound to have the effect of chopping them to pieces, destroying much of their vitality. One thing seems certain: however wrongheaded the results of synthetic interpretation have sometimes been, no one has ever accused such readings of lacking significant generalizations. By contrast, wholesale abandonment of the synthetic approach would threaten to turn Machiavelli scholarship into a study of more and more about less and less.[27]

There are some proponents of the genetic approach who resemble the scholars plying the synthetic mode of analysis in their willingness to offer a major generalization about Machiavelli's thought. Quite unlike the method of the synthetic interpreters, however, is the insistence of these geneticists that generalization be based upon a meticulous examination of the chronology of Machiavelli's writings. Included in this group of advocates of the genetic approach are Federico Chabod, Hans Baron, and Felix Gilbert, three of the most illustrious names among Machiavelli scholars. Implicitly or explicitly, they are scholars who believe that since the synthetic approach has yielded a multiplicity of interpretations of Machiavelli's meaning, some of which are transparently unhistorical, the most promising way to achieve a disciplined overview of his work is to set aside preconceived notions of his meaning and then to follow the indisputably historical procedure of tracing his intellectual development.

Despite the great investigative skill and dialectical subtlety that these formidable scholars have invested in genetic research, they have gone wrong from the beginning; wrong even in their own terms, for they have failed to purge their minds of preconceptions, as promised. Much of their genetic research is decisively shaped by the "realism/idealism" reading set forth in many synthetic interpretations—a reading, as we have previously argued, that is guilty of the historical fallacy of imposing upon Machiavelli a dichotomy we face today but which was never experienced by him.

One need not read between the lines to discover how much Federico Chabod, Hans Baron, and Felix Gilbert accept the realism/idealism conceptualization. Power politics versus humanism, realism versus idealism are dichotomies openly stated by these scholars and explicitly the reason why their work poses its most urgently felt genetic question: what was the order in which Machiavelli wrote *The Prince* and the *Discourses*? If his thought evolved from the *Discourses* to *The Prince*, we are asked to conclude that, originally an idealist, Machiavelli learned from political experience that the responsible leader had better set his dreams aside and get down to the business of becoming a master of power politics. If, on the other hand, Machiavelli wrote the *Discourses* after *The Prince*, we are told the proper inference is that he was originally a power politician but later, out of office and at liberty to read the classics, became an idealistic admirer of ancient republican liberty.

As reconstructed by Chabod, the chronology of Machiavelli's writings moves from the *Discourses*, a work of republican idealism, to disillusionment with republican possibilities in Italy, and from there to the "realism" of *The Prince*:

> The Republic yielded place to the Principate; the people, capable of dictating its wishes and of leaving its own impress on the State, gave way to the single man with his individual energy and the resources of his own ability; the vision of past glory—a vision clouded by nostalgic regret—was replaced by the theoretical prospect of Italy's political recovery.[28]

So much is Chabod's outlook shaped by the realism/idealism distinction that he invents a Machiavelli growing away from the idealism and humanism of the *Discourses* in order to explain how the same man could be the power politician of *The Prince*.

Chabod's thesis,[29] initially articulated in 1925, has been extraordinarily influential, especially among Italian scholars. In 1961 it was, however, forcefully challenged outside Italy by Hans Baron, who built a powerful case for the alternative chronology and counterthesis that "the course of [Machiavelli's] development was not one from the *Discourses* to the *Prince*, but from the *Prince* to the *Discourses*—from a treatise on the Renaissance principate to the most penetrating Renaissance treatise dealing with a republic."[30] At stake in the battle between Chabod and Baron over the chronology of Machiavelli's works was the question of whether Machiavelli fits into an old interpretation of the Renaissance, still in vogue when Chabod was writing, according to which its political thought was preeminently a chapter in the history of nascent absolutism; or was Machiavelli to figure as a chapter in Baron's now generally and rightly accepted account of Florentine humanism, according to which a major strand of Renaissance political thought belongs squarely within the camp of republican ideology, known also as civic humanism. Today almost no one doubts Baron's contention that Machiavelli was fundamentally republican in his political outlook.

At stake additionally in Baron's refutation of Chabod was the false question of whether Machiavelli, as a thinker whose most mature statement of his views was *The Prince*, should be regarded as a prophet of "realism;" or, as a thinker whose *Discourses* postdate *The Prince*, should be deemed a champion of "idealism" and "humanism." In this regard, Baron's essay shared the master assumption underpinning Felix Gilbert's essay, published several years earlier, which also argued that the *Discourses* followed *The Prince* in Machiavelli's development and that this discovery constituted a major interpretive finding. To quote Gilbert's closing words:

> The . . . differences between *The Prince* and the *Discorsi* can be considered as a first sign of Machiavelli's inclination to accept orthodox humanism, and the contrast between the political realism of *The Prince* and the political idealism of the *Discorsi* would appear to be the result of an intellectual development rather than an expression of a tension in Machiavelli's mind. . . . [T]here is . . . an inner logic in this development: for there are few if any who, after having once stared unblinkingly into the face of what man is, have been

able to hold to that vision and have not escaped into dreaming of what he ought to be.[31]

Baron would like to follow Gilbert but hesitates, it being all too evident that the *Discorsi* contains numerous "Machiavellian" passages. Rather than consider the possibility that Machiavelli's humanism and power politics were one and the same, that humanism was itself incipiently Machiavellian, and that this was Machiavelli's discovery, Baron resorts to the argument that Machiavelli was of two minds, and fathered two intellectual legacies, one humanistic, the other antihumanistic.[32]

On the basis of our earlier examination of the *Discourses* (chapter II, above) it is obvious that to determine which came first, *The Prince* or the *Discourses*, is to explain little; if Machiavelli did in fact believe the greatest feats of power politics were the special preserve and glory of republics, it is drastically wrong to assume that proof the *Discourses* was written after *The Prince* would constitute evidence of a Machiavelli repenting of his Machiavellism. Since Machiavelli was a power politician in both *The Prince* and the *Discourses*, there is no point in asking whether he evolved toward or away from Machiavellism. Genetic research cannot solve a problem that never existed. Small wonder that Eric Cochrane ended his well-known 1961 article on the state of the literature with a resounding call for a renewed effort at synthetic interpretation.[33]

During the years that have passed since Professors Gilbert and Baron published their essays on the chronology of *The Prince* and *Discourses*, Machiavelli studies have taken a significant new turn. The recent findings of those engaged in genetic research point to the conclusion, as John H. Geerken summarizes this literature, that "the *Prince* and *Discourses* did not originate as studies of two different subjects (tyranny and republics), composed at two different times (1513 and 1517 respectively), but were in fact interdependent aspects of an organically unified outlook."[34] This finding within the camp of the geneticists is one of two new developments calling for a synthetic study of Machiavelli's works. The other is the progressive obliteration of the distinction between a prehumanist and a humanist Machiavelli. What the biographical labors of scholars have taught us in recent years is that Machiavelli was already a devotee of the *studia humanitatis* early in his life, long before he wrote any of his major works:[35] we now know, for instance, that his father had definite humanist interests, that the young Machiavelli studied Latin and copied some Lucretius, and that possibly as early as 1503 he made political use of Livy. We know, too, that when the aging Machiavelli composed his last major work, the *Florentine History*, he drew upon previous humanist histories of his city and made use of such typically humanist devices as general reflections placed at the beginning of each book and of invented dramatic speeches interspersed throughout the narrative. Clearly, Machiavelli neither grew into nor out of humanism, but was for all practical purposes always a humanist. Not even *The Prince* is an exception to this generalization, for harking back as far as Aristotle's admiration of the man too great to be bound by the laws, or Isocrates's eulogy of the leader who might yet liberate his countrymen from barbarians, "civic humanists" had had an on-again, off-again affair with the prince.[36] Before, during, and after *The Prince* Machiavelli was a humanist, so he neither evolved toward nor away from humanism, and hence it matters little whether the humanistic *Discourses* preceded or followed *The Prince*.

Assuming that *Del modo di trattare i popoli della Valdichiana ribellati* was written in 1503, the conventional date of composition cited by scholars,[37] we may go so far as to suggest that not only was Machiavelli, for all practical purposes, always a humanist, but his humanism was always Machiavellian. For in this presumably very early essay Machiavelli is already arguing that the lesson of Roman history, which Florence needs to learn, is that violence must be uncompromisingly used against rebellious cities whenever there is no equally efficient way to preserve a republican empire. Halfway measures were rightly disdained by the Romans, he asserts here as in the *Discourses*, later.

Applied to Machiavelli, the genetic approach discloses the continuity of his thought, and not only legitimizes but actually demonstrates the pressing need for a synthetic study of his works centered around the secretary's relationship to the tradition of humanism. It has been our objective to provide such a study, organized around the thesis that he was the great subversive of the humanist tradition. Instead of a Machiavelli struggling to salvage as much humanism as he can in a world of power politics, we have encountered a Machiavelli striving to transform humanism into power politics. In place of a Machiavelli too small to be a threat to the standard Machiavelli, which is what results from a diet of purely genetic research,[38] we have come face to face with a Machiavelli who is as dangerous as he intended to be.

"HUMANISM," understood as the tradition of the *studia humanitatis*, does more than link Machiavelli's various works to one another; it also links them to the neoclassical thought of his contemporaries and to the classical writings of the ancient Romans. It places his texts in their intellectual context, permitting the interpreter to venture significant generalizations about his thought that are free of false modernizations and based upon a realization of the full generalizing powers of historical method.

Understood as a humanist, Machiavelli converses not only with the ancients and with his contemporaries through the mouths of the ancients, but also with us today, with all of us who are tempted by one or another version of the standard Machiavelli. The Machiavelli who emerges from a full-scale investigation of his relationship to the *studia humanitatis* speaks to the proponents of the standard Machiavelli by demonstrating how ahistorical their readings are; he shows scholars how seriously they have erred in making him their Machiavelli, a thinker who speaks to them by addressing their problems, a man after their own humanistic hearts, their forerunner.

In one sense, of course, it might be said that to understand Machiavelli historically is, then, to realize he does not speak to us at all, that contemporary conversations are one-sided, with Machiavelli silent and modern humanists, misled by the historical continuity of the word "humanism," doing all the talking as they impose their views on Machiavelli. Yet in another sense an historically understood Machiavelli need not be a Machiavelli who, dead and finally buried, cannot speak to us. Rather might it be said that every time the humanism of today claims a noble ancestry reaching back to the Greeks and Romans, Machiavelli threatens to do to us what he did to his humanistic contemporaries: to speak to us by radically challenging our humanism. Once again he comes to life and attempts a transformation of the humanistic heritage into proto-Machiavellism.

A Machiavelli restored to his meaning is a usurper of our tradition, a devastating critic of our humanism who speaks to us with the voice of a humanist. Why we are eager to misread him is not so difficult to comprehend: it's "us or him," so we make him one of us—a humane and safe response to the threat he poses.

This is not to say there are no scholars engaged in the enterprise of measuring Machiavelli against the backdrop of classical, humanistic literature. Some are, and it is surely significant that, whatever their differences, Leo Strauss, Felix Gilbert, Quentin Skinner, and Isaiah Berlin agree that a Machiavelli thus understood is shocking. But each of these scholars, in one way or another, pulls up short of the mark, refuses to take the full measure of his potential insight, and circles back to formulations that reinforce the standard Machiavelli.

Strauss's central purpose, repeatedly stated, is to prove that Machiavelli radically challenged both classical and Christian thought.[39] This sounds promising, but it is an intellectual project conducted by investigative methods that invite disbelief. Wrapped in secrecy and mystery, Machiavelli's message, as construed by Strauss, is ours to glimpse only after a long, indirect, convoluted pursuit, in which the difference between a careful reading and a torturing of the text is sometimes difficult to discern. Why Machiavelli should have hidden his message from us is never explained, even though it obviously needs to be. A man living before the Counter-Reformation and notoriously outspoken, Machiavelli had neither cause nor inclination to conceal his opinions; so we are ill-advised to go on a hunt for a hidden meaning. Simply to recover the overt significance of "the lion and the fox," a significance readily understood by Machiavelli's contemporaries, reared on Cicero and Dante, is surely a more convincing way to demonstrate Machiavelli's attack on humanism and Christianity than is Strauss's overly subtle search for covert significations. All the notion of a hidden message accomplishes is to offer the proponents of the standard view the satisfaction of believing that if only by such means can Machiavelli be taken from them, there is no need to worry.

Vulnerable on methodological grounds, *Thoughts on Machiavelli* is questionable historically as well. So blinded is Strauss by the view, held today, rating Greek thought higher than Roman, that he assumes the ancient authors Machiavelli rebelled against must have been Plato and Aristotle, the very authors who, by Strauss's own admission, are almost never mentioned in Machiavelli's works.[40] For Machiavelli, for most humanists of the Renaissance, and for most educated persons down to the end of the eighteenth century, the classics were basically Latin rather than Greek, yet Strauss spends much time conjuring up a Machiavelli rejecting the thinkers who meant little either to him or to his audience. Coming upon Machiavelli's denigration of discussions of the ideal regime, Strauss treats this as a novel break[41] with the "Great Tradition," with "the classics," with "classical political philosophy," that is (to Strauss), with Plato and Aristotle, when all it amounts to is a repetition of a commonplace found in the Roman historians, Machiavelli's true sources. Noting that for Machiavelli moral excellence and moderation are far from synonymous, Strauss assumes Machiavelli has rejected Aristotle's doctrine of the mean,[42] when the explanation nearer at hand is that he was rejecting "the middle way," a cliche in Florentine ruling circles; or, more generally, he was noting that *virtus* and *gloria* call for actions great rather than compromising. Despite Machiavelli's Roman treatment of Roman matters, Strauss sets forth a Greek discussion of Roman history.

Misleading on Machiavelli's historical sources, Strauss is equally misleading in his comments on the historical influence of the secretary's writings. "Machiavelli breaks with the Great Tradition and initiates the Enlightenment,"[43] Strauss suggests. Surely he is wrong; for however much Machiavelli and the *philosophes* share a hatred of Catholicism, they diverge drastically on "virtue" and "glory." As humanitarians, the *philosophes* battled not only the fanaticism of the Church; they also did battle with the heroic ethos, combating it because it led to literal combat. Sometimes the *philosophes* substituted a moral vocabulary of "interest" and *amour-propre* for the language of "virtue"; sometimes they retained the terminology of virtue while moderating its demands or altering its meaning. It was left for the arch-enemy of the *philosophes*, the ex- and anti-*philosophe* Rousseau, to reinvoke the standards of Roman republican virtue. Machiavelli leads away from the Enlightenment, not to it.

From our point of view, Strauss's historical errors are perhaps less important than the excuses he unwittingly provides the advocates of the standard Machiavelli for dismissing out of hand the suggestion that Machiavelli is the great renegade of Western political thought. Not the least of Strauss's difficulties is that he becomes entrapped in the snare of his own polemical rhetoric. Knowing his academic audience delights in saving Machiavelli from his sinister popular reputation—from modern echoes of the Elizabethan horror of a Satanic Machiavelli and a Machiavellian Satan—Strauss professes himself a believer in "the old-fashioned and simple opinion according to which Machiavelli was a teacher of evil."[44] That is, he adopts a neo-Elizabethan tone and is particularly strident—and disingenuous—when he calls Machiavelli a "blasphemer" and then retreats from offering the reader a full-scale exposition of Machiavelli's attack on Christianity, on the grounds that to do so would be to collaborate in a sinful activity.[45] By such means Strauss does indeed provoke the outraged response he desires, but he also plays directly into the hands of his enemies. What more could Machiavelli's saviors ask than that an exceptionally able modern detractor can do no better than re-create the obsessive reaction of the Elizabethans, too Christian to be fair to Machiavelli? Instead of launching a telling challenge to the standard Machiavelli, Strauss sets its automatic defense mechanisms to work and gives them a new *raison d'être*.

In truth it is not Machiavelli's anti-Christian sentiments that trouble Strauss; it is his democratic and propagandistic views, at odds with the aristocratic and contemplative ideals of Greek political philosophy,[46] that Strauss can abide neither in Machiavelli nor in the *philosophes*, authors—Strauss hints—not of an Enlightenment but of an "Obfuscation."[47] Most readers who stay with Strauss long enough to realize he is not an easily dismissed old-fashioned Elizabethan will conclude he is a newfangled right-wing ideologue, whose views on Machiavelli need not be taken seriously by his fellow academicians, children of the Enlightenment and the political left. Or they will conclude that Strauss has done little more than confirm what they knew all along, that Machiavelli, a pre-*philosophe*, is a man made in our own image.

The scholarship of Felix Gilbert is a model of meticulous research, lucidity of argumentation, and effective methodology. To Gilbert's findings may be added those of Quentin Skinner, who has wisely adopted the intellectual procedure of Gilbert, the master of Machiavelli studies. Briefly put, that mode of investigation, which is ours as well, consists in situating Machiavelli historically within the tradition of the *studia humanitatis* and of measuring his originality by the extent to which he reworks that tradition. Our objection to Gilbert and Skinner is not that they have done anything wrong; it is that they have not realized the full significance of Machiavelli's rebellion against the humanists. The promise of their scholarship has yet to be fulfilled.

As long ago as 1939, Felix Gilbert published his brilliant essay on "The Humanist Concept of the Prince and *The Prince* of Machiavelli," demonstrating that what made Machiavelli's treatise on princely rule so provocative was its transformation of a Christian and humanist genre, the moralistic "mirror-of-princes" literature, into a platform for expounding the theses of power politics.[48] Ever since 1939 Machiavelli studies have cried out for an extension of this approach to the *Discourses* and other republican writings—something Gilbert has recognized is desirable[49] but which he, for all his many splendid contributions to our understanding of Renaissance political thought, has not undertaken.

Skinner's brief *Machiavelli* is Gilbert's approach applied to the *Discourses*, and in it Machiavelli figures—quite rightly—as a polemical author parodying and satirizing the writings of various Roman moralists. As always, Skinner's scholarship is impeccable, and no one will deny that he has written a useful and succinct account of Machiavelli's thought. It may be denied, however, that he has delivered the book promised in the opening pages. "Once we restore Machiavelli to the world in which his ideas were initially formed, we can begin to appreciate the extraordinary originality of his attack on the prevailing moral assumptions of his age,"[50] Skinner announces at the beginning of his book. At the end we are still waiting for the reading of Machiavelli that would give us an understanding of why Machiavelli has always been enlisted in the ranks of the greatest political thinkers. Enough of Machiavelli's vitality is placed on display so that he comes off as more than just one more Renaissance humanist and as no less a thinker than, say, James Harrington, an influential second-rater. But it is not at all clear why Skinner apparently accepts the widespread conviction that Machiavelli was a thinker of the highest intellectual caliber.

Anyone familiar with Skinner's essays on method will not be puzzled by the gap between his stated goal and his actual performance in *Machiavelli*. Against the textbook habit of supposing that the works of Plato, Machiavelli, or Hegel are the repositories of "perennial wisdom," Skinner has correctly responded that the questions a past thinker posed were not timeless, perennial questions but time-bound, historical questions, and that their purportedly "eternal" character rests on the fallacy of ripping the text out of context, using it as an authority when answering our present-day questions.[51] In short, Skinner has very ably criticized political theorists for not being historians. Lacking in his work, however, is a criticism of historians for not being political theorists: lacking is an adequate account of the theory-building resources of historical method; lacking also is an exposition of the conversations Machiavelli held not only with Italian humanists and ancient Roman authors but which he would gladly hold with us today if we but invited him to our studies as he once invited the ancients to his. To all intents and purposes, Skinner's Machiavelli is both minor and dead. Once upon a time Machiavelli spoke to his contemporaries and spoke in such a manner that he did not lose his individuality in the crowd of humanists. That is true but hardly the whole story. For if the humanitarian values of the Stoic tradition are the "foundation"* upon which "enlightened" modern ideologies are built, then Machiavelli has undermined us as well as his contemporaries by turning Stoicism into Machiavellism.

Another reason why Skinner's Machiavelli is not dangerous has

---

* It is worth noting that Skinner's study of the Renaissance bears the title *The Foundations of Modern Political Thought*.

to do with the notion, originally argued by Felix Gilbert, that Machiavelli satirized and parodied humanist literature. This is perfectly true and can be a very fruitful way of interpreting Machiavelli, as Gilbert proved in his famous article on *The Prince*. But in order to be as successful as they might, Gilbert and Skinner would first have to explain to the reader of today how powerful a thing satire once was. To us, unfortunately, "parody" suggests a mere playing with words, and "satire" a lighthearted criticism of persons and their follies. It was not always so—indeed, it was not so until quite recently. Gilbert and Skinner need to tell their audience what they take for granted: that satire has traditionally been much more than a literary device.[52]

In primitive societies—it has been observed—the satirist's words are thought literally to destroy, and sometimes do drive their victims to self-destruction.[53] In the advanced culture of classical Rome, satire was a highly developed art form, especially in the hands of Juvenal, a favorite of the Renaissance humanists and a frequent, directly cited presence in Machiavelli's writings.[54] Loathing, contempt, and disgust felt for a once-civic society reduced to a parade of pimps, haughty ex-slaves, vile and debauched women, homosexuals without shame, patrons without taste, Greeks without integrity, and soldiers without courage or discipline, fill the pages of Juvenal, who drove no one to suicide but left the lasting impression that Roman society in general was suicidal.[55]

Something of Juvenal's spirit may be detected in those passages of the *Florentine History* devoted to battlefield scenes and written in the elevated style of the humanists, but which terminate with the report that only one man died, and he from falling off his horse, or—in another instance—a total of three died, and they of suffocating in the mud.[56] Even more of Juvenal's caustic bite may be discerned in Machiavelli's insistence upon crediting the pathetic Ciompi with the wisdom in the ways of power politics that he denied was ever the glory of the Florentine ruling class (chapter III, above). In the largest sense it was thanks to Juvenal's lessons in satire that Machiavelli could be comfortable with the moralistic Roman vocabulary of virtue and corruption, so little in accord with his unpuritanical temperament.

More than this or that Florentine social or political practice was parodied by Machiavelli; more than Florentine society looked at in the large was parodied. Nothing less than humanism itself was parodied and satirized, as Gilbert and Skinner say but the full significance of which they fail to drive home. Whereas satirists had always taken vice and corruption as their targets, Machiavelli did that and much more; he made virtue, traditionally the hanging judge of satire, his special target. Christian and Stoic virtue, at his doing, are the novel objects of the satirist's contempt and derision; and if it is virtue that is still doing the denouncing, the virtue speaking with the voice of an aged Roman censor is a youthful and shocking Machiavellian virtue. Wielding the satirist's vocabulary of virtue and corruption, Machiavelli fashions a revolution, a transvaluation of values, in which what had been called virtue—Christian and Stoic virtue—is henceforth deemed corruption, and what had been considered vice—Machiavellian politics—becomes virtue.

It is because they give an incomplete account of the depth of Machiavelli's repudiation of Christianity that Gilbert and Skinner stop short of communicating what Machiavelli's "satires" ultimately mean: that the world-view composed of Christian and Stoic values is to be not simply criticized but actively crushed and replaced by an alternative world-view. Because they correctly accept the view of today's historians that the humanists were Christians despite their admiration of pagan antiquity, and that an older interpretation of the Renaissance as a pagan era is mistaken,[57] Gilbert and Skinner are wary to a fault of spelling out the extent of Machiavelli's paganism.

Skinner takes pains to show that while for the humanists pagan *virtus* and Christian virtue were interchangeable, Machiavelli set them at odds with one another when he demonstrated the self-defeating nature of Christian values applied to politics. At one point Skinner even refers to Machiavelli's "anti-Christian scale of values,"[58] but we are never told what the author of the *Discourses* proposed to do about the problem Christianity presented; moreover, Skinner phrases his remarks in such a manner that we are wrongly led to believe Machiavelli was perhaps troubled by his findings, that he continued to cling to Christian values and would have preferred a world in which they and political wisdom were one and the same.

Outside *The Prince*, a work satirizing a Christian genre, Felix Gilbert finds nothing in Machiavelli aimed at Christianity. Sometimes Professor Gilbert finds Christian sentiments in the *Discourses*, Machiavelli's most stridently pagan work, by mistaking republican for Christian moral judgments. For instance, Gilbert places a standard civic denunciation of luxury under the heading of a "Christian condemnation of the sin of covetousness; striving for wealth takes on the character of original sin."[59] More justifiably, he cites *Discourses* I, 26, in which Machiavelli states that particularly brutal acts are neither Christian nor humane (*umano*). This discourse taken in isolation would certainly imply that Machiavelli was a Christian facing up to the factual truths of power. In reality, however, *Discourses* I, 26, so frequently cited in justification of Machiavelli, is dramatically over-ridden by *Discourses* III, 27, where Machiavelli recommends the violence the Romans used against rebels and condemns "men's feebleness in our day, caused by their feeble education . . . [which] makes them judge ancient punishments . . . inhumane [*inumano*]." By "education" he means, of course, what he meant from the opening pages of the *Discourses* and throughout the entirety of that work, namely "religion," a word he uses interchangeably with "education."[60] Christianity, humanitarianism, weakness, and ignobility are one and the same in *Discourses* III, 27, and they contrast sharply with Rome's willingness to kill those who stood in the way of her glory. A strong, virtuous republic will mimic the Romans; "but because such decisive actions have in them something great and noble a weak republic cannot carry them out."[61]

No one should expect Machiavelli's language to be perfectly free of Christian usages—that would be asking him to have accomplished the impossible task of purging the cumulative effect of one-and-a-half millennia from his mind. Neither *Discourses* I, 26, nor any other "aside" proves Machiavelli was Christian, especially not when we take into account that in all the passages directly addressed to Christianity and strategically located in that commentary at the beginning of each of its three books, Machiavelli resoundingly denounced Christianity. At every privileged location in the *Discourses* he uncompromisingly condemned all Christianity, not just the corrupt Christianity of the papacy but Christianity in general, the religion that is corrupt even when renewed and restored to its original, pure message, the religion corrupt because deemed corrupt when forced to answer to pagan virtue, the only true virtue (chapters III and VI, above).

Anyone tempted to argue that for Machiavelli the rejection of Christianity was somehow hedging or forced upon him by the unfortunate facts of political life would do well to reread *Discourses* II, 2. There, Christian and pagan religion are placed side by side, compared and contrasted, for the purpose of heaping as much contempt upon Christianity as Machiavelli could muster. Christianity, he observes, is dear to those who suffer, yet it does nothing to alleviate our maladies; it is weak where paganism is strong; humble, small, and feeble where paganism is bold, great, and magnificent; delicate, mild, and passive where paganism is fierce, awesome, and domineering. Unlike paganism which seizes the world and makes for a history worth remembering, Christianity abdicates the world and condemns it to the use of the worst elements of the human kind, the prelates and corrupt politicians whose history is one of what to avoid and what to condemn. Unlike paganism, religion of manly men, doers of great deeds,

Christianity robs virtue of its virility and makes women of men. Machiavelli did not explain how the slavish Christians triumphed over the masterful pagans; he did not write the *Genealogy of Morals*—but he did juxtapose Christianity and paganism in terms even Nietzsche could not surpass. For both Machiavelli and Nietzsche the crux of history is the struggle of "Rome vs. Israel, Israel vs. Rome."[62]

It is of course true that in the eighteenth chapter of *The Prince* Machiavelli separates virtue from utility, "being" from "seeming," just as Christians do, before recommending a generous dose of "seeming" in politics and arguing for the political necessity of judging even the virtues in terms of their consequences. But given his lack of Greek and the demands of his rhetorical situation, this is only to be expected. Machiavelli had not the philological means of recovering the utterly un-Christian Greek moral vocabulary that fused virtue with result and sanctioned dissembling as an aspect of virtue; and he would not have used the Greek vocabulary even if he could, for then he would have spoken directly past his contemporaries (chapter VI, above). Better to start with the Stoic and Christian notions of virtue and then demonstrate their inadequacy; better to make of virtuosity in power politics the most indispensable virtue, than to suffer the self-defeating irrelevance of rendering oneself unintelligible and rhetorically impotent by being a perfect, pre-Stoical pagan. Machiavelli preferred reinterpreting the word "sin," making it mean an abdication of political responsibility, to losing a Christian sanction for un-Christian deeds. He deemed it preferable to destroy Christianity and Stoicism from within, where a powerful battle against them could be waged, to taking harmless slaps at them from without, where aggression could take no effect.[63]

Fated to address the religion he despised, Machiavelli could speak neither a post- nor a pre-Christian language. A paganism rebelling against many centuries of Christianity cannot be a paganism pure, simple, and naive. This is the lesson in Christian/

pagan polemics brought home by a study of Machiavelli's thought; but it is a lesson drastically misunderstood if we conclude that Machiavelli was, in spite of everything, still a Christian.

By now it should be obvious that the concept of satire, even if exploited to its full interpretive potential, cannot reveal what is most remarkable in Machiavelli's thought. The more the satirist's indignation reaches beyond an attack on certain persons, places, or things to a denunciation of society in general, the closer he moves to the literature *de contemptu mundi*, that is, to a contempt for the world so deeply felt that it must issue in resignation, quietism, and a disunity of theory and practice. By contrast, Machiavelli's condemnation of Christian civilization was total, yet he intended to unite theory and practice by a seizure of the papacy followed by a reinterpretation of Christian doctrine "according to *virtù*" instead of *ozio*. He intended, furthermore, to arm the rulers of Florence with a revised version of the humanist education that was already theirs; he proposed a humanism that would continue to take Rome as its authority but which would interpret the history of the immortal city according to *virtù*, not *ozio*—a *virtù* assured by a substitution of a Machiavellian for a Stoical reading of Roman deeds. With the people armed in a citizens' army, the rulers armed with Machiavellian ideology, and the papacy in bondage, there was no limit to the greatness that might await Florence, despite the lateness of the hour.

Who would dare say that what Feuerbach and Marx did to Hegel or what Nietzsche did to humanism and Christianity can be satisfactorily explained by saying they wrote satires? And yet we say this of Machiavelli when no less was at issue in his case than in theirs.

The illustrious name of Isaiah Berlin rounds out our survey of scholars who have attempted to discover Machiavelli's originality and significance by studying his writings in relation to classical and Christian thought. Berlin's interpretation, at once broadly conceived and well-controlled, ties Machiavelli both to the pagan and Christian traditions preceding his work and to the Christian and post-Christian thought of the centuries following his death. His is a Machiavelli who is neither historically dead and buried nor ripped out of context—a Machiavelli speaking to the ancients and to the moderns, yesterday's moderns and today's.

Congratulations are due Professor Berlin for disproving the notion that Machiavelli, a pagan, was troubled by the problems bedeviling modern liberals, heirs of a Christian past. One may well question, however, whether Berlin is correct in his contention that Machiavelli's unintended legacy to us is a lesson in liberalism. First he throws out the standard Machiavelli, then he restores it.

Berlin's thesis, briefly considered, is an antithesis to Croce's understanding of Machiavelli as a kind of early liberal moralist, a man anguished by the knowledge that ethics and politics mix poorly, and convinced damnation awaits him when he acts politically. In answer, Berlin notes that however troubled Croce may have been by the demon of power, Machiavelli's thought is singularly free of such anguish—free because Machiavelli did not, like a modern liberal, have to suspend morality in order to be Machiavellian; he simply had to assert the tenets of pagan morality, a social morality quite different from the personal morality of Christianity. Whatever favors the interests of the community is good in pagan morality; therefore, a pagan statesman is at peace with himself, no matter how Machiavellian his deeds, for he knows morality is on his side and that immortality, not damnation, awaits him. Confronted with two moralities, one Christian, one pagan, Machiavelli chose the latter and in so choosing was relieved of the problems of both Christian and liberal statesmen, political manipulators of persons born with souls or inalienable rights, or both.

So far we can find nothing to blame and much to praise in Berlin's formulations. It is the next phase of his argument that is objectionable. Having denied that Machiavelli suffered anguish, Berlin goes on to contend that Machiavelli causes us anguish by forcing a choice between two incompatible moralities, one oriented toward public life, institutional needs, and the demands of social existence, the other oriented toward individual personality, the desire for innocence, the yearning for a self untarnished by compromises struck with society. Less what Machiavelli meant than what he means to us is disturbing, for it is our lot to want both of these moralities when we can have only one. Machiavelli forces us to choose between two sets of ends, neither of which we wish to relinquish but both of which we cannot have, since they are mutually exclusive and irreconcilable. A perfect Christian or humanist is a political victim and so is his cause; a perfect politician, even a politician of the highest moral aspirations, is only half a moral person. Without realizing it, Machiavelli prepared this terrible recognition scene for us.[64]

"The Originality of Machiavelli" contains all the charm, wit, and vigorous intelligence that one associates with the name of Isaiah Berlin. Nevertheless, Berlin's explanation of Machiavelli's present-day significance is highly misleading, as is his portrayal of Machiavelli's connection to pagan and Christian thought. A much more provocative and violent thing than Berlin realizes, Machiavelli's paganism was designed to destroy part of the pagan tradition (Stoicism) and all of Christianity. Not the mutual coexistence of alternative moralities but the birth (or rebirth) of one world-view and the death of another was Machiavelli's intent—an intention quite incompatible with modern liberalism, the ideology of tolerance, pluralism, and compromise. Berlin forgets what he knows so well, that the postrevolutionary liberals Benjamin Constant[65] and Fustel de Coulanges[66] had no choice but to do everything in their power to bury Machiavelli, the ancients, and civic virtue. If Machiavelli forces a choice upon us, as Berlin suggests, it is between the compromising and compromised morality of liberals and the uncompromising morality of Machiavelli, the man who hated the middle way.

After asserting that Machiavelli cleanly separated pagan from Christian morality and chose the former, Berlin backslides and before long starts presenting a Machiavelli who opted for the middle way, especially where Christianity is concerned. "Words like *buono, cattivo, onesto, inumano* [good, bad, honest, inhumane], etc. are used by [Machiavelli] as they were in the common speech of his time, and indeed of our own,"[67] Berlin notes, and concludes that Machiavelli did not despise Christian values in and of themselves. It may be objected that words such as "good" and "honest" are also normal usage among pagan authors, and that these linguistic expressions therefore probably have less to do with Christianity than with the functional prerequisites of any and all societies, Christian, pagan or otherwise: no society is conceivable in which everyone is constantly dishonest and immoral.[68] Furthermore, "good," as Machiavelli uses the word, although superficially it may look Christian, is frequently only a way station on the road to *virtù*. Machiavelli admired the "good" men he observed in the German republics of his day and disdained the "bad" men of the Italian cities, because "good" men are the best materials from which to fashion "virtuous" citizens—virtuous in the pagan sense.[69]

When all is said and done, Berlin's Machiavelli is not so very different from Croce's on the issue of religion. "Machiavelli does not formally condemn Christian morality"; "he does not seek to correct the Christian conception of a good man"[70]—these and many similar statements coming from Berlin's pen sound like Croce in English translation, except that Croce's Machiavelli responds to the irrelevance of Christianity with bad humor, Berlin's with good humor. Croce's Machiavelli painfully brackets off Christian values when politicking; Berlin's Machiavelli, deeming Christian values politically inept, painlessly ignores them. The differences between these two images of Machiavelli are subtle and the similarities are obvious: neither Machiavelli is the author of the violent denunciation of Christian values found in *Discourses*

II, 2, of the attack in *Discourses* III, 1 on the contemptible weakness of original, reformed Christianity, or of the diatribe in the second book of the *Art of War* against Christianity, the religion responsible for the bloodless wars of modern times.

The fire and ice of Machiavelli's statements on Christianity are absent from the interpretation of Isaiah Berlin; also missing is the inversion and subversion of Latin literature that characterizes Machiavelli's thought—his device for turning Stoicism into Machiavellism. As treated by Berlin, "paganism" is a concept so monolithic, so undifferentiated, that it encourages the reader to conflate Plato's contemplative, Aristotle's gentlemanly, Cicero's Stoical, and Livy's militant republic. Equally disappointing, Berlin repeatedly writes sentences in which Machiavelli is placed side by side with Cicero, his fellow pagan and hence—it is implied—his friend.[71] Some three centuries ago James Harrington performed the transubstantiation of the satanic Machiavelli of the Elizabethans into a respectable figure fit for English consumption by confounding—in the same paragraph of *Oceana*—Machiavelli's thoughts on empire with Cicero's.[72] *De Officiis*, which Machiavelli had deliberately abused for his own subversive purposes, was mistakenly used by Harrington to make Machiavelli a neo-Ciceronian, and thus to rob him of much of what made his republican thought provocative. How frustrating it is to find in Isaiah Berlin a similarly revised Machiavelli.

Berlin's essay addresses the question of Machiavelli's relation to paganism and Christianity without so much as hinting at the Florentine's radical restructuring of the one or his radical attack on the other. We should not be surprised, then, if in spite of a promise that the radical nature of Machiavelli's challenge to us, today, will be accounted for, we in truth are offered a Machiavelli who is our solace and comfort. At first Berlin argues that Machiavelli teaches us, without intending to do so, the irreconcilability of ultimate values (e.g., Christian and pagan), the impossibility of rationally proving the superiority of one set of values over another—a bitter fruit for us to harvest from two-and-a-half millennia of Western philosophy. But is this really what troubles us in Machiavelli? Most of us long ago made our peace with the absence of moral certitude, so long ago that Machiavelli could hardly shock us if this were all his position implies. On second glance, Berlin himself is far from shocked, he is positively cheered, by the prospect of yet another illustration of the implausibility of a rationally demonstrable *summum bonum*—a point made in so many of his essays. Like many another liberal, Berlin has seen quite enough of moral certainty. "Such certainty is one of the great justifications of fanaticism, compulsion, persecution." On the other hand, once uncertainty is accepted as a fact of life "the path is open to empiricism, pluralism, toleration, compromise."[73] How can Berlin, the liberal, seriously claim to find Machiavelli shocking, when he makes his man an unwitting teacher of liberalism?

Two patterns are evident in the findings of those scholars who measure Machiavelli against the yardstick of pagan and Christian thought. Those who are historically specific in their research (Gilbert and Skinner) moderate Machiavelli's innovations vis-à-vis his intellectual predecessors and keep him locked up in the past, where he can do us no harm. Those who venture more generalized arguments sometimes seriously miscontrue (Strauss), sometimes lose altogether (Berlin), his highly innovative response to classical and Christian traditions, and annex him to our "enlightened" liberal ideology. In either pattern, he is a safe Machiavelli.

VIEWED in perspective, Berlin's essay is one more variation on the standard Machiavelli. It takes its place alongside the other variants—realism versus idealism, the end justifying the means, the autonomy of politics, the economy of violence, the argument from necessity—and shares with them the ideological tactic of removing Machiavelli from his status as a repulsive symbol in the Christian imagery of the Elizabethans, only to relocate and rehabilitate him as a sympathetic symbol in the mythology of liberalism and other humanistic creeds. Machiavelli, who complained so bitterly that Fortuna had dealt with him unfairly during his lifetime, would have even more reason to bemoan his fate, should the message ever be delivered to him in the underworld that among the living he is a servant of the values he denounced as debilitating, effeminate, and self-destructive. After spending a lifetime absorbing the imagery of Dante and Cicero into a vision of power politics, Machiavelli's reward is that his name has been reabsorbed, by the professors, into the "great tradition" of humanitarian ideologies, be they Stoical, Christian, enlightened, liberal, or Marxist.

To demythologize Machiavelli, to save him from his saviors, is to engage in an enterprise literally "radical," one that takes us to the "roots" of the Western tradition, to our very origins, upon which Machiavelli commented so memorably. It is to have our heritage usurped or identified as our nemesis. Compared to this, Marx's indictment of liberalism, even when that attack was at its most shrill, was an unthreatening experience—an occurrence that never left the familiar and friendly world of "humanism."

Few of us will feel cheated of what is ours by a rediscovery of Machiavelli's repudiation of Christianity; some will actually applaud his anti-Christian stand, thinking it a step toward enlightenment and humanism. However, almost all of us need feel the sting of his transformation of humanism into what we regard as anything but humanism. Machiavelli did this to the Romans, to his contemporaries, and he does it to us if we live up to our professed belief that all opinions must be heard, and heard in good faith.

There is a violence to Machiavelli's intellectual pronouncements running exactly parallel to the violence he saw as the central feature of politics—a violence pertaining to the realm of ideas,

even if those ideas are never put into practice. Political foundations, he insisted, are violent, as are all returns to the beginning,
all rededications to virtue; and the same is true of Machiavelli's
writings: they, too, are violent, they take the established symbols
of the classical tradition—the symbols common to all educated
persons through the French Revolution and still not dead today—
and transform them into something explosive, while all the time
continuing ostensibly to abide by the accepted intellectual tradition and, indeed, claiming that tradition as their sanction. As
a theorist of subversive methods, Machiavelli advised the politician to preserve the old names and symbols, even as he builds
a new world:[74] this is precisely what Machiavelli the political
theorist does with our cultural heritage, our foundations. He tries
to draw us into a position where every return to our cultural
foundations, every conversation with the ancients, is a resurrection of Machiavelli and Machiavellism.

It was our ancestors, we wish to believe, who constructed the
foundations of Western culture and then nurtured it as we still
nurture it today. Ancestor-worship is something that never goes
completely out of style; humanists of today, commonly enough,
do not rest content until they have made their humanism the
latest statement of a tradition reaching back to the Greek and
Roman classics. Tracing our pedigree continues to be a considerable comfort, as it already was in the days of Homer. For as
long, then, as there continues to be a desire for a noble genealogy
of our morals, the past will not die; and for that long too the
path will be open for radically disenchanted thinkers, whether
named Machiavelli or Nietzsche, to subvert our genealogy by
showing that those who stood at the beginnings were as noble,
strong, and terrible as we are ignoble, weak and domesticated.[75]

Historians can destroy Machiavelli, of course, by saying that
his reading of Rome was inaccurate, but then they destroy Livy's
Rome, too, which was equally mythical; worse, the historians,
if they attack Machiavelli on historical grounds, will be destroying

myth itself, the storehouse of those images and symbols without which there is no "great tradition" transmitted from generation to generation. Machiavelli can indeed be destroyed by the kind of history that, failing to appreciate how deeply an intellectual tradition rests on historical myths, leaves us with books "of historical interest only."

Our heritage, our culture, our values, myths, symbols, and images are what is at stake in a reading of Machiavelli that does not bury him in a dead past. He is admittedly *ours*, as those who make him just like us imply; only, it must be added, his being ours even though he challenges us to the core, makes him exceptionally subversive. He does not speak past us, from another culture; he does not offer one more "paradigm" in a world of incommensurable paradigms;[76] he cannot be disposed of by speaking of the diversity and riches of Western culture, or of a particular "moment" in history,[77] or of an ethical pluralism that—in a last stand of the Whig interpretation of history—teaches us tolerance and liberalism. He challenges us from within our world, in our language, wielding our myths to his own advantage; and the challenge he poses is total. Doubtless that is why the scholars are so eager to have the "great tradition" swallow and digest him.

NOTES

Chapter I

1. E.g., J. H. Whitfield, *Machiavelli* (New York, 1975), pp. 74-75: "The problem of the reconciliation of the *Prince* and the *Discorsi* is the prime problem in the examination of Machiavelli."
2. *Discorsi*, 1, 10.
3. *Discursus florentinarum rerum post mortem iunioris Laurentii Medices* in *Tutte le opere*, pp. 24-31.
4. The reputation of Machiavelli in Elizabethan England has been accounted for in various studies. For a brief but able and lively treatment see Mario Praz, "Machiavelli and the Elizabethans," *Proceedings of the British Academy*, 13 (1928), 49-97. A more extended investigation may be found in Felix Raab, *The English Face of Machiavelli* (London, 1964).
5. See Zera S. Fink, *The Classical Republicans* (Evanston, Ill., 1945) for an early study of Machiavelli and neorepublicanism; for a noteworthy recent study see J.G.A. Pocock, *The Machiavellian Moment: Florentine Political Thought and the Atlantic Republican Tradition* (Princeton, 1975).
6. Garrett Mattingly, *Renaissance Diplomacy* (Baltimore, 1964), p. 35. In "Machiavelli's *Prince*: Political Science or Political Satire?" *The American Scholar*, 27 (1958), 482-491, Mattingly argues that the intention of Machiavelli was to satirize princely rule.
7. James Harrington, *The Commonwealth of Oceana*, in *The Political Works of James Harrington*, ed. J.G.A. Pocock (Cambridge, 1977), p. 332. Fink's study pays proper attention to the link between republics and empire. *The Classical Republicans*, pp. 67, 80-83, 156, 172, 188. By and large the recent literature does not do so.
8. *Il Principe*, 3, 7.
9. Fredi Chiapelli, *Studi sul linguaggio del Machiavelli* (Florence, 1952); *Nuovi studi sul linguaggio del Machiavelli* (Florence, 1969); and *Machiavelli e la lingua fiorentina* (Bologna, 1974); J. H. Hexter, *The Vision of Politics on the Eve of the Reformation* (New York, 1973), Chs. 3-4; Whitfield, *Machiavelli*, Ch. 6, and *Discourses on Machiavelli* (Oxford, 1969), passim, but esp. Ch. 8.
10. Felix Gilbert, *Machiavelli and Guicciardini: Politics and History in Sixteenth-Century Florence* (Princeton, 1965).
11. Roberto Ridolfi, *The Life of Niccolò Machiavelli*, trans. Cecil Grayson (Chicago, 1963).
12. E.g., Giuseppe Prezzolini, *Machiavelli*, trans. Gioconda Savini (New

260 NOTES TO CHAPTER I

York, 1967); Felix Gilbert, "Machiavelli in Modern Historical Scholarship," *Italian Quarterly*, 14 (1970), 9-26 and "Machiavellism," *Dictionary of the History of Ideas*, ed. Philip P. Wiener (New York, 1973), 3:116-126.

13. Benedetto Croce, *Elementi di politica* (Bari, 1925), pp. 59-67. Cf. Federico Chabod, *Machiavelli and the Renaissance*, trans. David Moore (New York, 1965), pp. 116, 138, 140; Gennaro Sasso, *Niccolò Machiavelli: Storia del suo pensiero politico* (Naples, 1958), p. 291.

14. Maurice Merleau-Ponty, "A Note on Machiavelli," in *Signs*, trans. R. C. McCleary (Evanston, Ill., 1964), pp. 211-223.

15. Friedrich Meinecke, *Machiavellism: The Doctrine of Raison d'Etat and Its Place in Modern History*, trans. Douglas Scott (New York, 1965), Ch. 1. Carl J. Friedrich's argument that Machiavelli, since he was pagan rather than Christian, did not have to contend with a problem of reason of state, is an extension of Meinecke. *Constitutional Reason of State* (Providence, R.I., 1957), esp. pp. 65-66.

16. Isaiah Berlin, "The Originality of Machiavelli," in *Studies on Machiavelli*, ed. Myron P. Gilmore (Florence, 1972), pp. 147-206.

17. Meinecke, *Machiavellism*, p. 29.

18. Machiavelli to Francesco Vettori, 16 April 1527, no. 321 in *Tutte le opere*.

19. Francesco Guicciardini, *Considerazioni sopra i Discorsi del Machiavelli*, in *Scritti politici e Ricordi*, ed. R. Palmarocchi (Bari, 1933). Translated into English by C. and M. Grayson under the title *Considerations on the 'Discourses' of Machiavelli*, in *Selected Writings* (London, 1965), p. 92.

20. Jacob Burckhardt, *The Civilization of the Renaissance in Italy*, trans. S.G.C. Middlemore (New York, 1958), p. 229.

21. Hans Baron, *The Crisis of the Early Italian Renaissance* (Princeton, 1966); Eugenio Garin, *Italian Humanism: Philosophy and Civic Life in the Renaissance*, trans. Peter Munz (Oxford, 1965); Eugene F. Rice, Jr., *The Renaissance Idea of Wisdom* (Cambridge, Mass., 1958), Ch. 2. J. H. Whitfield, *Petrarch and the Renascence* (New York, 1943), also separates the humanists from the despots. However, he does so by arguing, in effect, for the autonomy of the intellectual realm vis-à-vis politics, whereas Baron, Garin, and Rice point to republican humanists. See the first chapter of Whitfield's study.

22. Quentin Skinner has argued against Hans Baron that civic ideology existed long before the events in and around 1400. *The Foundations of Modern Political Thought: The Renaissance* (Cambridge, 1978). For our purposes the important question is not when did "civic humanism" emerge, but what is "civic humanism"?

23. Baron, *Crisis*, pp. 387-403.

24. *Istorie Fiorentine*, IV-VI.

25. Ibid., III, 25.

26. Ibid., VII, 19.

27. Baron, *Crisis*, p. 14; cf. Burckhardt, *Civilization*, p. 107.

28. *Discorsi*, II, 2.

29. Ibid., I, 58.

30. Baron, *Crisis*, p. 402.

31. *Istorie Fiorentine*, IV, 19. Note that Machiavelli believed the social structure of Lucca made a republican government natural to her. *Discorsi*, I, 55.

32. Paul Oskar Kristeller, *Renaissance Thought: The Classic, Scholastic, and Humanist Strains* (New York, 1961), pp. 111, 121.

33. Ibid., p. 139; cf. Whitfield, *Petrarch and the Renascence*: "Humanism as it developed from Petrarch to Valla and Alberti establishes an attitude which remained valid in Europe, *mutatis mutandis*, until the French Revolution," p. 165.

34. Neal Wood, "Machiavelli's Humanism of Action," in *The Political Calculus: Essays on Machiavelli's Philosophy*, ed. Anthony Parel (Toronto, 1972), Ch. 2.

35. Joseph A. Mazzeo, *Renaissance and Revolution* (New York, 1965), Ch. 3, has subtitled his essay on Castiglione, "The Self as a Work of Art."

36. Castiglione, *Il libro del Cortegiano* (Milan, 1972), IV, 27. Translated by Charles S. Singleton under the title *The Book of the Courtier* (New York, 1959).

37. *Arte della Guerra*, end of Book II.

38. *Istorie Fiorentine*, V, 1.

39. Donald J. Wilcox's *The Development of Florentine Humanist Historiography in the Fifteenth Century* (Cambridge, Mass., 1969) is valuable as a corrective to Burckhardt's denigration (*Civilization*, p. 247) of the historical writings of the humanists. But since Wilcox's work is in the mold of Hans Baron, it largely omits the topic of imperialism. Neither the imperialism of Machiavelli nor that of Bruni or of the humanists in general has been adequately treated in the interpretive literature.

40. *Istorie Fiorentine*, e.g., II, 6, 15; III, 29.

41. Giovanni Villani, *Cronica* (Florence, 1844-45), VIII, 36. My translation.

42. Ibid., XI, 92-94.

43. Lewis Coser, "Ideology and Conflict," Ch. 6 of *The Functions of Social Conflict* (New York, 1956).

44. Burckhardt, *Civilization*, pp. 117-118.

45. Garin, *Italian Humanism*, pp. 43-45; Skinner, *Foundations*, pp. 56, 74; F. Gilbert, *Machiavelli and Guicciardini*, pp. 92, 151-152.

46. Jerrold E. Seigel, *Rhetoric and Philosophy in Renaissance Humanism* (Princeton, 1968), p. 253. See also Ernst Robert Curtius, *European Literature and the Latin Middle Ages*, trans. Willard R. Trask (Princeton, 1953), "Outdoing," pp. 162-165.

47. Villani, *Cronica*, XI, 92. My translation.

48. See the opening sentences of Bruni's *Historiarum Florentini Populi*. The translation is by Renée Neu Watkins, *Humanism and Liberty: Writings on Freedom from Fifteenth-Century Florence* (Columbia, S.C., 1978), p. 27.

49. Quoted by Baron, *Crisis*, pp. 377-378.

50. On the contrast of the medieval city of traders with the ancient community of warriors see Max Weber, *The City*, trans. Don Martindale and Gertrud Neuwirth (New York, 1958).

51. The chronicler Enrico Dandolo, comments Eric Cochrane, "sought to demonstrate the folly of imperialism and the superiority of merchant ships, which made money, to warships, which cost money." *Historians and Historiography in the Italian Renaissance* (Chicago, 1981), p. 64.

52. Baron, *Crisis*, pp. 183-184. A useful complement to Baron's account of Dati may be found in Louis Green, *Chronicle into History: An Essay on the Interpretation of History in Florentine Fourteenth-Century Chronicles* (Cambridge, 1972), Ch. 4.

53. *Istorie Fiorentine*, preface.

54. Ibid.: "Nella guerra che si fece contro a Filippo Visconti duca di Milano, avendo a fare esperienzia della industria e non delle armi propie, perché le avieno in quelli tempi spente. . . ."

55. F. Gilbert, *Machiavelli and Guicciardini*, p. 129.

56. Ibid., p. 151.

57. Lauro Martines, *Power and Imagination: City-States in Renaissance Italy* (New York, 1979), pp. 174-175, has noted the emergence of political classes in the fifteenth century and an increasing tendency after mid-century to "put political and business careers in opposition." We may draw the inference that the anticommercial "prophets of force" of Machiavelli's period were not created overnight.

58. Baron, *Crisis*, pp. 390-391.

59. The most subtle and sophisticated example of this style of reasoning is C. B. Macpherson, *The Political Theory of Possessive Individualism: Hobbes to Locke* (Oxford, 1962).

60. See Albert O. Hirschman, *The Passions and the Interests: Political Arguments for Capitalism before its Triumph* (Princeton, 1977). I have argued elsewhere that Montesquieu was a particularly striking example of a humanist who used economic thought to tame the heroic ethic. *Montesquieu and the Old Regime* (Berkeley, 1976).

61. Alfred von Martin, *Sociology of the Renaissance* (New York, 1963), pp. 65-70. This book, in its employment of the concept of the *Zeitgeist*, is in the tradition of Hegel. But since von Martin understands the *Zeitgeist* of the Renaissance as an expression of the interests of the bourgeoisie, he is also deeply indebted to Marxist thought.

62. Sheldon Wolin, *Politics and Vision* (Boston, 1960), Ch. 7.

63. Herbert Butterfield, *The Statecraft of Machiavelli* (New York, 1962), p. 76.

64. Castiglione, *Book of the Courtier*, II, 8.

65. Livy, *History*, VIII, 7; *Discorsi*, II, 16; III, 34.

66. This is the message of the *Arte della Guerra*.

67. Hannah Arendt, *The Human Condition* (Chicago, 1958), esp. Ch. V.

68. E.g., Skinner, *Foundations*, pp. 86-89.
69. Quoted by Garin, *Italian Humanism*, p. 56.
70. Sallust, *The War with Catiline*, trans. J. C. Rolfe (Cambridge, Mass., 1965), VIII.
71. M. L. Clarke, *The Roman Mind* (New York, 1968), p. 35.
72. Livy, *History*, trans. Henry Bettenson (Baltimore, 1976), XXXI, 44.
73. Ibid., VII, 32 (my translation); *Discorsi*, III, 38.
74. *Arte della Guerra*, end of Book IV.
75. *Discorsi*, I, 16.
76. Michael Walzer, *Regicide and Revolution* (Cambridge, 1974), p. 28.
77. *Il Principe*, 18.
78. Allan H. Gilbert, *Machiavelli's Prince and Its Forerunners* (Durham, N.C., 1938).
79. Felix Gilbert, "The Humanist Concept of the Prince and *The Prince* of Machiavelli," *The Journal of Modern History*, 11 (December, 1939), 449-483.
80. *Il Principe*, 15. In this instance I have not followed Allan Gilbert's translation.
81. J. R. Hale, *Machiavelli and Renaissance Italy* (New York, 1960), p. 30.
82. Skinner, *Foundations*, pp. 180-186.
83. *Discorsi*, I, 4.
84. Ibid., I, 6: "Quelle inimicizie che intra il popolo ed il senato nascessino, tollerarle, pigliandole per uno inconveniente necessario a pervenire alla romana grandezza."
85. In Livy, Machiavelli's chief source on the Roman republic, the notion of war as a diversion from internal conflict is a recurring theme. E.g., *History*, II, 28, 32; IV, 1, 58. Cf. *Discorsi*, I, 6.
86. See his rendering of Roman history in the first book of his *Historiarum Florentini Populi*.
87. *Discorsi*, I, 6.
88. Baron, *Crisis*, pp. 144, 314.
89. Butterfield, *Statecraft*, p. 44.
90. Pocock, *The Machiavellian Moment*, pp. 217-218.
91. Neal Wood, "Machiavelli's Concept of *Virtù* Reconsidered," *Political Studies*, 15 (June 1967), 159-172, p. 170; "Introduction" to *The Art of War*, trans. Ellis Farnsworth (New York, 1965).
92. The notion of a hidden message has been propounded by Leo Strauss in *Thoughts on Machiavelli* (Seattle, Wash., 1969). In the same vein is Harvey C. Mansfield, Jr., *Machiavelli's New Modes and Orders* (Ithaca, N.Y., 1979).
93. On glory see Russell Price, "The Theme of *Gloria* in Machiavelli," *Renaissance Quarterly*, 30 (Winter 1977), 588-641.
94. The literature on Machiavelli's uses of the word *virtù* is voluminous. I shall cite only a few articles. Neal Wood, "Machiavelli's Concept of *Virtù* Reconsidered" (already cited in note 91); I. Hannaford, "Machiavelli's Concept of *Virtù* in *The Prince* and *The Discourses* Reconsidered," *Political Studies*, 20

(1972), 185-189; John H. Geerken, "Homer's Image of the Hero in Machiavelli: A Comparison of *Areté* and *Virtù*," *Italian Quarterly*, 14 (1970), 45-90; Russell Price, "The Senses of *Virtù* in Machiavelli," *European Studies Review*, 3 (1973), 315-345; John Plamenatz, "In Search of Machiavellian *Virtù*," in *The Political Calculus*, ed. Parel.

95. Cicero, *De Officiis*, I, 16. 50.

96. Ibid., I, passim.

97. Ibid., trans. Harry G. Edinger (Indianapolis, 1974), III, 6. 28.

98. *La Vita di Castruccio Castracani da Lucca*, in *Tutte le opere*, p. 626.

99. *Discorsi*, II, 2.

100. *Tusculan Disputations*, trans. J. E. King (Cambridge, Mass., 1950), II, 18. 43.

101. *Discorsi*, III, 10.

102. Ibid., II, 2.

103. Ibid., II, preface: "Sarò animoso in dire manifestamente quello che io intenderò di quelli e di questi tempi; acciocché gli animi de' giovani che questi mia scritti leggeranno, possino fuggire questi, e prepararsi ad imitar quegli, qualunque volta la fortuna ne dessi loro occasione." Cf. *Discorsi*, I, 33, 46, 60. Several speakers in the dialogue *Dell'Arte della Guerra* are young men.

104. Aristotle, *Nicomachean Ethics*, I, 3.5.

105. *Il Principe*, 25.

106. *Discorsi*, II, 2.

107. Ibid.

108. Friedrich Nietzsche, *Beyond Good and Evil*, trans. Walter Kaufmann (New York, 1966), Pt. 2, no. 43.

109. The only work in which Machiavelli does not speak of "the common good" is, significantly, *Il Principe*.

110. Cf. John Neville Figgis, *Political Thought from Gerson to Grotius, 1414-1625* (1907; reprint ed., New York, 1960), p. 110: "It is impossible to understand Machiavelli without comparing him with Nietzsche whose *Uebermensch* is but Machiavelli's man of *virtù* stripped of those public ends which make even Cesare Borgia less odious."

Chapter II

1. *Discorsi*, I, 9.

2. Ibid., III, 17.

3. Ibid., I, 2; *Arte della Guerra*, I, p. 311.

4. *Discorsi*, I, 58.

5. Ibid., I, 20.

6. Ibid., I, 58; III, 34.

7. Ibid., I, 29.

8. Ibid., I, 58.

9. Ibid., I, 30.
10. Ibid., II, 2.
11. Ibid., I, 58. My translation. Allan Gilbert is not wrong to translate "il bene commune" and "il bene proprio" in terms of "property," but the context calls, I think, for a distinction between public and private interest.
12. *Il Principe*, 5.
13. *Arte della Guerra*, II, p. 332.
14. *Discorsi*, I, 20. Cf. Livy's long digression comparing the Roman leaders favorably to Alexander the Great. *History*, IX, 17-19.
15. *Discorsi*, II, 2.
16. Ibid., I, 43.
17. *The Complete Essays of Montaigne*, trans. Donald M. Frame (Stanford, 1958), II, 7. Cf. Aristotle, *Politics*, trans. Ernest Barker (New York, 1962), 1279a-1279b: "It is possible for one man, or a few, to be of outstanding excellence; but when it comes to a large number, we can hardly expect a fine edge of all the varieties of excellence. What we can expect particularly is the military kind of excellence, which is the kind that shows itself in a mass."
18. *Discorsi*, II, 2.
19. Ibid.
20. Polybius, *Histories*, VI, 11-18; *Discorsi*, I, 2. For a noteworthy treatment of Polybius, see Kurt von Fritz, *The Theory of the Mixed Constitution in Antiquity* (New York, 1954).
21. *Discorsi*, I, 3-6.
22. Ibid., I, 2, 34.
23. Ibid., I, 17, 55.
24. Ibid., I, 37.
25. Ibid., I, 22, 24.
26. Ibid., I, 51.
27. Ibid., III, 25; *Arte della Guerra*, V, p. 360.
28. *Discorsi*, III, 25; II, 7.
29. *Arte della Guerra*, I, p. 307.
30. *Discorsi*, II, 18.
31. *Arte della Guerra*, II, p. 326. "Perché lo esercito animoso non lo fa per essere in quello uomini animosi, ma lo esservi ordini bene ordinati. . . ."
32. Livy, *History*, VIII, 7; *Discorsi*, II, 16; III, 34.
33. *Discorsi*, II, 25.
34. Sallust, *The War with Catiline*, VII.
35. Castiglione, *The Book of the Courtier*, II, 8.
36. *Discorsi*, III, 28; cf. Francesco Guicciardini, *Ricordi* (Milan, 1951), second series, 32: "La ambizione non è dannabile, né da vituperare quello ambizioso che ha appetito d'avere gloria co' mezzi onesti ed onorevoli; anzi sono questi tali che operano cose grande ed eccelse. . . ."
37. *Discorsi*, I, 2.
38. Ibid., III, 25. My translation.

39. Aristotle, *Politics*, 1283b and throughout the third book; 1332b.
40. *Discorsi*, III, 25; I, 36.
41. Ibid., I, 60.
42. Ibid., III, 29; II, 18; *Arte della Guerra*, II, p. 321.
43. Meinecke, *Machiavellism*, p. 32.
44. *Il Principe*, 6.
45. Ibid., 17; *Discorsi*, I, 3, 9, 29, 37; II, preface.
46. *Discorsi*, I, 47.
47. Ibid., I, 58.
48. Ibid., I, 44.
49. Ibid., I, 5; *Il Principe*, 9.
50. *Il Principe*, 6, 9, 26; *Arte della Guerra*, VII, p. 388; *Discorsi*, I, 11, 16-18, 35, 45, 55; III, 8.
51. *Discorsi*, I, 1, 11; *Il Principe*, 2, 7.
52. *Arte della Guerra*, VII, p. 388.
53. Cf. Charles S. Singleton, "The Perspective of Art," *The Kenyon Review* 15 (Spring 1953), 169-189.
54. *Discorsi*, I, 11-14; *Arte della Guerra*, IV, p. 354; VI, p. 370; VII, p. 388.
55. Machiavelli ranks the founders of religion even higher than the founders of republics. *Discorsi*, I, 10.
56. Ibid., II, 9.
57. Machiavelli did not understand that to Livy *fortuna* meant destiny, not chance or accident. In his own quasi-religious way, Livy believed as strongly as Machiavelli that Roman empire was inevitable.
58. *Discorsi*, II, 1.
59. Ibid., I, 29.
60. Ibid., II, 2.
61. Polybius, *Histories*, trans. W. R. Paton (Cambridge, Mass., 1966 and 1967), VI, 2; I, 1.
62. *Discorsi*, I, 4, 6.
63. Ibid., I, 6.
64. Ibid., II, 19.
65. Ibid., II, 3.
66. Ibid, I, 6.
67. Ibid., II, 24.
68. Ibid., II, 3.
69. Ibid., III, 31; *Arte della Guerra*, I, p. 312.
70. Felix Gilbert, "Bernardo Rucellai and the Orti Oricellari: A Study on the Origin of Modern Political Thought," *The Journal of the Warburg and Courtauld Institutes*, 12 (1949), 101-131; and "The Venetian Constitution in Florentine Political Thought," in *Florentine Studies*, ed. Nicolai Rubinstein (London, 1968), pp. 463-500.
71. *Discorsi*, I, 5.
72. Ibid., I, 36.
73. Ibid., I, 55.

74. Polybius, *Histories*, VI, 7-8; *Discorsi*, I, 2.
75. *Discorsi*, II, 19.
76. Ibid., I, 6; *Istorie Fiorentine*, I, 29.
77. *Arte della Guerra*, I, p. 312.
78. Aristotle, *Politics*, 1294b; Polybius, *Histories*, VI, 11.
79. Rarely does a city run the full Polybian cycle of regimes, returning to one-man rule. Its usual fate is to be conquered during one of its periods of corruption, whether under tyrannical, oligarchical, or democratic rule. *Discorsi*, I, 2.
80. Ibid., II, 17.
81. Ibid., II, 6.
82. *Il Principe*, 5.
83. Ibid., 3.
84. *Discorsi*, II, 1; cf. *Discorsi*, II, 6 and *Il Principe*, 3.
85. *Discorsi*, I, 27, 30; III, 27.
86. *Il Principe*, 8.
87. *Discorsi*, I, 26, 30; II, 23.
88. Ibid., II, 23.
89. Ibid., II, 19. The Romans were "sanza alcuno esemplo."
90. Ibid., II, 32.
91. Ibid., II, 4.
92. Ibid., II, 13.
93. Ibid., I, 2.
94. Ibid., II, 2.
95. *Il Principe*, 15.
96. *Discorsi*, II, 2, the opening sentence.
97. Ibid.; *Arte della Guerra*, II, p. 332.
98. *L'Asino*, Ch. 5.
99. *Discorsi*, II, 19.
100. See Chapter II, note 36.
101. Cf. the tears shed by Marcellus for Syracuse. Livy, *History*, XXV, 24.
102. *Arte della Guerra*, II, p. 332.
103. Plato, *Republic*, 423; Aristotle, *Politics*, 1324b-1327a; 1333b-1334b.
104. *Discorsi*, I, 37; II, 19; III, 24, 49.
105. Bossuet and Montesquieu, who for their different reasons were out to refute Machiavelli in his own terms, made the causal link between expansion and corruption that Machiavelli shied away from. See Hulliung, *Montesquieu and the Old Regime*, Ch. 6.
106. *Discorsi*, I, 6.
107. Ibid., II, 8; III, 16.
108. Ibid., II, 9, 19, 23.
109. Ibid., I, 6.
110. For a different view see Giorgio Barberi Squarotti, *La forma tragica del 'Principe' e altri saggi sul Machiavelli* (Florence, 1966).
111. Maurice Merleau-Ponty, *Humanism and Terror*, trans. John O'Neill

(Boston, 1969), pp. 24, 62, 64, 66 on the problem of dirty hands as the rebirth of tragedy.

Chapter III

1. See Machiavelli's letter of 9 March 1498 to Ricciardo Becchi, no. 3 in *Tutte le opere*, for a skeptical view of Savonarola. A more charitable estimate of the prophet's significance may be found in the *Discorsi*, I, 11, 45. See also Donald Weinstein, "Machiavelli and Savonarola," in *Studies on Machiavelli*, ed. Gilmore, pp. 251-264.

2. *Il Principe*, 6.

3. *Discorsi*, I, 52.

4. Machiavelli to a lady, post 16 September 1512, no. 195 in *Tutte le opere*.

5. *Discorsi*, III, 30.

6. Ibid., III, 3.

7. Ibid.

8. *Discorso fatto al magistrato dei dieci sopra le cose di Pisa* in *Tutte le opere*, pp. 3-5.

9. E.g., *Il Principe*, 13, 20; *Discorsi*, I, 38; II, 24; III, 16, 27, 48.

10. *Del modo di trattare i popoli della Valdichiana ribellati* in *Tutte le opere*, pp. 13-16.

11. *Discorsi*, II, 23; III, 27.

12. On merchants as diplomats see Chabod, *Machiavelli and the Renaissance*, pp. 60-61. Machiavelli would not agree with Chabod's statement that "merchants . . . were diplomats by nature."

13. For some discerning comments on Machiavelli in office see Felix Gilbert, "L'ambiente politico fiorentino tra il '400 e il '500," *Terzo Programma*, 10 (1970), 7-15.

14. F. Gilbert, *Machiavelli and Guicciardini*, pp. 33-34 on the expressions commonly used in Florentine political circles. Machiavelli explicitly denounces the Florentine adage "to profit from the help of time" and contrasts it with ancient Roman practice in *Il Principe*, 3.

15. *Istorie Fiorentine*, I, 39; III, 1.

16. *Decennale Primo* in *Tutte le opere*, p. 950.

17. *Arte della Guerra*, II, pp. 332-333.

18. *Discorsi*, preface.

19. Ibid., III, 1.

20. For a succinct account of the conventions of humanist historiography see F. Gilbert, *Machiavelli and Guicciardini*, Ch. 5.

21. *Istorie Fiorentine*, V, 1.

22. Allan Gilbert translates "questo guasto mondo" as "this corrupt world." Since Machiavelli does not here, as elsewhere, use the adjective "corrotto," I have substituted the term "wasted." Also possible are "spoiled," "tainted," "marred."

23. Machiavelli to Francesco Vettori, 16 April 1527, no. 321 in *Tutte le opere*.
24. *Istorie Fiorentine*, II, 6.
25. Ibid., II, 15.
26. Ibid., III, 29.
27. Ibid., II, 6.
28. Ibid., preface.
29. Ferdinand Schevill, *History of Florence* (New York, 1936), passim.
30. *Istorie Fiorentine*, V, 1.
31. For a denunciation of petty Machiavellism in the *Arte della Guerra*, see *Tutte le opere*, VII, p. 388.
32. *Discorsi*, II, 13.
33. *Istorie Fiorentine*, III, 11.
34. *Discorsi*, I, 55.
35. Ibid., III, 1.
36. Ibid., I, 55.
37. Cf. Machiavelli's comment in *Il Principe*, 4, that feudal monarchies suffer invasion fostered by their own unruly nobles.
38. *Istorie Fiorentine*, III, 1.
39. Ibid., II, 11-12, 22.
40. Ibid., II, 17.
41. Ibid., II, 2-10.
42. Ibid., II, 11-15.
43. Cf. Weber, *The City*, pp. 153-154.
44. *Istorie Fiorentine*, III, 5.
45. Ibid., IV, 9.
46. Ibid., IV, 7-14.
47. Ibid., IV, 1.
48. Ibid., II, 33.
49. Ibid., II, 34-35.
50. Ibid., II, 36; *Il Principe*, 17, 19; *Discorsi*, III, 26.
51. *Istorie Fiorentine*, II, 36.
52. Ibid.
53. Tacitus, *Histories*, trans. Clifford H. Moore (Cambridge, Mass., 1952), I, 16: "You are going to rule over men who can endure neither complete slavery nor complete liberty."
54. Note the theme of *Discorsi*, I, 25: "Chi vuole riformare uno stato anticato in una città libera, ritenga almeno l'ombra de' modi antichi."
55. *Istorie Fiorentine*, VII, 1.
56. Ibid., VIII, 8.
57. *Discorsi*, III, 28; *Istorie Fiorentine*, VII, 1-2.
58. *Discorsi*, III, 1.
59. *Istorie Fiorentine*, II, 38.
60. Ibid., II, 39.
61. Ibid., III, 5.

62. Thucydides, *Peloponnesian War*, III, 82-83.
63. Sallust, *The War with Catiline*, LII.
64. *Discorsi*, I, 11; *Arte della Guerra*, IV, p. 354; VI, p. 370.
65. *Istorie Fiorentine*, III, 5.
66. Ibid.
67. Ibid.
68. Ibid., IV, 7.
69. Ibid., II, 18, 40; III, 2, 14.
70. *Discorsi*, I, 30.
71. *Istorie Fiorentine*, III, 17.
72. Eric Cochrane has noted Bruni's reluctance to deal with the Ciompi episode. *Historians and Historiography in the Italian Renaissance*, p. 6.
73. Curtius, *European Literature and the Latin Middle Ages*, pp. 94-98.
74. *Istorie Fiorentine*, III, 13; *Il Principe*, 8.
75. *Istorie Fiorentine*, III, 13; *Discorsi*, I, 2; III, 25.
76. *Istorie Fiorentine*, III, 13; *Il Principe*, 3.
77. *Il Principe*, 7.
78. *Istorie Fiorentine*, III, 13; *Il Principe*, 15.
79. *Istorie Fiorentine*, III, 13; *Arte della Guerra*, V, p. 359.
80. *Istorie Fiorentine*, IV, 6; cf. V, 33.
81. Ibid., II, 25. My translation.
82. *Discorsi*, preface; I, 39; III, 43.
83. Felix Gilbert has argued that the *Istorie Fiorentine*, if finished, would probably have given expression to the hope, based on notions of cyclical history, that better times were ahead for Florence. "Machiavelli's *Istorie Fiorentine*: An Essay in Interpretation," in *Studies on Machiavelli*, ed. Gilmore, pp. 75-99. Gilbert's interpretation is aimed against the view that the *Istorie Fiorentine* is a work of despair.
84. *Arte della Guerra*, I, p. 304.
85. *Discursus florentinarum rerum post mortem iunioris Laurentii Medices* in *Tutte le opere*, pp. 24-31.
86. Tacitus, *Histories*, IV, 8.
87. See the discussion of Machiavelli's uses of Tacitus in Kenneth C. Schellhase, *Tacitus in Renaissance Political Thought* (Chicago, 1976), Ch. 4.
88. *Arte della Guerra*, VII, p. 389.
89. E.g., *Istorie Fiorentine*, III, 25; V, 5.
90. *Discorsi*, I, 12.
91. Ibid., II, 4.
92. For an antidote to the nineteenth-century view, consult Felix Gilbert, "The Concept of Nationalism in Machiavelli's *Prince*," *Studies in the Renaissance*, I (1954), 38-48.
93. Whitfield, *Machiavelli*, p. 70.
94. Machiavelli to Francesco Guicciardini, 17 May 1526, no. 299 in *Tutte le opere*.
95. Guicciardini, *Considerations on the 'Discourses' of Machiavelli*, p. 81.

96. F. Gilbert, *Machiavelli and Guicciardini*, pp. 105-115.

97. "When the Rucellai, the Vettori, the Guicciardini write about the fifteenth century as the lost paradise . . . , what else are they doing but drawing from the fact of the victory of the foreigners the conclusion that a national policy, a policy of cooperation among the Italian powers, could have been successful . . . ?" F. Gilbert, "The Concept of Nationalism in Machiavelli's *Prince*," p. 46.

98. Machiavelli to Francesco Vettori, 10 August 1513, no. 211 in *Tutte le opere*.

99. *Il Principe*, 11.

100. Ibid., 20.

101. On Vettori the power politician, see F. Gilbert, *Machiavelli and Guicciardini*, pp. 249-250.

102. *Istorie Fiorentine*, VII, 23.

103. Francesco de Sanctis, *History of Italian Literature*, trans. Joan Redfern (New York, 1931), p. 573.

Chapter IV

1. Alessandro Parronchi, "La prima rappresentazione della 'Mandragola,' " 64 (1962), 37-86; Theodore Sumberg, " 'La Mandragola': An Interpretation," *Journal of Politics*, 23 (1961), 320-340.

2. See J. R. Hale's introduction to *The Literary Works of Machiavelli* (Oxford, 1961) for a plea that Machiavelli's plays and letters be treated as works of art rather than as material to be ransacked for political content.

3. *Discorso o dialogo intorno alla nostra lingua* in *Tutte le opere*, p. 929.

4. *Clizia*, prologue.

5. *Discorso o dialogo*, p. 929; Marvin T. Herrick, *Italian Comedy in the Renaissance* (Urbana, Ill., 1966), p. 21.

6. *Discorsi*, III, 6; *Mandragola*, I, 1.

7. *Discorsi*, I, 26.

8. On the morality of social roles in classical thought see Alasdair MacIntyre, *A Short History of Ethics* (New York, 1966), Ch. 2. His work draws heavily upon the writings of A.W.H. Adkins, especially *Merit and Responsibility: A Study in Greek Values* (Oxford, 1960). For a recent restatement of the morality of social roles, see Dorothy Emmet, *Rules, Roles and Relations* (Boston, 1975).

9. *Mandragola*, I, 1.

10. *Clizia*, II, 4.

11. Marvin T. Herrick, *Comic Theory in the Sixteenth Century* (Urbana, Ill., 1964), p. 131.

12. Cf. Henri Bergson, *Le rire* (Paris, 1940).

13. Hobbes, *Leviathan*, Chs. 11, 13.

14. The notion that the Renaissance witnessed the birth of the individual was central to Jacob Burckhardt's splendid study, *The Civilization of the Ren-*

aissance in Italy, and has remained influential ever since. On the notion of a switch in Machiavelli's thought from a medieval theory of a *corpus immobile* (motionless body) to a modern theory of a *corpus vorans* (devouring body) see Wolin, *Politics and Vision*, Ch. 7. Pierre Mesnard also stresses perpetual change as characteristic of Machiavelli's conception of the world. *L'essor de la philosophie politique au XVI' siècle* (Paris, 1969), Ch. 1.

15. *Mandragola*, I, 3.

16. Hale, *Machiavelli and Renaissance Italy*, pp. 22-23: "Sins of the flesh he comprehensively condoned. Sexual faithfulness was not considered by him, nor by his nearest friends, as a necessary part of marriage; infidelity impaired neither duty nor affection. . . . Man's inclinations became wrong when they threatened the welfare of the state as a whole. . . ."

17. Machiavelli to Francesco Vettori, 10 December 1513, no. 216 in *Tutte le opere*.

18. *Arte della Guerra*, I, p. 302.

19. Machiavelli to Francesco Guicciardini, post 21 October 1525, no. 291 in *Tutte le opere*.

20. I cannot agree with Giorgio Barberi Squarotti's contention that Machiavelli treated matters of theory in the sublime style, matters of practice in the comic style. "Il Machiavelli fra il 'sublime' della contemplazione intellettuale e il 'comico' della prassi," *Lettere Italiane*, 21 (1969), 129-154. The choices Machiavelli made between the high and the low styles were dictated by subject matter—affairs of state being treated in the sublime style, affairs of the heart in the comic style. Such was the normal view in classical thought.

21. For a stimulating discussion of Ovid and courtly love see C. S. Lewis, *The Allegory of Love* (Oxford, 1936), Ch. 1.

22. Aldo D. Scaglione, *Nature and Love in the Late Middle Ages* (Berkeley, 1963), convincingly develops this interpretation of Boccaccio.

23. Ibid., p. 81.

24. See, e.g., the stories of the fourth day of the *Decameron*.

25. Machiavelli to Francesco Vettori, 31 January 1515, no. 239 in *Tutte le opere*.

26. See note 103 in Chapter I (above).

27. *Clizia*, prologue.

28. *Mandragola*, IV, 9.

29. *Clizia*, I, 2.

30. Ovid, *Amores* I, 9. 1-20.

31. Herrick, *Italian Comedy in the Renaissance*, Ch. 5.

32. Johan Huizinga, *Homo Ludens* (Boston, 1955), p. 12.

33. *Clizia*, I, 2.

34. Huizinga, *Homo Ludens*, p. 11.

35. Ibid.

36. Ibid., p. 8.

37. In ancient Roman comedy, adulterous wives were a forbidden topic. The neo-Roman comedy of the Renaissance, which drew heavily upon Boccaccio for

its stories, frequently dealt with women committing adultery. Douglas Radcliff-Umstead, *The Birth of Modern Comedy in Renaissance Italy* (Chicago, 1969), pp. 33-35, 46, 64, 242.

38. Machiavelli to Luigi Guicciardini, 8 December 1509, no. 170 in *Tutte le opere*. Trans. J. R. Hale, *The Literary Works of Machiavelli* (Oxford, 1961).

39. Machiavelli to Francesco Vettori, 3 August 1514, no. 230 in *Tutte le opere*.

40. Note the date of Machiavelli's letter to Luigi Guicciardini, cited above in note 38: December 8, 1509, which is to say, during the period of his public service to the Florentine republic.

41. Francesco Vettori to Machiavelli, 16 January 1515, no. 238 in *Tutte le opere*. My translation.

42. Machiavelli to Francesco Vettori, 5 January 1514, no. 219 in *Tutte le opere*.

43. *La Vita di Castruccio Castracani da Lucca*, p. 627 in *Tutte le opere*.

44. George Eckel Duckworth, *The Nature of Roman Comedy* (Princeton, 1952), Ch. 6.

45. *Clizia*, prologue.

46. *Mandragola*, I, 2.

47. Ibid., I, 3.

48. Ibid., II, 4.

49. Aristotle, *Poetics*, 1448a.

50. *Mandragola*, IV, 1.

51. Ibid., III, 1.

52. Ibid., III, 10.

53. Ibid., III, 4.

54. Ibid., III, 2.

55. Ibid., III, 11.

56. Ibid., III, 9.

57. Ibid., IV, 6.

58. Ibid., V, 4.

59. Ibid., V, 2.

60. *Clizia*, IV, Canzone.

61. Herrick, *Italian Comedy in the Renaissance*, p. 81; Squarotti, *La forma tragica del 'Principe' e altri saggi sul Machiavelli*, p. 67.

62. *Mandragola*, IV, 4.

63. Plautus, *The Ghost* in *The Rope and Other Plays*, trans. E. F. Watling (Baltimore, 1964), p. 52.

64. De Sanctis, *History of Italian Literature*, p. 576: "Not a single incident in this play arises from chance."

65. Quoted by Herrick, *Comic Theory in the Sixteenth Century*, p. 73.

66. *Discorsi*, III, 35; *Istorie Fiorentine*, IV, 7; VIII, 22.

67. De Sanctis, *History of Italian Literature*, Ch. 15.

68. There are only two references to adultery in the *Discorsi*, and they add up to very little (I, 10, 18). "Come per cagione di femine si rovina uno stato,"

III, 26, is not concerned with adultery. Rather, its aim is to warn political rulers against the folly of forcibly seizing other men's women.

69. *Clizia*, I, I.

70. Machiavelli to Francesco Vettori, 31 January 1515, no. 239 in *Tutte le opere*.

71. Erich W. Segal, *Roman Laughter* (New York, 1971), gives a systematic and delightful statement of this view.

72. Herrick, *Comic Theory in the Sixteenth Century*, passim.

73. *Il Principe*, 15.

74. Segal, *Roman Laughter*, Ch. 5.

75. *Mandragola*, V, 4.

76. Ibid., V, 6.

77. *Arte della Guerra*, I, p. 315; II, pp. 323-324.

78. Ibid., I, p. 308; cf. p. 306.

79. Ibid., VI, p. 370.

80. Castiglione, *Il libro del Cortegiano*, IV, 51-73.

81. On court politics as sexual politics see Walzer, *Regicide and Revolution*, p. 33.

82. Castiglione, *Il libro del Cortegiano*, III, 51.

83. Leon Battista Alberti, *I libri della famiglia*, translated into English by Guido A. Guarino under the title *The Albertis of Florence* (Lewisburg, Penn., 1971), p. 138.

84. Ibid., p. 110.

85. Ibid., pp. 51, 109.

86. Ibid., pp. 108, 110.

87. Elizabeth Rawson, *The Spartan Tradition in European Thought* (Oxford, 1969).

88. *Arte della Guerra*, I, p. 304.

89. Although Machiavelli believed nature is "variable," he also thought nothing more common than for human personality to rigidify. E.g., *Discorsi*, III, 9. Perhaps this is why he describes Lorenzo de Medici's combination of political prudence with lovemaking as a rare union of two different persons in one man. *Istorie Fiorentine*, VIII, 36. Or perhaps his position in this late passage is simply inconsistent with his earlier statements on the connections between human nature, politics and love.

Chapter V

1. See the discerning comments of Eugenio Garin on Petrarch's understanding of the significance of conversation. *Italian Humanism*, Ch. 1.

2. Machiavelli to Francesco Vettori, 10 December 1513, no. 216 in *Tutte le opere*.

3. Plato, *Republic*, 347. Plato set forth several arguments urging the phi-

losopher to accept political office, none of which—it may be argued—was thoroughly convincing.

4. See the tenth book of the *Nicomachean Ethics*.

5. Cicero, *De Officiis*, I, 6. 19; I, 20-21; I, 43. 153; III, I. 1.

6. Sallust, *The War with Catiline*, III. 2.

7. E.g., *Lettere*, nos. 242, 247, 248 in *Tutte le opere*.

8. *Il Principe*, 20.

9. Polybius, *Histories*, XII, 28. 2-3.

10. *Discursus florentinarum rerum post mortem iunioris Laurentii Medices* in *Tutte le opere*, pp. 30-31.

11. *Il libro del Cortegiano*, IV, 47-48.

12. Polybius, *Histories*, VI, 47. 7-10.

13. Livy, *History*, trans. Frank Gardner Moore (Cambridge, Mass., 1950), XXVI, 22.

14. *Il Principe*, 15.

15. E.g., Plato, *Laches*, 182e; Aristotle, *Politics*, 1271b. Rawson, *The Spartan Tradition in European Thought*, Ch. 5.

16. On the similarity of Machiavellian *virtù* to ancient pagan virtue see Geerken, "Homer's Image of the Hero in Machiavelli: A Comparison of *Areté* and *Virtù*."

17. *Discorsi*, I, 10.

18. *Istorie Fiorentine*, V, 1.

19. Tacitus, *Annals*, trans. John Jackson (Cambridge, Mass., 1937), IV, 32.

20. Augustine, *City of God*, III, 9.

21. Aristotle, *Politics*, 1279a-1279b.

22. Polybius, *Histories*, VI, 5.5-9.11.

23. *Discorsi*, I, 2.

24. Polybius, *Histories*, VI, 12.

25. Plato, *Republic*, 414-415.

26. Polybius, *Histories*, VI, 56. 6-15.

27. Aristotle, *Politics*, 1280a; 1289b-1293a; 1304b-1306b.

28. Von Fritz, *The Theory of the Mixed Constitution in Antiquity*, pp. 30, 74, 333.

29. Ibid., p. 339.

30. Aristotle, *Politics*, Bks. VII-VIII.

31. "To the Greeks," writes M. L. Clarke, "freedom meant an equal sharing of the management of the affairs of the city; for the Romans it was rather the enjoyment by the individual of certain rights." *The Roman Mind* (New York, 1968), p. 14. Polybius initiated the new turn of thought when he designated punishment as the bond of society and stressed the importance of contracts. *Histories*, VI, 14. 3-5 and VI, 17.

32. Aristotle, *Politics*, 1282b.

33. See the discussion of the emergence of justice and law in *Discorsi*, I, 2. Note also that Machiavelli showed not the slightest interest in the myth that all Roman law was a clarification of the original Twelve Tables. Continuity is

accounted for, in his thought, by periodic "renewals," noteworthy for their violence.

34. Plato, *Republic*, 571. Trans. Jowett.

35. Exceptionally interesting on the Oedipus myth, its transformation from Homer to Sophocles, and the social and psychological reasons underlying this transformation is E. R. Dodds, *The Greeks and the Irrational* (Berkeley, 1966), Ch. 2. He does not deal with Plato's use of Oedipus, however.

36. Plato, *Republic*, 548.

37. Ibid., 551.

38. Dante Germino has argued that "the psyche for Machiavelli can best be represented as a horizontal field of conflicting drives rather than, as for Plato, a hierarchical ordering of faculties. . . ." See his essay "Machiavelli's Thoughts on the Psyche and Society" in *The Political Calculus*, ed. Parel, Ch. 3, esp. pp. 80-81. I am inclined to the contrary view that Machiavelli simply lost Plato's psychological insights and lacked sufficient psychological penetration to offer an alternative. I agree with Isaiah Berlin's comment on Machiavelli: "His psychology is often excessively primitive." See Berlin's essay "The Originality of Machiavelli," p. 199.

39. In Plato's thought this tyrant is the monster of dream life become the factual reality of politics. Typically, Roman thought lost sight of this psychological conception while retaining Plato's equation of democracy with tyrant-breeding anarchy.

40. It is misleading to refer to Sallust as an advocate of "Roman radicalism"—an unfortunate expression used by Charles Norris Cochrane in his admirable *Christianity and Classical Culture* (Oxford, 1940), p. 17. Sallust's point was not that the nobles should be denied positions of leadership, but rather that their ranks should remain forever open to those *novi homines* (self-made men) who merited political promotion. See D. C. Earl, *The Political Thought of Sallust* (Cambridge, 1961), Ch. 3.

41. Sallust, *The War with Catiline*, VIII. 2–IX.

42. Livy, *History*, trans. B. O. Foster (Cambridge, Mass., 1948), VIII, 22. 8; cf. XXXI, 44. 3.

43. Ibid., XXXVI, 15. For the Greek eulogy of Thermopylae see Herodotus, *The Persian Wars*, VII, 202-229.

44. For an interpretation of Thucydides' *History of the Peloponnesian War* as an historical rendering of the themes of Greek tragic drama, see the exceptional book of F. M. Cornford, *Thucydides Mythistoricus* (London, 1907).

45. Polybius, *Histories*, VI, 51. 3–52. 4.

46. Ibid., II, 56.

47. "As a people, the Romans lacked a tragic sense of life." Herbert J. Muller, *The Spirit of Tragedy* (New York, 1965), p. 114.

48. M.L.W. Laistner, *The Greater Roman Historians* (Berkeley, 1966), p. 95. P. G. Walsh, *Livy: His Historical Aims and Methods* (Cambridge, 1961) notes

that Livy downplayed evidence of Roman savagery, p. 101. Thus Livy both made Rome less evil than she was and her enemies more evil than they were.

49. E.g., *Istorie Fiorentine*, V, 11.

50. Machiavelli to Francesco Vettori, 26 August 1513, no. 214 in *Tutte le opere*.

51. Only in *The First Decade*, which tells the story of Florentine and Italian reverses during the first ten years of foreign invasion, does Machiavelli's face approach the expression found on the mask of tragedy.

52. Sallust, *The War with Jugurtha*, XLI; Polybius, *Histories*, VI, 18; XXXI, 25; XXXII, 13.

53. *Discorsi*, I, 18; III, 16.

54. Laistner, *The Greater Roman Historians*, p. 131.

55. Tacitus, *Annals*, IV, 33.

56. *Discorsi*, I, 16, 19, 58; III, 1. *Il Principe*, 19. *Ritratto di cose di Francia* in *Tutte le opere*, pp. 55-63.

57. *Il Principe*, 4.

58. Machiavelli to Francesco Vettori, 10 August 1513, no. 211 in *Tutte le opere*.

59. Machiavelli to Francesco Vettori, 10 December 1514, no. 233 in *Tutte le opere*.

60. Machiavelli to Francesco Vettori, 10 August 1513, no. 211 in *Tutte le opere*.

61. Francesco Vettori to Machiavelli, 20 August 1513, no. 212 in *Tutte le opere*.

62. Machiavelli to Francesco Vettori, 26 August 1513, no. 214 in *Tutte le opere*.

63. Ernst Cassirer, *The Myth of the State* (New Haven, 1963), p. 154.

64. E.g., Leonardo Olschki, *Machiavelli the Scientist* (Berkeley, 1945), p. 58.

65. E.g., Wood, "Machiavelli's Humanism of Action," p. 34.

66. Plato, *Republic*, 562-570; 573-580. Aristotle, *Politics*, 1313a-1314a.

67. *Il Principe*, dedication; *Discorsi*, dedication.

68. *Discorsi*, preface to the first book.

69. See Frank Manuel, *Shapes of Philosophical History* (Stanford, 1965) and Karl Löwith, *Meaning in History* (Chicago, 1949).

70. Polybius, *Histories*, VI, 9. 10-12. An explicit comparison of political to seasonal change is made by Tacitus, *Annals*, III, 55.

71. *Discorsi*, I, 39.

72. *Arte della Guerra*, III, p. 343.

73. See Myron P. Gilmore, "The Renaissance Conception of the Lessons of History," in *Humanists and Jurists: Six Studies in the Renaissance* (Cambridge, Mass., 1963), Ch. 1.

74. Guicciardini, *Ricordi*. Translated into English by Mario Domandi under the title *Maxims and Reflections of a Renaissance Statesman* (New York, 1965), C, 110.

75. Garin, *Italian Humanism*, is an influential example of the view that the Renaissance was an important step toward the development of historicist thought.

76. Guicciardini, *Maxims and Reflections*, B, 114.

77. Nevertheless, modern historians looking for the seeds of historicism have found some of them in Guicciardini. E.g., F. Gilbert, *Machiavelli and Guicciardini*; Pocock, *The Machiavellian Moment*; Vittorio De Caprariis, *Francesco Guicciardini: dalla politica alla storia* (Bari, 1950). Their arguments are persuasive if Guicciardini is viewed from historical hindsight, a perfectly justifiable procedure. My point is that Guicciardini never consciously abandoned the classical subsumption of history under the category of nature. We are fascinated with the way in which circumstances pushed his naturalism toward historicism; he was not.

78. Guicciardini, *Maxims and Reflections*, C, 35.

79. Ibid., C, 9.

80. E.g., *Il Principe*, 3.

81. Guicciardini, *Maxims and Reflections*, B, 35. Cf. Herbert Butterfield's remarks on "The Machiavellism of the Study" in *The Statecraft of Machiavelli* (New York, 1962), Pt. 3, Ch. 3.

82. Guicciardini, *Maxims and Reflections*, B, 61.

83. Sydney Anglo, *Machiavelli* (New York, 1969), pp. 244-249.

84. Guicciardini, *Maxims and Reflections*, C, 182.

85. Mattingly, *Renaissance Diplomacy*, Ch. 26.

86. E.g., *Lettere*, nos. 204, 205, 211, 214, 233, 235, 294, 296 in *Tutte le opere*.

87. *Il Principe*, 25.

88. *Discorsi*, II, 1.

89. Guicciardini, *Maxims and Reflections*, C, 136. In one of his last letters a frustrated Machiavelli complained that "it is no marvel if in a crazy time the crazy come out well." This is not the mood of his major works. Rather, it is a momentary note of exasperation. Machiavelli to Francesco Guicciardini, 5 November 1526, no. 315 in *Tutte le opere*.

90. Boccaccio, *Decameron*, II, 9; III, 5; VIII, 7, 10; IX, 8.

91. Guicciardini, *Considerations on the 'Discourses' of Machiavelli*, p. 77.

92. Ibid., p. 101.

93. Ibid., pp. 110-112.

94. Ibid., p. 89.

95. Ibid., p. 114.

96. Ibid., p. 101.

97. Ibid., p. 113.

98. Ibid., p. 82.

99. Ibid., p. 113.

100. Ibid., p. 92.

101. Guicciardini, *Maxims and Reflections*, C, 48; B, 95.

102. Ibid., C, 107.

103. *Discorsi*, II, 2.

104. Vettori shared with Guicciardini an acceptance of power politics as a fact of life. See note 101 in Chapter III (above).

105. Guicciardini, *Maxims and Reflections*, C, 114.

106. Friedrich Nietzsche, *The Use and Abuse of History*, trans. Adrian Collins (Indianapolis, 1957), p. 14. A more literal translation of *Vom Nutzen und Nachteil der Historie für das Leben* is *The Advantage and Disadvantage of History for Life*.

107. Georges Sorel, *Reflections on Violence*, trans. J. Roth and T. E. Hulme (New York, 1961).

108. Polybius, *Histories*, I, 1. 2.

Chapter VI

1. *Discorsi*, preface.

2. Seigel, *Rhetoric and Philosophy in Renaissance Humanism*, Ch. 8.

3. E. Cochrane, *Historians and Historiography in the Italian Renaissance*, p. 17.

4. On antiquarian history see Nietzsche, *The Use and Abuse of History*, pp. 17-20.

5. Alberti, *The Albertis of Florence*, p. 30.

6. Ibid., p. 265.

7. Leonardo Bruni, *Laudatio Florentinae urbis* in Hans Baron, *From Petrarch to Leonardo Bruni* (Chicago, 1968), pp. 245, 256, 258.

8. Ibid., p. 244: "Quamobrem ad vos quoque, viri Florentini, dominium orbis terrarum iure quodam hereditario ceu paternarum rerum possessio pertinet."

9. Seigel, *Rhetoric and Philosophy in Renaissance Humanism*, Ch. 8.

10. Ibid.

11. *Discorsi*, dedication.

12. F. Gilbert, "Bernardo Rucellai and the Orti Oricellari: A Study on the Origins of Modern Political Thought," p. 127. The limited power of chancellors in general, humanists or not, has been noted by Nicolai Rubinstein, "Machiavelli and the World of Florentine Politics," in *Studies on Machiavelli*, ed. Gilmore, pp. 3-28, esp. pp. 8-9.

13. E. Cochrane, *Historians and Historiography in the Italian Renaissance*, pp. 9, 116, 221-222.

14. Seigel, *Rhetoric and Philosophy in Renaissance Humanism*, Ch. 8.

15. F. Gilbert, *Machiavelli and Guicciardini*, p. 129.

16. Nietzsche, *The Use and Abuse of History*, p. 15.

17. Ibid., p. 16.

18. Weber, *The City*.

19. F. Gilbert, *Machiavelli and Guicciardini*, pp. 151-152.

20. *Clizia*, II, 4.

21. E.g., Hale, *The Literary Works of Machiavelli*, pp. xxi-xxii.

22. See Segal, *Roman Laughter*, pp. 53-56.

23. See J. H. Hexter, *Reappraisals in History: New Views on History and Society in Early Modern Europe* (New York, 1963). For the claim by a scholar of our day that "classical societies were to some extent market societies" see Macpherson, *The Political Theory of Possessive Individualism*, p. 67. The difficulty with Macpherson's statement is that the concept of a "market society," applied to most everything on either side of the Middle Ages, becomes the night in which all cows are black.

24. *Clizia*, prologue.

25. R. M. Ogilvie, *Roman Literature and Society* (New York, 1980), p. 29, observes that the scenes of Plautus "are not confined to Athens but take place in a universal city which comprises the Roman, Greek and Carthaginian worlds equally."

26. On abstraction in Machiavelli's comedies see Squarotti, *La forma tragica del 'Principe' e altri saggi sul Machiavelli*, pp. 43-103.

27. *Istorie Fiorentine*, I, 5.

28. Ibid., I, 9, 23.

29. On the violence of despots and the instability of despotic regimes, see Burckhardt, *Civilization*, Pt. 1, Chs. 1-4. The conspiracies, poisonings, and assassinations discussed by Sallust and Tacitus encouraged Machiavelli to conflate ancient and Renaissance politics.

30. Note the comment of Francesco de Sanctis: "Here is the whole basis of Machiavelli's speculations: the corruption of the Italian race, indeed of the Latin race, and the healthfulness of the Germanic race." *History of Italian Literature*, p. 541.

31. "If he went to France with Caesar, he went to Germany with Tacitus." Ridolfi, *The Life of Niccolò Machiavelli*, p. 103. See Caesar, *Gallic War*, Bk. VI and Tacitus, *Germania*. For a modification of Ridolfi's statement see Schellhase, *Tacitus in Renaissance Political Thought*, p. 67.

32. *Discorsi*, III, 43.

33. Francesco Guicciardini to Machiavelli, 18 May 1521, no. 263 in *Tutte le opere*.

34. On foundation in Roman thought see Hannah Arendt, "What is Authority?" in *Between Past and Future* (New York, 1963), Ch. 3.

35. Especially in *L'Asino*.

36. *Discorsi*, I, 9.

37. *Il Principe*, 2: "E nella antiquità e continuazione del dominio sono spente le memorie e le cagioni delle innovazioni. . . ."

38. Machiavelli to Giovan Battista Soderini (?), 13-21 September 1506 (?), no. 116 in *Tutte le opere*; cf. *Discorsi*, III, 9.

39. *Art of Love*, end of the first book.

40. The essential work is Curtius, *European Literature and the Latin Middle Ages*.

41. The essential work is Erich Auerbach, *Mimesis: The Representation of Reality in Western Literature*, trans. Willard R. Trask (Princeton, 1953).

42. See *Discorsi*, I, 24, for Machiavelli's subordination of the family to the city.

43. Of interest but mistaken, in my opinion, is Peter E. Bondanella's contention that Machiavelli mixed styles. The principal evidence in support of his argument is the letter of Machiavelli to Vettori, 31 January 1515, no. 239 in *Tutte le opere*, half of which treats sex and seduction, half politics and public life. Yet even here the evidence overwhelmingly indicates that Machiavelli held the literary standards of the Latin classics sacred: he self-consciously divided his letter in two and apologized for discussing love and politics in the same letter. Machiavelli did indeed believe what he asserted in this letter, that variable Nature sanctioned a life moving back and forth between love and politics. But as a literary artist Machiavelli always treated these two activities separately, and as a moralist he rank-ordered politics above love—in good classical fashion. Peter E. Bondanella, *Machiavelli and the Art of Renaissance History* (Detroit, 1973), p. 130.

44. Mazzeo, *Renaissance and Revolution*, Ch. 3.

45. Burckhardt's formula of "the state as a work of art," although modified by historical research showing that the *Signorie* were the end result of a gradual historical development, remains accurate as a designation of Machiavelli's view of the state.

46. See notes 50-53 in Chapter II (above).

47. Ridolfi, *The Life of Niccolò Machiavelli*, p. 210.

48. Machiavelli to Francesco Vettori, 10 December 1513, no. 216 in *Tutte le opere*.

49. See especially the stories of the fourth day of the *Decameron*.

50. Radcliff-Umstead, *The Birth of Modern Comedy in Renaissance Italy*, is useful on the question of audience.

51. Martines, *Power and Imagination*, p. 185.

52. Nicia is very impressed by the nonsensical words spoken by Callimaco in Latin. *Mandragola*, II, 2.

53. Burckhardt, *Civilization*, Pt. 2, Ch. 4.

54. *Mandragola*, prologue.

55. Castiglione, *Il libro del Cortegiano*, II, 57, 83.

56. Ibid., II, 13.

57. Johan Huizinga, *Men and Ideas*, trans. James S. Holmes and Hans van Marle (New York, 1970), p. 291: "The folk tale does not admonish to virtue and lament vice, but relates successful 'tricks.' "

58. *Discorsi*, III, 25.

59. Plamenatz, "In Search of Machiavellian *Virtù*," suggests Machiavelli shows us "only a part of life," p. 176.

60. I agree with the words of Ernst Cassirer: "However paradoxical it may sound, we must say that in this case our own modern historical sense has blinded

us and prevented us from seeing the plain historical truth. Machiavelli wrote not only for Italy nor even for his own epoch, but for the world. . . ." *The Myth of the State* (New Haven, 1946), p. 126.

61. *De Officiis*, I, 29. 103-104.

62. On humanist historiography see F. Gilbert, *Machiavelli and Guicciardini*, Ch. 5; E. Cochrane, *Historians and Historiography in the Italian Renaissance*, passim; and Wilcox, *The Development of Florentine Humanist Historiography in the Fifteenth Century*.

63. As Eric Cochrane has noted. *Historians and Historiography in the Italian Renaissance*, p. 6.

64. Baron, *Crisis*, pp. 61-64.

65. *Discorsi*, I, 1, 49; *Istorie Fiorentine*, II, 2.

66. *Discorsi*, I, 1.

67. Ibid., II, 1. This may be a case of using one classical author against another, Polybius against Plutarch. "The progress of the Romans," wrote Polybius, "was not due to chance and was not involuntary, as some among the Greeks choose to think, but . . . by schooling themselves in such vast and perilous enterprises it was perfectly natural that they not only gained the courage to aim at universal dominion, but executed their purpose." *Histories*, I, 63.

68. Tacitus, *Annals*, III, 65.

69. For an examination of the slippery term "realism" see Johan Huizinga, "Renaissance and Realism" in *Men and Ideas*, pp. 288-309. Note particularly the following comment: "The language of Joinville or Villani was, in the final analysis, more realistic than that of Machiavelli, however realistic the thought of the latter may have been," p. 301.

70. "Have not all readers of Machiavelli felt how his heroes have no inside?" Singleton, "The Perspective of Art," p. 180.

71. Walsh, *Livy*, calls attention to "the fortune of the Roman people—a conception which has no connotation of chance, but has a close connection with the Stoic destiny," p. 95. Cf. p. 50 on the Stoic coloring of virtually all Roman historiography.

72. E.g., Livy, *History*, IV, 31-32; V, 27, 36.

73. Ibid., XXXIII, 30, 33; XXXIV, 32, 41, 58; XXXVI, 17, 34; XXXVII, 35; XXXIX, 25; XLV, 18.

74. *Il Principe*, 5.

75. As students of Roman historiography have repeatedly noted. E.g., Walsh, *Livy*, p. 223; Laistner, *The Greater Roman Historians*, p. 71.

76. *De Officiis*, III, 4. 18.

77. Ibid., III, 12. 49-50.

78. *Discorsi*, II, 4, 13.

79. *De Officiis*, III, 3. 11; III, 11. 49.

80. *Il Principe*, 18.

81. Compared to the original Stoic position, Cicero's effort to merge the honorable with the useful may be viewed as a step in the direction of Machiavelli.

See Marcia Colish, "Cicero's *De Officiis* and Machiavelli's *Prince*," *Sixteenth Century Journal*, 11 (1978), 81-93. Yet Machiavelli's position should not be viewed as an incremental development, but as a radical departure, a subversion of Cicero's writings. See Felix Gilbert, "The Humanist Concept of the Prince and *The Prince* of Machiavelli," for proof that the humanists both prepared the way for Machiavelli and served as his target.

82. Livy, *History*, v, 27; *Discorsi*, iii, 20.
83. Livy, *History*, ix, 20; *Discorsi*, ii, 21, 25.
84. *Il Principe*, 18.
85. See Livy, *History*, i, 53, on Roman deceit as un-Roman.
86. Sallust, *The War with Catiline*, xi; *The War with Jugurtha*, iv.
87. *The War with Catiline*, x.
88. Ibid., liv.
89. Quoted by Skinner, *Foundations*, p. 47.
90. Alberti, *The Albertis of Florence*, p. 305.
91. Ibid., p. 145.
92. *Il Principe*, 18. Cf. Sallust, *The War with Catiline*, v.
93. *Discorsi*, ii, 13.
94. Xenophon, *Cyropaedia*, trans. J. S. Watson and Henry Dale (London, 1855), i, 6. 27.
95. Ibid., i, 6. 22.
96. Guicciardini, *Considerations on the 'Discourses' of Machiavelli*, p. 113: "I have not Xenophon quite fresh in my memory, but I think he instructs Cyrus in prudence and industry . . . but not in fraud."
97. Livy, *History*, trans. B. O. Foster (Cambridge, Mass., 1948), ix, 11. Cf.: xxxiv, 23, 49; xxxv, 44, 46; xxxvi, 41; xxxvii, 25; xlii, 52; xliv, 24.
98. Ibid., xxiv, 38. My translation.
99. Ibid., xlii, 11. My translation.
100. Curtius, *European Literature and the Latin Middle Ages*, pp. 85-86. F. Gilbert, *Machiavelli and Guicciardini*, p. 158n.
101. "I am ready to take the man by force, not by fraud," says Neoptolemus. He then asks Odysseus "You think it no shame . . . to speak falsehoods?", and receives the reply, "No, if the falsehood brings deliverance." Sophocles, *Philoctetes*, in *The Complete Plays of Sophocles*, trans. Richard Claverhouse Jebb (New York, 1967).
102. Virgil, *Aeneid*, trans. W. F. Jackson Knight (Baltimore, 1956), ii, 390.
103. *Discorsi*, ii, 4, 13.
104. *Istorie Fiorentine*, vi, 17.
105. Ibid., vi, 29.
106. D. C. Earl notes that in Sallust the concept of *virtus* is not restricted to one field of activity or to one social class. *The Political Thought of Sallust*, p. 31.

107. "Neither *areté* nor *virtù* is tied to any one kind of action, but can characterize every activity. It is not *what* is done that is designated by *areté* and *virtù*, or *who* does it, but *how* it is done." Geerken, "Homer's Image of the Hero in Machiavelli: A Comparison of *Areté* and *Virtù*," p. 48.

108. A.W.H. Adkins, *Moral Values and Political Behavior in Ancient Greece* (New York, 1972).

109. MacIntyre, *A Short History of Ethics*, p. 90.

110. F. Gilbert, "The Humanist Concept of the Prince and *The Prince* of Machiavelli," 449-483.

111. *Arte della Guerra*, II, p. 321; *Discorsi*, II, 18.

112. *Discorsi*, III, 29. Felix Gilbert notes that the Florentines regarded internal conflict as the fruit of "sins." *Machiavelli and Guicciardini*, p. 36.

113. Francesco de Sanctis sees in other writers of the Renaissance "a complete divorce between the man and the writer"; but not in Machiavelli. *History of Italian Literature*, p. 558.

114. Allan Gilbert's translation of "che hanno interpretato la nostra religione secondo l'ozio, e non secondo la virtù" as "who have interpreted our religion according to sloth and not according to vigor" is unfortunate since it obscures the classical terminology that is critical for understanding this very vital passage.

115. *Il Principe*, 26.

116. *Discorsi*, III, 30.

117. Ibid., I, 19.

118. Ibid., I, 26.

119. *Prima legazione alla corte di Roma*, 30 in *Tutte le opere*, p. 518.

120. *Il Principe*, 25; *Discorsi*, I, 27; III, 9, 44.

121. Machiavelli thought it possible that nepotism would transform the papacy into a hereditary monarchy. *Istorie Fiorentine*, I, 23.

122. Machiavelli to Francesco Vettori, 20 June 1513, no. 205 in *Tutte le opere*.

123. *Discorsi*, I, 12; *Istorie Fiorentine*, I, 23.

124. *Discorsi*, III, 1.

125. Ibid., I, 12.

126. Burckhardt, *Civilization*, Pt. 2, Ch. 3.

127. *Istorie Fiorentine*, VI, 29; VII, 27, 32.

128. Alberti, *The Albertis of Florence*, p. 145.

129. *Discorsi*, I, 27.

130. Dante, *Inferno*, VI, XVI.

131. *Discorsi*, I, 10.

132. *Istorie Fiorentine*, III, 7.

133. Max Weber, "Politics as a Vocation," in *From Max Weber: Essays in Sociology*, ed. H. H. Gerth and C. Wright Mills (New York, 1958), p. 126.

134. Machiavelli to Francesco Guicciardini, 16 April 1527, no. 321 in *Tutte le opere*.

135. *Mandragola*, IV, 1.

136. Ridolfi, *The Life of Niccolò Machiavelli*, pp. 249-250. Many scholars take this story seriously, and no one takes seriously the story—an eighteenth-century fabrication—that Machiavelli died a pious death. See Eugenia Levi, "Nota su di un falso Machiavelliano," *Pensiero Politico*, 2 (1969), 459-463, and Sergio Bertelli, "Nota al Testo" in the Salerno edition of Machiavelli, *Opera Omnia*, vol. 5.

137. *Belfagor* contains another vision of a comic Hell. *Favola* in *Tutte le opere*, pp. 919-923.

138. Dante, *Inferno*, trans. Dorothy L. Sayers (New York, 1977), III.

139. *Tutte le opere*, p. 1005.

140. *Discorsi*, I, 38; II, 15, 23; III, 27.

141. *De Officiis*, I, 13. 41.

142. *Inferno*, XI.

143. Ibid., XVII.

144. Ibid., XXVI.

145. Thomas More, *Utopia*, trans. Paul Turner (Baltimore, 1965), pp. 109-116.

146. *Il Principe*, 18.

147. *Discorsi*, II, 2.

148. E.g., Livy, *History*, IV, 59; XXIV, 38; XXVII, 16; XXVIII, 2, 20; XXX, 8.

149. E.g. *Aeneid*, IX, 339, 560-566; X, 454-456, 708-716, 723-728; XI, 811; XII, 6, 103, 716, 750-755.

150. On Machiavelli's relationship to Seneca see Neal Wood, "Some Common Aspects of the Thought of Seneca and Machiavelli," *Renaissance Quarterly*, 21 (1968), 11-23; and Quentin Skinner, *Machiavelli* (New York, 1981), pp. 25, 29, 36, 45-46. Cicero seems to me Machiavelli's primary target among the Roman moralists, Seneca a secondary target.

151. Compare Thucydides, *History*, V, 85-116, with Machiavelli, *Del modo di trattare i popoli della Valdichiana ribellati* and *Discorsi*, II, 23; III, 27.

Chapter VII

1. E.g., *The Prince and Other Works*, ed. Allan H. Gilbert (Chicago, 1946), pp. 12ff.

2. Robert Michels, *Political Parties*, trans. Eden and Cedar Paul (New York, 1962).

3. Milovan Djilas, *The New Class* (New York, 1957).

4. Merleau-Ponty, *Humanism and Terror*.

5. *Discorsi*, I, 18.

6. "Machiavelli is the first important political realist." Edward Hallett Carr, *The Twenty Years' Crisis, 1919-1939* (New York, 1964), p. 63.

7. Some scholars believe Machiavelli's "realism" was an effort simply to

understand the "is" of politics, instead of concentrating on the "ought." In this view Machiavelli was a scientific observer of politics rather than a moralist. I have already registered my dissatisfaction with this version of the realism/idealism interpretation in Chapter V (above).

8. E.g., Augustine, *City of God* and Reinhold Niebuhr, *Christian Realism and Political Problems* (New York, 1953).

9. E.g., Peter Gay, *The Enlightenment: The Rise of Modern Paganism* (New York, 1967), pp. 285-287.

10. Wolin, *Politics and Vision*, Ch. 7.

11. *Discorsi*, II, 10; see F. Gilbert, "L'ambiente politico fiorentino tra il '400 e il '500," p. 14.

12. "Machiavelli is worth more than Kant." Merleau-Ponty, *Humanism and Terror*, p. 104.

13. Whitfield, *Machiavelli*, p. 67.

14. *Discorsi*, I, 6.

15. Ibid., I, 2, 3; II, 10, 12; III, 6. *Arte della Guerra*, II, pp. 332-333.

16. *Discorsi*, III, 12; *Arte della Guerra*, IV, p. 354.

17. *Discorsi*, I, 38. The senators acted, whenever possible, on the basis of choice rather than necessity, and permitted the rulers of subject cities to act out of choice only when "necessity" would have driven them to rebellion against the Roman yoke.

18. Already in the seventeenth century the liberal philosopher John Locke faced this problem when he argued strongly for tolerance but refused to tolerate those Catholics who gave their loyalty to a foreign prince, the pope. *A Letter Concerning Toleration* (Indianapolis, 1955).

19. On the need of constitutional thought to incorporate generous doses of *raison d'état* see Friedrich, *Constitutional Reason of State*.

20. Merleau-Ponty, *Humanism and Terror*.

21. It is, of course, true that Machiavelli occasionally betrays his most radical thoughts and returns to formulations close to those of Guicciardini and Vettori, and close to ours today. *Discorsi* III, 40 and 41 sanction fraud when it is necessary but deny that fraudulent acts can ever win one "glory." Machiavelli has momentarily forgotten that in *Discorsi* II, 4 and 13 he claimed that Roman fraud was essential to her magnificent "greatness." But this inconsistency does not undo what is remarkable in Machiavelli's thought. Both Guicciardini and Vettori recognized that Machiavelli's thought, while it may have begun like theirs, went far beyond them to radical formulations they could not accept.

22. Whitfield, *Machiavelli*, p. 68, assumes that to prove Machiavelli was concerned about "honor" and "glory" is to defend him.

23. See note 65 in Chapter V (above).

24. Thucydides, *The Peloponnesian War*, trans. Richard Crawley (New York, 1951), V, 105.

25. *Istorie Fiorentine*, V, 11.

26. Quentin Skinner, "Meaning and Understanding in the History of Ideas," *History and Theory*, 8 (1969), 3-53, p. 20.

27. I have argued elsewhere that Montesquieu is another case of a thinker whose major works can and should be studied synthetically. "Montesquieu's Interpreters: A Polemical Essay," *Studies in Eighteenth-Century Culture*, 10 (1981), 327-345. The decision as to whether the genetic or synthetic approach should be emphasized will vary from thinker to thinker and can never be made in advance.

28. Chabod, *Machiavelli and the Renaissance*, p. 41.

29. Ibid., Ch. 2.

30. Hans Baron, "Machiavelli: The Republican Citizen and the Author of 'The Prince,' " *The English Historical Review*, 76 (1961), 217-253, p. 253.

31. Felix Gilbert, "The Composition and Structure of Machiavelli's *Discorsi*," *Journal of the History of Ideas*, 14 (1953), 136-156, p. 156.

32. Baron, "Machiavelli: The Republican Citizen and the Author of 'The Prince,' " p. 251 n.

33. Eric Cochrane, "Machiavelli: 1940-1960," *The Journal of Modern History*, 33 (1961), 113-136, p. 136.

34. John H. Geerken, "Machiavelli Studies Since 1969," *Journal of the History of Ideas*, 37 (1976), 351-368, p. 357.

35. Recent contributions to the study of Machiavelli's biography include the following: Chiappelli, *Nuovi studi sul linguaggio del Machiavelli*; Gian Roberto Sarolli, "The Unpublished Machiavelli," *Review of National Literatures*, 1 (1970), 78-92; Nicolai Rubinstein, "Machiavelli and the World of Florentine Politics."

36. Aristotle, *Politics*, 1284a. Cf. C. Cochrane, *Christianity and Classical Culture*, p. 110: "In seeking to trace the genesis of the cult [of the Caesars], we must begin by insisting that, so far from being foreign or exotic, it was rooted in theories of human nature more or less explicit in Classicism."

37. Allan Gilbert has questioned this date. *Machiavelli: The Chief Works and Others*, p. 161. His argument, that the year cited by scholars rests merely on the date of the events addressed in this essay, overlooks Machiavelli's statement that he is speaking of what happened during "l'anno passato" (*Tutte le opere*, p. 14)—that is, 1502, the year of Florentine troubles in the Valdichiana. It seems to me, therefore, that the burden of proof is upon Gilbert if he wishes to challenge the conventional date. He has set forth no such proof.

38. One other type of genetic research that wrongly trivializes Machiavelli's writings is that which posits personal reasons for his most significant utterances. This is the geneticism guilty of the "genetic fallacy"—the assumption that an author's thought need not be taken seriously if it had something to do with his personality. Various of Machiavelli's contemporaries initiated this process of answering Machiavelli through a refusal to take him seriously when they dismissed him as a man compulsively driven to argue the opposite of commonly held opinions. See F. Gilbert, *Machiavelli and Guicciardini*, pp. 164-165. Gilbert's own remark that Machiavelli was eager to attract attention by holding

extraordinary views (ibid., p. 165) is itself a piece of genetic research which, however accurate, flirts with the genetic fallacy.

39. Strauss, *Thoughts on Machiavelli*, pp. 59, 120, 232, 242-243.

40. Ibid., pp. 224, 290.

41. Ibid., p. 296.

42. Ibid., p. 238.

43. Ibid., p. 173.

44. Ibid., p. 9.

45. Leo Strauss, "Machiavelli and Classical Literature," *Review of National Literatures*, I (1970), 7-25, p. 17; *What is Political Philosophy?* (Glencoe, Ill., 1959), p. 41.

46. Strauss, *Thoughts on Machiavelli*, pp. 127, 173, 294.

47. Ibid., p. 173.

48. See Chapter I (above) for a discussion of this outstanding article.

49. Felix Gilbert, *History: Choice and Commitment* (Cambridge, Mass., 1977), p. 472.

50. Skinner, *Machiavelli*, p. 2.

51. Skinner, "Meaning and Understanding in the History of Ideas." Polemically, this essay is an adaptation of Herbert Butterfield, *The Whig Interpretation of History* (New York, 1965), to intellectual history. Philosophically, Skinner is restating the viewpoint of R. G. Collingwood. E.g., Collingwood, *An Autobiography* (Oxford, 1939).

52. For a general historical survey see Gilbert Highet, *The Anatomy of Satire* (Princeton, 1962).

53. Robert C. Elliott, *The Power of Satire: Magic, Ritual, Art* (Princeton, 1960), passim.

54. E.g., *Discorsi*, II, 19; III, 6.

55. For a general study see Gilbert Highet, *Juvenal the Satirist* (Oxford, 1954).

56. *Istorie Fiorentine*, IV, 6; V, 33. F. Gilbert, *Machiavelli and Guicciardini*, pp. 237-238.

57. Jacob Burckhardt presented the Renaissance as an un-Christian and even pagan era in his *The Civilization of the Renaissance in Italy*, Pt. 6. Subsequent scholarship has moved away from Burckhardt's position. I suspect, without being able to offer proof, that scholars will eventually uncover pockets of militant paganism within the Renaissance.

58. Skinner, *Foundations*, p. 184.

59. F. Gilbert, *Machiavelli and Guicciardini*, p. 176.

60. *Discorsi*, preface.

61. Ibid., III, 27.

62. Friedrich Nietzsche, *The Genealogy of Morals*, trans. Francis Golffing (New York, 1956), p. 185.

63. The *Exortatione alla penitenza* (*Tutte le opere*, pp. 932-934) does not prove Machiavelli was pious. It merely proves what was never in question, that

Machiavelli was willing to participate in the rituals of Florentine society. See *The Prince*, ed. Robert M. Adams (New York, 1977), p. 123.

64. Isaiah Berlin, "The Originality of Machiavelli." See also Geerken, "Machiavelli Studies Since 1969," pp. 365-368.

65. Benjamin Constant, *De la liberté des anciens comparée à celle des modernes*. In *Oeuvres Politiques de Benjamin Constant* (Paris, 1874), pp. 258-286.

66. Fustel de Coulanges wrote his famous book *The Ancient City* (New York, n.d.) in order to save Frenchmen from the revolutionary implications of their classical education. See his "introduction" to *The Ancient City*, and his "Inaugural Lecture" in *The Varieties of History*, ed. Fritz Stern (Cleveland, 1956), pp. 179-188.

67. Berlin, "The Originality of Machiavelli," p. 173.

68. Alasdair MacIntyre, *A Short History of Ethics*, p. 95.

69. Machiavelli frequently commented on Germany. E.g., *Rapporto delle cose della Magna; Discorso sopra le cose della Magna e sopra l'Imperatore; Ritratto delle cose della Magna* in *Tutte le opere*, pp. 63-71. *Discorsi*, I, 55; II, 19.

70. Berlin, "The Originality of Machiavelli," p. 173.

71. Ibid., p. 163.

72. Harrington, *The Commonwealth of Oceana*, p. 323. Harrington's imperialism was a direct continuation of Machiavelli; his understanding of imperialism as a matter of making the world safe for Protestantism was anything but Machiavellian.

73. Berlin, "The Originality of Machiavelli," p. 205.

74. *Discorsi*, I, 25.

75. Judith N. Shklar, "Subversive Genealogies," *Daedalus*, 101 (1972), 129-154.

76. Thomas S. Kuhn, *The Structure of Scientific Revolutions* (Chicago, 1962).

77. The language of a "moment" in history is the language of historicism. In Machiavelli studies it is best known for its place in the title of J.G.A. Pocock's *The Machiavellian Moment*.

INDEX

Library of Congress Cataloging in Publication Data

Hulliung, Mark.
Citizen Machiavelli.

Bibliography: p.
Includes index.
1. Machiavelli, Niccolò, 1469-1527—Political science.
2. Political science—History. 3. Humanism. I. Title.
JC143.M4H78 1983   320'.01'0924   83-42562
ISBN 0-691-07661-8

Mark Hulliung is Associate Professor
of Politics at Brandeis University and the author of
Montesquieu and the Old Regime (California).